UNDERSTANDING PLATO'S *REPUBLIC*

UNDERSTANDING PLATO'S *REPUBLIC*

Gerasimos Santas

WILEY-BLACKWELL

A John Wiley & Sons, Ltd., Publication

This edition first published 2010
© 2010 Gerasimos Santas

Blackwell Publishing was acquired by John Wiley & Sons in February 2007. Blackwell's publishing program has been merged with Wiley's global Scientific, Technical, and Medical business to form Wiley-Blackwell.

Registered Office
John Wiley & Sons Ltd, The Atrium, Southern Gate, Chichester, West Sussex, PO19 8SQ, United Kingdom

Editorial Offices
350 Main Street, Malden, MA 02148-5020, USA
9600 Garsington Road, Oxford, OX4 2DQ, UK
The Atrium, Southern Gate, Chichester, West Sussex, PO19 8SQ, UK

For details of our global editorial offices, for customer services, and for information about how to apply for permission to reuse the copyright material in this book please see our website at www.wiley.com/wiley-blackwell.

The right of Gerasimos Santas to be identified as the author of this work has been asserted in accordance with the UK Copyright, Designs and Patents Act 1988.

Library of Congress Cataloging-in-Publication Data

Santas, Gerasimos Xenophon.
Understanding Plato's Republic / Gerasimos Santas.
    p. cm.
  Includes bibliographical references and index.
  ISBN 978-1-4051-2010-4 (hardcover : alk. paper) – ISBN 978-1-4051-2018-0 (pbk. : alk. paper) 1. Plato. Republic. I. Title.
  JC71.P6S26 2010
  321'.07–dc22

                                              2009033123

A catalogue record for this book is available from the British Library.

Set in 10/12.5pt Galliard by SPi Publisher Services, Pondicherry, India
Printed and bound in Malaysia by Vivar Printing Sdn Bhd

1 2010

To all the students who helped me teach the *Republic*

Contents

Preface

This book is the result of what I have learned from teaching Plato's *Republic* for half a century in colleges and universities (Hamilton College 1958–61, UC Berkeley 1961–2, Brandeis University 1962–6, Wellesley College 1966–8, Johns Hopkins University 1968–9, Salzburg 1984, Stanford 1980–1, UC Irvine 1969–2008). In large introductory courses, with freshmen, sophomores, and upperclassmen from nearly all majors, students reading the book were intrigued, mystified, delighted or appalled, but never bored. Upper division and graduate students always found the book engaging, always something to argue about – support, refute, compare, or built upon. During all this time, while the "canon" was being revised or downgraded in many curriculum wars in colleges and universities across the world, in the classroom the *Republic* held up as a true classic, a book that is always contemporary.

The present work is not a commentary or a comprehensive discussion of all the topics in the *Republic* – worthy projects that would be much larger. It is intended to help the reader understand the main argument of Plato's masterwork – that we are all better off or happier leading just lives in a just society, and even better off being just (rather than unjust) persons in unjust societies. It also discusses the fundamental ideas used to build up Plato's controversial theories of what a just society is and what a just person is, and to support the main argument – his theories of virtue and good, the analogy between just society and just person, the analysis of the human soul, Plato's theory of forms and his high standard of knowledge, especially the difficult knowledge of good necessary for governing ourselves and others well. Two significant consequences – mixed blessings – of Plato's meritocratic theory of justice are also discussed: his revolutionary and pleasing proposals for the equality of women and his disturbing but instructive criticisms of direct democracy and desire satisfaction theories of good. And throughout the book there are comparisons to contemporary theories of justice and the human good, especially the diametrically opposite theories of John Rawls (whose *Theory of Justice* I taught alongside the *Republic* many times in the last quarter century).

Many students taking my courses have helped me understand Plato's concepts and theories, especially when they took the side of Socrates' opponents in the *Republic*. Many graduate students, in seminars, writing dissertations, or helping me teach the book, led me to revise opinions. And colleagues, in conferences and colloquia where earlier drafts of several chapters were presented, helped me understand and appreciate other interpretations and many difficult parts of the *Republic*. I thank all of them, and especially Georgios Anagnostopoulos, Mariana Anagnostopoulos, Hera Arsen, Hugh Benson, Chris Bobonich, Jim Bogen, Gerald Cantu, G.R.F. Ferrari, Mike Ferejohn, Rachana Kamtekar, David Keyt (who made important comments on several chapters), Mark McPherran, Fred Miller, Deborah Modrak, Terry Penner, Ron Polansky, A.W. Price, Chris Rowe, Christopher Shields, Alejandro Santana, Jason Sheley, Rachel Singpurwalla, Nick Smith, Joshua Weinstein, John Whipple, Nick White, and Charles Young. None of these good people is of course responsible for any of my mistakes or interpretations.

1

Introduction
The Style, Main Argument, and Basic Ideas of the Republic

> *For it is no ordinary matter we are discussing, but about how we must live.* (*Republic:* 352d[1])
> *At the center of his [John Rawls'] thought about this history [of moral philosophy] is the idea that in the great texts of our tradition we find the efforts of the best minds to come to terms with many of the hardest questions about how we are to live our lives.* (Barbara Herman[2])

Plato wrote the *Republic* about the same time he founded the Academy, when he had some distance from his master, Socrates, and had began to develop answers of his own to Socratic and other questions. Justly regarded as the most comprehensive masterwork of his middle years, it discusses some of the most fundamental questions of philosophy; and remarkably it succeeded in setting the agenda for many questions in ethics, political philosophy, moral psychology, education, art, epistemology and metaphysics.

Beyond introducing some main questions of philosophy, it presents important alternative answers to these questions and reasoned debates of such answers by vigorous proponents and passionate opponents on all sides. It even sets out alternative conceptions of philosophy itself: a Socratic conception of philosophy as a reasoned examination of our own and others' beliefs about how we should live, and a more comprehensive and constructive effort to build theories that can help us understand the world around us and our place in it. The *Republic* exhibits both conceptions, arguably in fruitful and harmonious combination.

1   The Dialogue Style and the Characters

The *Republic* may be the most wonderful philosophy book ever written for any reader. Plato's masterful use of dialogue, his easy conversational style, his use of analogies, metaphors, similes, allegories and myths, take the reader into philosophy almost imperceptibly, leading her from the concrete to the abstract, causing her to question ideas she took for granted and to wonder about the new ideas in the book.

Plato's sketch and use of character add to the intrinsic interest of the large issues debated. Socrates' questions are answered by characters who are star examples of the ideas they defend. With a foot in the grave, fearful of having cheated anyone and ready to make amends, the wealthy old man Cephalus thinks of justice as honesty in word and deed. His more confident son, the war-like leader Polemarchus, takes justice to be something that benefits allies and harms foes. A harsh fighter – "this wolf before … me" – Thrasymachus argues that justice in societies exists for the benefit of rulers, and the rest of us are better off being unjust if we can get away with it. Plato's brothers, Glaucon and Adeimantus, two good men, are shaken by the debate and want Socrates to make them believe in justice again, a justice which, they propose, would be agreed by all and be better for all than a lawless state of nature.

"The most just man who ever lived," Socrates is willing to carry the fight for justice to the ends of the earth, even to just reward and punishment after death. In the *Republic* he is Plato's star example of the philosopher. Not only the critical thinker of the early dialogues – and he is that in the first book of the work, fearless and willing to die for the right to examine our lives; but also a constructive philosopher who never stops searching for the truth about justice and our good, and who dares to put forward unpopular proposals for governing and for the equality of women, and to reveal obscure visions of a cosmic good.[3]

The *Republic*'s dialogue style serves many purposes. The oppositions to Socrates' views are presented vividly and dramatically by persons who live their ideas. Socrates can examine persons' lives as well as their theories. The other characters have a chance to defend their views and to raise objections to Socrates' constructive theories. They may represent the ideas and ideals of Plato's contemporaries, who may be closer to the reader, remarkably even the modern reader, than what Plato puts in the mouth of Socrates. Through the other characters, the reader is often represented, her objections considered. By staying in the background, never identifying himself with any of his characters, Plato fosters the impression that he is staging a debate about how to live that presents all the alternatives fairly.[4] The series of dialogues that make up the work perhaps mirrors a conception of philosophy as thinking out and discussing reasoned alternative answers to important questions about human life, and is an invitation to all readers to participate and make a rational choice among the alternatives.

In every page of the *Republic* we have at least four voices: the author, at least two characters, and the reader. For example, in the dialogue with Thrasymachus, we have:

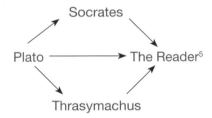

The reader might take Socrates' side, play Thrasymachus, work up a third view of her own, criticize the way Plato conducts the debate, or even just sit back and enjoy the whole show.

All this has made the book very popular indeed – perhaps the most popular philosophy book ever written.[6] But it is not an easy book, not at all. The very literary features and the style that make the book so popular can also mislead the reader and camouflage the difficulties of the ideas it expounds and defends. What reader can fail to appreciate the Allegory of the Cave? To think that she too is in a world of shadows and conflicting opinions, and longs to get out into the light and know the meaning of life? But this very allegory is supposed to illustrate the Platonic journey that only a few can complete, from ignorant perception to true opinion, to knowledge of mathematics, of Platonic Forms and finally of the Form of the Good, about which Socrates had just made the most obscure remarks in the whole Platonic corpus. The allegory by itself is so suggestive and apparently self-contained that teachers sometimes assign it without requiring the student to read the passages in the previous two books, which contain the theories of knowledge and opinion, appearance and reality, and the form of the good – the very theories the allegory is supposed to illustrate!

The ideas of the book are more difficult than the style might suggest. And Plato's philosophical tools – intricate refutations, inductive and deductive arguments, following out the implications of a hypothesis, thought experiments, abstract theories, analyses of important concepts – all these take hard work to understand; though they are beautifully integrated with the literary devices, and this makes for exciting reading.

A reader might also notice that Plato's dramatic style enables him to illuminate certain things and leave others in shadows, to voice some problems and be silent about others – the "artful chiaroscuro" so characteristic of his writing. We don't know whether he wrote in this way naturally, or by deliberate choice, in uncertainty, or sometimes in ignorance.

Should we try to light up the shadows and voice the silences? In contemporary philosophy this is done all the time; most confidently in the case of arguments that seem to be missing one or more premises – we add premises (which hopefully are not obviously false) necessary to make the argument valid, and attribute them to the author, using a principle of charity; occasionally we are lucky to find the missing premises elsewhere in the author's writings and then we are more confident that he believed them.[7]

But with other kinds of shadows and silences, interpretation is more problematic. When a theory is very incomplete, as Glaucon's social contract theory of justice is, for example, how do we complete it? We can try the argument route if we can arrange the propositions of the theory so that some are premises and some conclusions; but we cannot do this always or conclusively. Or we notice that Plato has Socrates criticize Thrasymachus' theory of justice persistently for many pages, but does not similarly criticize the theories of Plato's brothers, and Plato does not tell us why he did not unleash his star critic on his brothers. What can we make of this silence?

Adding to difficulties but also to excitement can be comparisons of competing ideas to Plato's own, beyond the oppositions that Plato himself sets up, in the history of later important books on the same subjects. The difficulty is to avoid gross anachronisms when we make such comparisons. However great, the *Republic* is a pioneering work embedded in its own historical, philosophical and literary context. And Plato did not have the benefits of subsequent philosophy. But we do; and we can make some comparisons to competing ideas in other important authors on justice, happiness, goodness, ideals of human knowledge and their role in governing, and speculations about utopian institutions. These can set up exciting contemporary dialogues between Socrates, later philosophers, and the reader. Such comparisons, whether to John Rawls or John Stuart Mill, can also help us understand both the limits and the greatness of the *Republic*.

2 The Main Argument and Plot of the *Republic*

Plato discusses many subjects in the *Republic*: the uses and misuses of wealth, competing theories of what justice is, rival conceptions of human happiness, the relation of justice to happiness, early and advanced education, religion and theology, private property, the other virtues of cities and of individuals, the human soul and human motivations, gender, the monogamous family, good and bad governing, good and bad constitutions, knowledge and opinion, appearance and reality, goodness itself, the nature and value of art and its place in society, even reward and punishment in the after life, and many more. The reader can easily get lost and the work itself can appear without unity and coherence. Did Plato have a design for the work, a grand plan that orders its many subjects?[8] And does the *Republic*'s dramatic plot follow the plan?[9]

Fortunately, Plato gives us several signposts along the way that support positive answers to these questions. Most noticeably, at the end of Book I, Socrates tells us that they have been discussing three questions, which he orders in a certain way, and expresses his dissatisfaction with their discussion so far: "So now the whole conversation has left me in the dark; for so long as I do not know what justice is, I am hardly likely to know whether or not it is a virtue, or whether it makes a man happy or unhappy" (*Republic*: 354). The last question is discussed repeatedly from beginning to end, most significantly in Books I, II, IV, IX and X. So we know this is a central question that drives the whole investigation. The first question is also discussed in all these books and more, and Socrates has just told us that it is the first question to be answered in the order of investigation. We know then that these are two central questions that motivate the whole work.[10]

The question whether justice is good for us and makes us happy, has more breadth and depth than might at first appear. At a very practical, concrete level it seems to pose the choice between acting justly and acting unjustly, or more holistically a choice between leading a just or unjust life. This choice arises in the experience of living, since sometimes it seems that what justice requires is contrary to our good, and then we may reasonably ask why we should do what we believe to be just.[11] This is indeed a question that the work pursues from beginning to end, and its argument, that we are better off being just, is choice guiding concretely and practically.

But Plato also presents us with three rival major answers to the first question of the work on what justice is: the partial justice of Thrasymachus, the more egalitarian justice of Plato's brothers, and the unusual conception of justice for societies and human souls that Socrates advocates. It is difficult to escape the implication that Plato means for us, the readers, to choose among these three answers. Thus the *Republic* poses for us not only the practical and concrete choice between just and unjust action – or a just and unjust life – but also the more theoretical and philosophically challenging choice among three kinds of justice.

Moreover, Plato points out that the two choices are interdependent: we cannot reasonably choose between justice and injustice (of actions or lives) unless we first know what justice is or until have made a choice among the known and rival conceptions of justice.[12] It may well be that in a society governed by Thrasymachus' justice some might be better off sometimes doing what is unjust in that society; whereas in a society that satisfies the principle of justice favored by Socrates, one might always be better off doing what is just in that society. The *Republic* is a great work also because it challenges us to make informed and rational choices not only between just and unjust actions or lives, but also among different kinds of just societies. The work reveals that the reach of justice is far greater and reaches deeper than we might commonly think.[13]

Later, in Books V, VI and VII, we read that knowledge of the Platonic form of the good is necessary for understanding the good of justice and of the other social and individual virtues, for understanding our good, and for governing well. But this knowledge is very difficult and far more valuable than sense perception and opinion; and it is possible only if there are unchangeable universals or archetypes – the Platonic Forms.

In the *Republic*, Platonic Forms have to play two very demanding roles. They have to make possible a very high standard of human knowledge – "infallible" knowledge. And they have to make such high knowledge possible for the good, the beautiful, and the just – the very things that Plato tells us are the most disputed and hard, if not impossible, to measure.[14] And yet these high demands seem necessary for a utopian government – an "epistocracy" – whose basis for political power is knowledge of the good. Very few talented individuals can attain knowledge of the form of the good after a long education in the sciences and Platonic dialectic.

In these middle books we see that Plato thinks these theories of knowledge (epistemology) and of reality (metaphysics) are a necessary foundation for the ethics and political philosophy his Socrates defends in the rest of the work. A far cry, this, from John Rawls who argues that we can have a theory of justice (and, we might add, of goodness as rationality)[15] without metaphysics, in "Justice as Fairness: Political, not Metaphysical" (Rawls 1985).

Thus we know that the *Republic* is centrally about justice and our good, and about the knowledge of the good required for understanding and bringing justice, happiness, and good government into our lives and our societies. If we can discover what justice is, learn what the good or goodness is, and find out how justice is good for us, we can then soundly design the political and social arrangements that approximate these ideals, and we can plan the education that would make us just and happy persons.

The *Republic* proposes many revolutionary reforms of existing institutions: public and strictly planned education, complete separation of political and military power from property and wealth, the equality of women, limits to the monogamous family, public control of art and the media, and many others. But discussions of these institutions and other subjects are subordinate to the advancement of the ideals of justice, knowledge, and the good – and this is the key to understanding the unity and coherence of the work. The book's greatness is to be found in the blending of this unity and coherence of large ideas that appeal to reason with masterful discussions of significant details and stories, myths, similes, metaphors and allegories that pull in the reader's emotions.[16]

The dramatic plot follows the philosophical grand design, though not always directly. Plato makes a writer's choice about what to reveal when – how to construct the philosophical drama. For example, primary education for the ideal city is outlined in Books II and III, before the virtues of the completely good city and of the good person are defined in Book IV, even though the education is designed to advance these virtues.[17] Nor do we learn until Books V, VI and VII that understanding and approximating in reality these ideals absolutely depend on knowledge of the form of the good – a very abstract good and a very demanding knowledge that only a few talented can attain after many years of higher education. Again, though the soul is analyzed into three parts in Book IV, the analysis does not become clear till it is put to work in analyzing unjust persons in Book VIII and Plato's discussion of the influence of art on character in Book X.

To understand the work we have to do more than read on attentively. We also have to look backward from time to time, re-think earlier passages and see the significance of the whole. Fortunately, these "anomalies" are usually signaled by Plato himself, as postponements, digressions, or returns to the main themes.[18] If we understand the grand philosophical plan of the work and the priorities among its many questions, we can still make sense of the whole work as coherent and unified. The philosophical plan and the dramatic plot are weaved together to make the book accessible, readable, and exiting.

3   The Fundamental Ideas of the *Republic*

We have just reviewed one way to understand the unity and coherence of the *Republic*: by its main argument, that we are better off or happier being just rather than unjust; and by the main things this argument presupposes or implies: several theories of justice (and a choice among them); competing conceptions of happiness (and a choice among them); Plato's theories of forms, of knowledge, and of the good. And there is a large consensus on the centrality of this argument.

Another way to understand the structure and coherence of the work, one that does not compete but rather complements understanding the main argument, is by identifying its basic ideas – the building blocks that explain everything else important in it. Some of these are argued for rather than taken for granted, and their importance becomes quite evident – they can be called "leading ideas" of the work. Others are taken for granted rather than argued for, and can be more difficult to notice, though once found they can be seen at work. They might be called "basic assumptions." The basic assumptions and the leading ideas can then be used to explain other important ideas of the work that belong to its superstructure.

Ideally, the use of this method would require that we spot all of Plato's basic assumptions, identify all his leading ideas and show how they can be derived from the assumptions, and finally show how the basic assumptions and the leading ideas explain the rest of Plato's ideas in that work. This is very ambitious and would take far more work and space.[19] Here we can offer only a sample of how the whole work might be thus understood. For each basic assumption or leading idea I take up below, I sketch other important ideas and themes it helps explain.

There are many basic assumptions in the *Republic*, taken for granted and without argument. Three in particular are worth mentioning here, since they play large yet almost unnoticed roles in Plato's theory of justice. Interestingly, all three first appear early in the work.

An important basic assumption in the *Republic* is Plato's theory of functional virtue and good, the idea that a virtue is a quality that enables something to function well, and that functioning well is an essential part of the good of the thing. This theory is stated without argument, in Book I, in the form of three definitions, but with convincing illustrations of functions from natural organs and from artifacts. It is more like an explicit basic (but complex) assumption.[20]

This theory is used in that first book to construct an argument that justice makes us happy.[21] It is used in Books II to IV to construct the completely good city, and to analyze and define the virtues of cities and persons. It is also used to distinguish between knowledge and opinion in Book V, in the analysis of unjust cities and persons in Book VII, and in the analysis of art in Book X. It is hard to doubt its importance textually; though it has not been recognized and discussed explicitly till recently.[22] Philosophically, it is even harder to doubt its importance, since it provides Plato with an account of good to build a theory of justice with in Book IV, before the account of the form of the good in Book VI. And we know that a theory of justice cannot be built without some account of the good; especially the justice of society (as distinct from the justice of persons) has to be concerned with how what is good and bad for its members is distributed, and so it has to suppose some account of what is good and bad. It is no accident that in the *Republic* there are disputes about happiness and our good alongside the disputes about justice. In Rawls the dependence of justice on good is quite clear and explicit, and equally clear that the account of the good his justice uses is his theory of primary goods.[23]

A second basic assumption is what Plato takes to be the primary subject of justice. Plato, no less than Rawls, knew that the concept of justice is applied to many things: societies, persons, social and individual actions, laws, constitutions, perhaps even desires and intentions. But he chose the first two of these for his investigation into the nature and benefits of justice (*Republic*: 368e), and did so without argument, apparently on the further basic assumption that if he discovers what a just society is and what a just person is, he can derive the other applications from these. But some argument may be needed. Rawls sees the same diverse applications of the concept of justice, but he makes a different choice about what he needs to investigate, namely the justice of the basic structure of society, and supposes that the justice of persons can be derived from the justice of society.[24] These different basic assumptions lead to very different investigations of justice in Plato and Rawls.

A third basic assumption Plato makes without argument is the equivalent of what Rawls calls "the natural lottery" assumption: that nature distributes at birth advantages and disadvantages – such as high or low intelligence, strong or weak spirit, physical strength, beauty, health or birth defects, and so on.[25] Plato's Socrates brings up this assumption at the beginning of his construction of a just city and gives it a big role in the first formulation of his principle of justice: because people are born with different abilities relevant to the cooperative production of the various things people need, not only should labor be divided, but persons with different inborn abilities should be matched to the labors for which their abilities best suit them (*Republic*: 369–70). Thus Plato's justice takes a stand on these natural inborn differences: she works them into the institutions of society; but not so with all inborn differences – Plato's justice blindfolds inborn gender differences. The myth of metals is an allegory in part symbolizing this assumption and its role in the just city (*Republic*: 414–15).[26]

An important leading idea of the *Republic* is the analogy Plato sets up between the virtues or vices of a person and the virtues or vices of a city-state, especially the analogy between a just person and a just soul. This is only stated and illustrated in Book II, but it is argued for in Book IV. The importance of understanding this analogy for understanding the rest of the work is unquestionable. The analogy is used in Book IV to deduce a definition of a just person from the definition of a just city-state that already Plato had constructed (and similarly to deduce the other virtues of persons from the corresponding virtues of the ideal city-state); in Book VIII, it is used again to construct parallels, and to find causal relations, between various unjust city states and unjust persons, and to characterize and rank both. Thus Plato puts normative ethics (the justice and the good of persons) and normative political philosophy (the justice and the good of city-states) on parallel tracks, supposes that we cannot understand either without the other, and finds several causal and other relations between the justice and the good of the one and the justice and the good of the other.[27] This analogy has received plenty of attention.[28]

A second leading idea is Plato's pioneering analysis of the human soul into reason, spirit, and appetite. In Book IV this tripartite division of the soul is explicitly argued for and not taken for granted. It is used immediately in the analyses and definitions of the four cardinal virtues of persons. In Book VIII it is used to analyze several types of unjust persons; in Book IX it is used to show that just persons enjoy a pleasanter life, at least in the most valuable pleasures; and in Book X it is used to determine the value of art and its place in society. Further, the analysis of the soul is presupposed in the theory of early education in Books II and III, and assumed in the "longer road" of the higher education of reason in Book VII. Without understanding Plato's analysis of the soul, none of these other ideas of his can be understood. The whole "moral psychology" of the *Republic* depends on Plato's analysis of the human psyche. No wonder it also has received so much attention.[29]

A third leading (and complex) idea in the *Republic* is Plato's "metaphysical epistemology":[30] his distinction between knowledge and opinion – that knowledge is "infallible" (free of error or falsehood) while opinion can contain errors and can be true or false; his further claim that such knowledge is possible only if there are Platonic forms, everlasting and unchanging universals or archetypes that enable us to sort out and to evaluate physical objects and works of art; and his further claim yet, that there is the universal form of the good that accounts for the value of forms and the lesser value of physical objects and works of art. He argues for this cluster of leading ideas in Books V, VI and VII, and their importance is also indisputable and much discussed.[31]

Plato uses this conception of knowledge, of forms, and the form of the good, to define the philosopher, as one who does not deny or confuse universals with their physical and artistic instantiations; to justify the paradox of the philosopher-king, that political power should be based on knowledge of universals and above all knowledge of the form of the good.[32] The incredibly demanding higher education of future rulers, in Book VII, is based on this cluster of leading ideas. And the extreme political elitism of Plato's ideal city – that only his philosophers can rule well – is also based on this cluster of leading ideas and on the natural lottery assumption, or an empirical part of it, that the extremely high intelligence required for ruling well is naturally distributed to very few at birth.

Even in this little rough and ready partial sketch, we can see that Plato indeed orders his ideas: some are very basic assumptions, others are argued for, and others yet belong to the super-structure that is built on the first two. A more complete ordering would reveal more fully the philosophical structure of the *Republic*.

But we must remember that Plato's ordering is not always explicit – sometimes apparent, sometimes hinted at, sometimes even hidden. And he may not have had a complete ordering of all his ideas in that work. Plato writes informally, dramatically, poetically, and artfully, using every device, weapon, or stratagem known to a writer, be he a poet, philosopher, psychologist, or storyteller.

Notes

1   All references to Plato's *Republic* in this book are to Stephanus pages, which are the same in all modern editions and translations of the *Republic*. Such page numbers are usually found in the margins. Thus, in the Cooper edition of *Plato: Complete Works*, "*Republic*: 352d" refers to the *Republic*, Stephanus page 352 (found in the margin), section d of that page. All translations are my own unless otherwise indicated, but heavily indebted to Shorey (1935) and Cornford (1941).

2   Rawls (2000).

3   For Plato's characters and their integration into the philosophical themes see O'Connor (2007) and Weiss (2007).

4   For different readings of the *Republic* due to its dialogue form, see Rowe (2006).

5   For Plato's readers see Yunis (2007).

6   For the history of the book, ancient and modern, see Introduction in Ferrari (2007).

7   See Cohen and Keyt (1992) for the classic discussion of the use of the principle of charity in interpreting Plato.

8   In an attempt to exhibit both the richness and the grand plan of the *Republic*, Cornford (1941), in his influential and most popular translation of the work in the twentieth century, offers an analytic table of contents to display the richness of its many subjects, and divides the work into five parts with headings to outline the grand plan that orders the subjects. Though one might disagree with Cornford's re-dividing the *Republic* (into five parts rather than the traditional ten books), his headings of parts and chapters are an invaluable guide to any reader.

9   For the integration of plot, character, and philosophy in the *Republic* see especially Rosen (2005), and Anton (2008).

10   The second question, whether justice is a virtue, does not appear very explicitly in the rest of the work, but the theory of function and virtue at the end of Book I answers the question of what a virtue is, and the theory of justice in Book IV answers the question whether justice is a virtue. See chapters 4 and 5 below.

11   See the Introduction in White (1979: 9–13), for a discussion of this question.

12   This is part of the point Socrates makes about the priority of what justice is over the other questions. For a different view see Penner (2005).

13   The reach and depth of justice is revealed again in Rawls (1971), "The Subject of Justice," (1971: 7–11), and well explained by Barry (1989: chapter 6).

14   In the *Euthyphro* (7a–7e), Socrates tells us that the arts of counting, measuring, and weighing can help us resolve many disputes, but not disputes about the good, the just, and the beautiful, implying that these cannot be resolved by the mathematical arts. For discussion see Irwin (1995) and Santas (2006b).

15   Rawls (1971: chapter VII, "Goodness as Rationality"): a goodness knowledge of which is far more accessible to ordinary human beings. But the rules of choice he proposes are largely rules for instrumental goods. Rawls acknowledges that disputes about ultimate ends are far harder to adjudicate and may be endless; fortunately, he thinks, agreement about ultimate ends is not necessary for agreement on justice. See his "Social Unity and Primary Goods" (Rawls 1982).

16   For discussion of the psychology of Plato's myths and allegories see J. Lear (2006).

17   See G. R. Lear (2006) for discussion of education to love of beauty and how it helps to become just.

18   Apparent and real digressions are noted by Penner (2006: 238–40) who also sets out the work's "Project as a Whole". Ferrari also notes that "the *Republic* itself makes a point of interweaving its themes – since it is replete with anticipations, suspensions, and transformations of its leading ideas" (2007: xx).

19   Rickless (2007: chapter 1), used this method to give a clear and orderly statement of *one* of the theories in the *Republic*, Plato's theory of forms. From a purely philosophical standpoint, this is an admirable way to understand a grand theory, though one that needs to be studied to be appreciated.

20   Strictly, the three definitions would be three basic assumptions.

21   That argument is found unsatisfactory by Socrates, but the theory itself is not. See Santas (2006a) for details.

22   See Santas (2001: 66–90, 11–17) and Santas (2006a), for tracking the use of the functional theory from Book I to X. For further arguments of its importance, see Coumoundouros and Polanski (2009).

23   Rawls (1971: 3–6 (The Role of Justice), 90–5 (Primary Goods as the Basis of Expectations), 142–5 (The Rationality of the Parties)).

24   Rawls (1971: 7–11, 433–40).

25   Rawls calls these advantages "natural" primary goods, as distinct from social primary goods – such as liberties and income and wealth – that society distributes through its basic institutions. Rawls notes that what the natural lottery distributes is neither just nor unjust, but what societies do with such distributions can be just or unjust (consider what societies do with, for example, color, gender, intelligence or beauty).

26   See Schofield (2007). In so far as the allegory of the metals is a symbol for the natural lottery assumption, it is no lie on Plato's part, noble or otherwise; Plato believed that people are born with unequal intelligence, spirit, and abilities for productive arts and trades; and we know that people are born with unequal IQ, and unequal abilities for mathematics, music, and so on. Of course, if the allegory or myth of metals is taken literally, that people are born with gold, silver, or iron in their souls, it is false, and young children might take it literally. See Jonathan Lear (2006).

27   Plato's most brilliant student, Aristotle separated ethics and politics, and did not take to Plato's analogy between the two, though he found other important relations between them. It is hard to find any subsequent theorists of justice and the good who have followed Plato in this analogy.

28   For example, Lear (1993), Williams (1997), Ferrari (2003), Santas (2001), Keyt (2006b), and many others. Since Popper's attack on the political philosophy of the *Republic*, some writers have downplayed the "dismal politics" of the work; this is understandable but not appropriate when we consider the work as a whole.

29   In the last fifteen years alone we have had several major works on it (Price 1995; Bobonich 2002; Lorenz 2005; Weinstein 2004).

30   See White (1992).

31   The literature on this cluster of ideas is immense; for some recent discussions see, e.g. Penner (2006) and Denyer (2007).

32   See especially Reeve (1988), and recently Denyer (2007) and Sedley (2007).

2

Is Justice the Interest of the Rulers? Is It Good for Us?
The Challenge of Thrasymachus

The conversations in the *Republic* take place in the house of Cephalus, a respected and wealthy old man with a foot in the grave, preoccupied with thoughts of death, and now frightened by childhood stories about punishment in the afterlife. When Socrates asks him about the burdens of old age and the uses of wealth, Cephalus naturally thinks of wealth as a means of restitution, if he has injured anyone in this life by lying or breaking a promise. Socrates puts these two rules in Cephalus' mouth as an account of what justice is and brings up counter examples to dispute it: Cephalus agrees that it would not be just to return a borrowed weapon to a man who has gone mad and is dangerous to himself or others, despite one's promise. The dialogue with the old man foreshadows many themes of the *Republic*, but the immediate point is that Socrates wants to know what justice is universally, something not provided by a list of rules that are sometimes right to break. Socrates wants greater generality that might explain the rules and their exceptions.[1]

Cephalus leaves to offer expensive sacrifices to the gods in the hope of a better afterlife, turning over the argument to his son Polemarchus, who appeals to the poet Simonides, for the view that justice is rendering to each man his due or what is appropriate to him. Socrates does not dispute the truth of this general saying, but he correctly asks what is due or appropriate to one, and Polemarchus replies that harm is due and appropriate to enemies, benefit to friends. The poets invoke the muses for inspiration, and Polemarchus appeals to the poets to tell us what justice is.

The dialogue with Polemarchus serves to raise important questions about justice: what is the subject matter of justice, war between nations, business transactions, the practices of the arts and sciences?[2] And what is the role of justice, what is justice for?[3]

It also presents an argument for the famous Socratic view that it is never just to harm a human being, not even in retaliation, not even an enemy (an argument for the view taken for granted in the *Crito*). Typically, Socrates uses three sets of analogies to argue for it: since harming horses or dogs means making them worse with respect to the excellence appropriate to horses or dogs, analogously with human beings; and since justice is the excellence appropriate to human beings, harming a human being would be making him/her less just or unjust. But horse riding experts do not make horse riders worse in riding by the art of horsemanship or music experts others less musical by the art of musicianship; analogously just men do not make other less just by the art (or virtue) of justice. Further, it is not the function of heat to do its opposite, to cool; analogously it is not the function of justice to do its opposite and make men unjust, or of good men to make men bad. So it cannot be the part of a just man to make another unjust, whether his enemy or not. The argument has its weaknesses: apparently too narrow a conception of harm: what about theft or damage to one's property or bodily harm or homicide? How are these harms excluded from the just man's conduct? Further, there are other virtues besides justice: it may seem nearly contradictory to have a just man make another man unjust, but why could not a just man make another cowardly? Can the argument be repeated for the other virtues? However, the argument foreshadows Platonic views argued later on: that harm might be primarily defined relative to the virtues, and that to cause a man to have injustice in his soul is the greatest of harms you can do to him.[4]

Socrates' dialogue with Thrasymachus broadens and deepens the investigation into the nature of justice. Thrasymachus' theory of justice applies the concept to whole societies and their political institutions, not only to individuals as the previous speakers mostly did. The subject of justice is broadened to fundamental political issues as well as ethics.[5] Further, it contains implicitly a conception of the major goods that Thrasymachus thinks make up human happiness, and a thesis about the relation of justice to happiness. It even displays a coherent and clear method for discovering what justice is. Plato has Socrates examine vigorously all these parts of Thrasymachus' almost complete conception of justice, and Thrasymachus defends it vociferously. Let us consider it step by step.

1   Why does Thrasymachus Think that Justice is the Interest of the Rulers?

At first Thrasymachus simply announces the essence of his view in an one line formula: "What I say is that justice is nothing but what is to the interest of the stronger" (*Republic*: 338).

Socrates immediately raises the first good question: who is the stronger? And Thrasymachus gives the best answer, broadening at the same time the subject of justice: "Don't you know that a state may be ruled by a tyrant, a democracy, or an aristocracy? Of course. And that the ruling element is always the stronger? Yes." The rulers in any one of these constitutions have the power of life, liberty, and property over their subjects. What can be greater strength than that?

In the next remarkable move, Plato has Thrasymachus give an argument *for* his formula,[6] which reveals the major grounds for it as well as a method of investigating the nature of justice:

> Don't you know then, said he, that some cities are governed by tyrants, in others democracy rules, in others aristocracy? Assuredly. And is it not this that is strong and has the mastery in each – the ruling party? Certainly. And each form of government enacts the laws with a view to its own advantage, a democracy democratic laws and tyranny autocratic and the others likewise, and by so legislating they proclaim that the just for their subjects is that which is for their, the rulers', advantage and the man who deviates from this law they chastise as a lawbreaker and unjust. This then, my good sir, is what I understand as the identical principle of justice that obtains in all states, the advantage of the established government. This holds power, so that if one reasons correctly, it works out that the just is the same everywhere, the advantage of the stronger. (*Republic*: 338e–339a, Shorey translation)

Thrasymachus begins with an elucidation of the stronger in his initial definition: the ruling party in each form of government, whether a tyranny, a democracy, or an aristocracy. Next, he asserts a big empirical generalization: that in all forms of government the ruling party enacts laws to its own advantage. Given the variety of constitutions included, the view allows that the laws may be different in content in different kinds of government (think of the different tax laws, for example, that such different regimes might enact), but claims that they all have this feature in common. Thrasymachus then brings in another premise (is it also an empirical generalization or is it a postulate?) that each form of government proclaims that justice consists in observing the laws it has enacted and (punishable) injustice in breaking these laws; again these laws may be different in different forms of government and so justice may be different in content in different states; but all these laws have in common that they determine what justice is in each state. Finally, from these three premises Thrasymachus concludes that justice is everywhere ("in all states") the same, the advantage of the stronger.

This argument reveals a method for finding out what justice is: on the assumption that the positive laws of a state determine completely what justice is in that state, the method consists in an empirical investigation of the aims of the laws and the motives and practices of legislators in each state, and then generalizing from the results to what is common (if anything) to the justice of all states. On the same assumption – let us call it the legal positivist assumption[7] – any one can perform this investigation and find out what the result is; it is an investigation which nowadays would be done by an empirical political scientist studying comparative government. We might ask, for instance, what justice is in Norway, and suppose that the complete answer will be found in its constitution and laws.

Of course, we must not confuse the method with the particular result Thrasymachus claims would be discovered if the method were applied. Plato does not have Thrasymachus actually do the empirical research necessary to support his result. No evidence from a study of different actual states is offered for the truth of Thrasymachus' empirical generalization. It is perhaps generally thought that tyrants legislate for their own advantage, a benevolent dictator being a rather unusual and unreliable exception. Perhaps the same might be thought of aristocracies, if French revolutions are any evidence. These two cases might account for the fact that generally readers of the *Republic* think of Thrasymachus' view as a very realistic and powerful challenge to other theories of justice.

But is Thrasymachus' generalization true of democracies? Were not *all* citizens rulers in ancient direct democracies, all of them members of the Assembly, each with one vote? Does not the distinction between ruler and subject disappear in the case of ancient participatory democracy?[8] Perhaps even in this case Thrasymachus' generalization might apply, if we think of democracies as constitutions in which the poor rule against the rich and of democratic rule as majority rule (this seems to be the way Plato thinks of democracy in *Republic*, Book VIII; and Aristotle, *Politics*, Book III, chapters 8 and 9). So too in democracies, Thrasymachus might argue, the majorities made up of the poor legislate to their own advantage and against the rich. Perhaps we can begin to see here the importance of a large middle class for the stability and even the justice of modern representative democracies.

But the fact still remains that no evidence gathered from actual investigation of ancient states is offered by Thrasymachus for his generalization that in all states the rulers legislate for their own advantage. Aristotle apparently did such an empirical study of some 158 different ancient constitutions and apparently found that in some cases Thrasymachus' result does indeed obtain, and called such constitutions "deviant" or "perverted." But he disagreed with Thrasymachus' generalization that all constitutions have this common feature of aiming at the advantage of the ruling party; and he certainly disagreed with Thrasymachus' positivist assumption since he argued that none of the deviant constitutions are just. Plato himself foreshadows Aristotle's conclusion in the *Laws* (Book IV, 714–15 and Book III, 697).[9]

2   Socrates' Refutations of Thrasymachus' Premises

Now we must remember that the empirical generalization becomes relevant to Thrasymachus' conclusion only on the assumption that justice is identical to the positive laws of societies; so if we want to find out what justice is we must investigate the laws of each society, the aims of the laws and the practices of legislators. Socrates' first argument (*Republic*: 339) is against this positivist assumption and confirms its crucial importance. He points out that rulers or legislators might sometimes make a mistake in supposing that a particular law they enact would be to their own advantage; in such a case acting in accordance with such a mistaken law would be both just (by the positivist assumption) and also unjust (by Thrasymachus' formula of justice as the advantage of the ruler). This is correct, and it is an internal criticism of Thrasymachus' view, using his own premises, and a new premise to which he agrees and which seems incontrovertible, that rulers can and do sometimes make mistakes about what laws are to their own interest.

But this criticism has a more general validity: so long as laws are thought of as means to some end, such empirical mistakes are possible, whether the end is the advantage of the ruler or the advantage of every citizen or the common interest. Thus the positivist assumption would be incorrect, even if as a matter of fact legislators aimed at common advantage or the advantage of every citizen (as Plato himself thinks they should (*Republic*: 420bc)); even in that case it would be incorrect to claim that the positive laws of society completely determine what is just. The possibility of such mistakes shows that laws *can* be unjust, so long as laws are means to ends and no matter what the ends are. Plato has succeeded in opening up an important logical gap between the positive laws of societies and justice; an empirical study of the positive laws of societies and the aims and practices of legislators might still be instructive and relevant to finding out what justice is, but it would not completely determine the nature of justice. Plato takes this result for granted in the rest of the work, for example when he argues for the justice of the equality of women, which was against the positive laws of every known society.

Thrasymachus is given an opportunity to repair the damage from the first argument (*Republic*: 340). He rejects a possible option of altering his initial formula; to justice is what the rulers *think* is to their advantage. He does not say why he rejects this option, but we can see that it allows too tenuous a connection between justice and a ruler's advantage; in a possible case of a ruler who makes too many relevant mistakes in legislating, the justice of his positive laws would be no more to his advantage than to his disadvantage. And since rulers can come to power in a wide variety of ways – inheritance, brute force, election, luck – who can say that unintelligent, uneducated or simply stupid rulers would be unusual? This option changes Thrasymachus' view too much and constitutes no defense of it.

Thrasymachus does not deny that human beings can make mistakes about means to ends. Rather he argues that when rulers make such mistakes they are not the stronger: he now adds knowledge of what laws are good for rulers (at least freedom from such mistakes) to his previous condition, political power, as joint necessary conditions for being the stronger (*Republic*: 340). He adds knowledge to political power – reasonably enough – for is not knowledge itself power? The result is an idealized notion of ruler as one who is a de facto ruler and possesses the relevant knowledge (makes no relevant mistakes) – an idealized notion of the art of ruling. This, of course, escapes the objection of Socrates' first argument: the laws which de facto rulers enact when they make a mistake no longer count as constituting justice. The contradictory result is avoided.

But there may not be any such idealized rulers (de facto rulers who never make the relevant mistakes) and, if so, Thrasymachus' formula of what justice is, with the idealized notion of a ruler, would have no application to any existing state; a disastrous consequence for his view, since now there would be no states with such rulers to study and no empirical generalization forthcoming.

Thrasymachus might try to avoid this disastrous consequence by referring to actual rulers and further selecting only those laws they enact without mistakes as being the laws that constitute justice; so now one would study aims of the laws and the practices of actual legislators when they make no mistakes and generalizing from the results. But this study would be at best very difficult: there would be great uncertainty about which laws constitute justice since neither the investigators nor the rulers themselves might know when they are making a mistake or when laws they enacted might turn out to be contrary to their interest. Further, how are the subjects of such rulers to know which of the enacted laws were correctly enacted and hence just? This may be an intolerable uncertainty for such a regime with respect to compliance and stability.[10]

But Thrasymachus' idealized notion of ruler does allow Socrates to examine Thrasymachus' formula of justice free of the relevant mistakes. Suppose we could determine when actual rulers make no relevant mistakes in legislating. Would Thrasymachus' original formula of justice be true in such cases? Would justice be the advantage of idealized rulers, or actual rulers in so far as they make no relevant mistakes? In his second argument against Thrasymachus Socrates takes up this question, since Thrasymachus has now added knowledge to de facto political power as another necessary condition for being the stronger.

Socrates now builds an argument by analogy, intended to show that Thrasymachus' other premise, the empirical generalization would be false under these conditions. If ruling, on Thrasymachus' own reformed view of an idealized de facto ruler making no relevant mistakes, requires knowledge of what is to the rulers' interest, and if ruling is thus an idealized art that contains no relevant mistakes, then we can compare it to other arts such as medicine and navigation in so far as they can be thought idealized also, and thereby test Mr Thrasymachus' empirical generalization.

Socrates suggests and Thrasymachus agrees that medicine and the physician, in so far as they make no mistakes about the body, are the stronger party and the human body of the patient the weak party: "That is the reason why the art of medicine has now been invented, because the body is deficient" (*Republic*: 341e). Similarly, in navigation, the pilot, in the ideal case of making no mistakes, is the stronger party and the passengers the weaker party, since he knows what is safety at sea and they don't. Then, Socrates suggests, the physician qua physician aims at healing the patient, since qua physician he has no need of healing and the patient qua deficient body does have such need; similarly, the pilot qua pilot aims at the safety of the passengers at sea (and, incidentally, his own safety when he happens to be a passenger). These are the functions of these arts and the reasons for their existence: being perfect, as idealized in making no mistakes, they seek to make up the deficiencies of their imperfect or deficient subjects. Similarly, since ruling is an art, idealized in making no mistakes, and rulers are the stronger party and subjects the weaker, Socrates draws the conclusion that the function of ruling is not to promote the interest of the rulers (except incidentally as in the case of the pilot) but of those the rulers have charge over, the ruled.

Of course Socrates' argument by analogy uses an idealized conception of the arts, since it is testing Thrasymachus' modified view with the notion of an idealized ruler; and Socrates gives the idealized notion a basis, a rationale for inventing and using the arts in the first place. We prize the arts for their needed knowledge and in so far as they are making no mistakes.

It should be noted that this argument does not show that Thrasymachus' empirical generalization is false of merely de facto rulers, that actual rulers do not make laws to their own advantage; to show *that* we would need an actual empirical investigation of actual rulers' legislative aims and practices by political scientists doing comparative government across nations and historical periods.

But if Thrasymachus were to revert to his original notion of the stronger as a merely de facto ruler, Socrates' first argument would come into play and disarm any empirical generalization in Thrasymachus' favor: even if Thrasymachus' generalization turned out to be true of merely de facto rulers, it still would not follow that justice *is* the advantage of the stronger, but at most that what merely de facto rulers *think* is their advantage and so at most what they *think* justice is. And why would anyone suppose that justice is identical with what such rulers think justice is? After all they are fallible about means to ends, like the rest of us. And their subjects are bound to think differently on what justice is, since such rulers' justice is systemically contrary to their, the subjects', interest.

Sometimes it is said that Thrasymachus' formula amounts to the view that "might makes right." But this is a bit too simplistic and covers up different notions of "might." To begin with, we have might as de facto political power, and then might as de facto political power *and* knowledge about what is to one's own good. Then again, since Thrasymachus applies justice to three main constitutions, we can see that in his view "might" can refer to importantly different powers. In a tyranny might can refer to the successful violence and stealth of one man; in an aristocracy might can refer most likely to the power of the wealth of the few. But in a democracy, especially the ancient participatory democracies, might can refer to the collective consent (by vote) of the citizens who are both rulers and ruled. We might object to the might of violence and stealth creating justice; and to the might of wealth creating justice. But would we similarly object to the might of citizens creating justice by legislating for themselves?

In sum, we see that Plato presents Thrasymachus' conception of justice as a reasoned view of what justice is, put together by successive elucidations of who is the stronger (first, actual rulers, and then actual rulers who make no relevant mistakes), by the positivist assumption that justice is constituted by the positive laws of states, and by an allegedly true empirical generalization that legislating rulers in all states enact laws to their own advantage. Thrasymachus' formula of justice is the conclusion from all three these premises; and since one of them is clearly an empirical generalization, we can see that this part of Thrasymachus' view depends on an empirical investigation of actual laws; in that sense Thrasymachus' method for discovering the nature of justice is empirical.

Seeing clearly the argument and the method by which Thrasymachus reached his formula of what justice is enables us to avoid confusions and to assess the formula critically, by examining its basis, the premises and the reasoning by which the conclusion is reached. We can tell, for example, how one premise, the empirical generalization, might be confirmed or shown to be false by examining the legislative practices of each state or form of government. Socrates' disputing of the positivist assumption is fruitful too. By treating laws as means to ends and appealing to human fallibility about means to ends, Socrates opens up some logical space between positive law and justice – we can't, and don't want to, suppose that laws are always just, no matter what ends laws are supposed to serve. Our empirical political scientists can still do interesting empirical investigations of the justice embedded in each form of government, but it has to be on a weaker assumption, that what a state (or its leaders) *thinks* justice is can be found in its constitution and laws, an assumption that leaves it open that a state (or at least its rulers) might be mistaken and its justice is really injustice. Thrasymachus' super conclusion, that justice is the interest of the ruling party, will never follow from such an investigation; but at most, that what is *thought* everywhere (at least by rulers) to be justice turns out to be the interest of the ruling party – a disturbing enough conclusion. By opening up some logical space between justice and positive laws Plato was able to dispute the justice of many existing positive laws even if they were universally present in all societies. And this opened the way for his more open-minded investigation of justice in the rest of the work.

It is also important to see clearly what has remained unchallenged by Socrates' refutations: the empirical generalization that actual rulers make laws to their own advantage. Even it is not always true, but true only too often (as Aristotle confirmed), it poses a recurring political problem: how to guard against abuses that result from the combination of self-interest (natural to all human beings) and political power. Plato's rigidly controlled educational programs, and his radical proposals of a complete divorce of political power from private property and even private family in his ideal city, show that he was acutely aware of this fundamental political problem still to be solved.[11]

3   Is [the] Justice [of Thrasymachus] Good for Me?

This question,[12] which drives the *Republic*, makes its first appearance in Thrasymachus' heated defense of his view (*Republic*: 343a–344d) against Socrates' argument from analogy. First, he brings up a counter analogy, the art of the shepherd: "in politics the genuine ruler regards his subjects exactly like sheep, and thinks of nothing else, night and day, but the good he can get out of them for himself" (343b). Socrates is so naïve, he says, that he does not know that "justice and the just are in reality the other man's good – the advantage of the stronger and the ruler and harmful to the one who obeys and serves." (243c)[13]. Further, "the just man always comes out at a disadvantage in his relations with the unjust": first, in the dissolution of a partnership the just man always comes off worse than an unjust partner; then, in paying taxes the just will contribute more from an equal estate than the unjust; and even when he holds office the just man will let his affairs go into disorder, make no profit from his office, and will displease his friends by his unwillingness to serve them contrary to justice, while to the unjust office holder all the opposite advantages accrue (343e).

Finally, he says that the easiest way to see how much more profitable it is to be unjust rather than just is to consider injustice on a large scale, a "complete [or perfect] injustice" which makes the wrongdoer "most happy": this is tyranny, "which both by stealth and by force takes away what belongs to others, both sacred and profane, both private and public, not little by little but at one swoop" (344a). Unlike small-time lawbreakers who usually get caught and punished, tyrants, in addition to taking the property of citizens, "kidnap and enslave the citizens themselves," and when they do that "they are pronounced happy and blessed ... For it is not the fear of doing but of suffering injustice that calls forth the reproaches of those who revile injustice. Thus, Socrates, injustice on a sufficiently large scale is a stronger, freer, and more masterful thing than justice, and as I said in the beginning, the just is the advantage of the stronger, while the unjust is what profits oneself and is his advantage" (344bc).

Some readers have thought that in this speech Plato has Thrasymachus change his mind or be inconsistent about what justice is, his remarks on tyranny being the chief evidence. On his view, how can the tyrant be unjust, indeed the most unjust of men, and tyranny the complete or perfect injustice?[14] As we have seen in Thrasymachus' earlier remarks, the tyrant's laws, at least when he makes no mistakes in legislating to his own advantage, constitute justice, no less than aristocracy's laws or democracy's laws. But if the tyrant is the most unjust, we seem to have the paradox of the most unjust of men enacting laws, even when not making relevant mistakes, which constitute justice. How can the greatest injustice, by its own operation, produce its opposite, justice?

I think it would be a grave flaw in our author, Plato, if he had Thrasymachus change his account of what justice is, or present him as having an inconsistent account of what justice is, without adequate reason. And no adequate reason has been given for the present imputed change or inconsistency. When earlier Socrates found an inconsistency in Thrasymachus' account, Plato has Thrasymachus explicitly modify his view, to a ruler who makes no mistakes, to avoid it. Plato has given no signal of any new inconsistency, and indeed he has Thrasymachus reaffirm his original formula of what justice, as the advantage of the rulers, is at the end of this speech (344c).

Still, we have a good question about Thrasymachus' present remarks on the injustice of tyranny and tyrants. I think Thrasymachus' view has room for an adequate answer without inconsistency. First, we notice that Thrasymachus' view is elliptical on an important point: are rulers subject to the laws they make or are they above the law? Well, Thrasymachus can give a variable and probably true answer to this question: in democracies rulers are subject to the laws, in aristocracies perhaps not, and in tyrannies for sure not. In participatory democracies the citizens are both rulers and ruled (both at once in the Assembly, rulers by rotation in the Council and by lot in Jury Courts); since there is no (at least permanent) distinction between rulers and ruled, the laws apply to all (at least citizens) equally. But in tyrannies some are rulers and some subjects; none are both at once, and ruling is not available simply by being a citizen, by elections, or by rotation and lotteries; the tyrants make laws for their subjects, not for themselves. If so, tyrants cannot be unjust by breaking their own laws, the laws they have themselves enacted without mistakes; the laws do not apply to them; they are above the law. But that still leaves it open that they became unjust when they were subjects and trying to become tyrants, by breaking the laws of the existing regime, be it the laws of democracy or aristocracy or even another tyranny. And this is just what the text suggests (344b): men become tyrants by breaking the existing laws on a large scale – taking citizens' property and enslaving them – and getting away with it by "stealth or violence." Would be tyrants become unjust in the same way as anyone else becomes unjust in Thrasymachus' view: by breaking existing laws in one's society (Polus' portrait of a tyrant is essentially the same, in *Gorgias*: 471ad).

The difference from ordinary subjects who break existing laws is that future tyrants do it on a large scale and get away with it – successful injustice with the greatest prizes: property and wealth, power, freedom from others' rule, and even newly found praise and admiration by citizens and foreigners alike. These, on Thrasymachus' view, are the great good things of life, the possession of which makes a man happy. In the opening pages of Book IV Socrates will challenge the importance of these goods and this account of happiness, and disagreements about goods and happiness will be put in play in addition to the disagreements about justice.

Within Thrasymachus' view we must always keep in mind that unjust conduct by a citizen can be nothing but conduct contrary to the positive laws of his country, and just conduct nothing but conduct consistent with the existing positive laws. This is a direct implication of his legal positivist assumption. The injustice of the tyrant has to conform to this.

Socrates goes on to dispute Thrasymachus' analysis of the shepherd analogy and defends his argument by analogy, by making a distinction between the function of an (presumably idealized) art and the need or desire of the practitioner to make a living by practicing it; a physician might practice medicine in order to make a fortune, but this motive is not to be confused with the function of medicine – to heal and maintain health; even in this case the physician excels by healing, not by making money, even if he does make lots of it. A good physician is one who heals well, not one who makes a fortune, even if the two were perfectly correlated – which they are not. Similarly with ruling: the function of ruling is to promote the good of the subjects of ruling, not the rulers, even if many actual rulers go into it to benefit themselves. In "a city of good men," Socrates famously says, "immunity from office-holding would be as eagerly contented for as office is now" (347d).

But Thrasymachus' praise of injustice and his great admiration of the complete injustice of tyrants shift the dialogue to the other great issue of the *Republic*, the benefits and evils of justice and injustice. "This point then I by no means concede to Thrasymachus, that justice is the advantage of the stronger. But that we will reserve for another occasion. A far weightier matter seems to me Thrasymachus' present statement, his assertion that the life of the unjust man is better [for one] than that of the just" (347e).

Asked to say which is true and which he would choose, Glaucon replies that the life of justice is the more profitable, implying apparently that the choice between lives should be made on that ground. But how are they going to decide which is the true answer? One way, Socrates points out, is to "count and measure" all the goods that go with the life of justice, and all the goods Thrasymachus has listed on the side of injustice, in two set speeches; but then, he says, they would need judges to say which side won. He might have added that while counting the goods on each side might be contentious enough, measuring them would be even more difficult; they might measure wealth and property, but how would they measure and compare with each other power, freedom, health, peace of mind, and pleasure?[15] The alternative method, which Glaucon now chooses, is to proceed as before, Socratically: by question and answer and by using as premises in arguments only what is admitted by the participating interlocutors (*Republic*: 347e–348b).

Now it is no surprise to hear Thrasymachus say that the life of injustice is more profitable than the life of justice, especially injustice on a large scale and provided one gets away with it. From his reformed formula of what justice is, the advantage of the stronger (actual rulers who make no mistakes), we can infer directly that the subjects' being just is to the interest of actual rulers who make no mistakes; to the subjects themselves being just is no advantage, since being just means obeying the laws of the rulers who enacted those laws so that obedience to them is to the rulers' advantage. Though there may be cases where the subjects obeying such laws is to the advantage of both rulers and ruled (say, on safety and war issues), Thrasymachean laws have been designed to favor the rulers; so that in cases where the interests of the rulers and the ruled conflict – on divisions and distributions of property and wealth, paying taxes, and cases of relatively scarce resources – the subjects' just conduct will be to the advantage of the rulers and the detriment of the just subjects. Correspondingly, in all such cases, the injustice of subjects will be to their advantage, provided they can get away with.

Moreover, it is likely that the larger the injustice the greater the advantage gained; hence Thrasymachus' admiration for large scale injustices and the intelligence to get away with it, for the success of the would be tyrant in becoming a tyrant by force or stealth. Successful tyrants are Thrasymachus' heroes: they become tyrants by breaking the existing positive laws of their countries, they get away with their injustice, and get all the good things of life as a result.

But Socrates is surprised when he cannot get Thrasymachus to admit that justice is a virtue and injustice a vice. Had Thrasymachus admitted that, Socrates could have mounted an argument proceeding from the admiration generally felt for virtues to their benefits, and from the shame of vices to their bad results.[16]

> Is it likely, you innocent [Thrasymachus asks Socrates], when I say that injustice pays and justice does not pay? But what then, pray? The opposite, he replied. What, justice vice? No, but a most noble simplicity or goodness of heart. Then you call injustice badness of heart? No, but goodness of judgment. Do you also, Thrasymachus, regard the unjust as wise and good? Yes, if they are capable of complete injustice, he said, and are able to subject to themselves cities and tribes of men. (348cd)

This is a "harder stand," Socrates remarks, "and if you are going as far as that it is hard to know what to answer" (348e). Still, he tries bravely to refute Thrasymachus, once more relying on analogies between justice and the arts, such as music and medicine, to show that justice is a virtue and injustice a vice (349d–351a). Thrasymachus' unjust man admittedly tries to "outdo" or "overreach" both just men and other unjust men; but a musical man (an expert in composing or playing music) does not try to outdo other musical men but only unmusical men; and so with a physician; similarly a just man does not try to outdo other just men but only unjust ones. But the musical man and the physician are the ones who have knowledge and are good in matters of music or medicine; similarly then the just man is the one who has knowledge and is good in matters of justice, not the unjust man. So, justice falls under the head of knowledge and virtue, not injustice.

This is an argument by analogy and so cannot prove conclusively Socrates' conclusion. But even as an argument by analogy, it seems weak: the main notion Socrates uses, to outdo or overreach (*pleonektein*), can mean different things when applied to justice and the arts; Thrasymachus uses it to refer to getting and having more (than one's share, more than the just, and even other unjust men) of the good things of life – this is its standard use; whereas Socrates stretches its application to the arts to refer to outdoing or overreaching in the activities of healing or tuning a lyre. In the one case we have the notion of doing things well and doing them ill (the arts), in the other case we have the notion of not getting more good things (justice) and getting more than others (injustice). Moreover, the argument now puts in question what a virtue is, but fails to answer it: Thrasymachus and Socrates now disagree on what justice is and on whether justice is a virtue, but they and the reader may also be in the dark about what a virtue is. Plato perhaps signals the argument's difficulties by indicating that Thrasymachus is now admitting things he does not believe (350de).

Socrates next argues against another part of Thrasymachus' view that injustice is something "stronger" than justice (351a–352d). A city may be unjust in its relation to other cities and try to enslave other cities unjustly, Thrasymachus agrees, adding that this is what the best city that is completely unjust will do – now paralleling what he said about the completely unjust man. The question is, Socrates says, whether it is justice or injustice that enables a city, an army, a group of bandits, thieves, or any other group, to be successful in such an endeavor, or indeed in any action they attempt in common. He argues convincingly that if in any of these cases – city, army, group of thieves – the persons in it are unjust toward each other, they will fight and hate each other, whereas if they are just toward each other they will have harmony and friendship. But if so, injustice toward each other will make them less effective in their common endeavors, and justice more effective; it seems empirically true that internal dissent and conflict makes common endeavors more difficult while harmony and friendship makes such endeavors easier to carry out successfully (other things equal). So justice is stronger than injustice, in the sense that it is an enabling power, whereas injustice is a disabling quality.

Here, relative to any group of persons, we have a distinction between the group being just or unjust toward others outside the group and members of the group being just or unjust toward each other. Relative to city states, this, in effect, is a distinction between what we now call domestic and international justice.[17]

Socrates now applies the same distinction to an individual: an individual can be just or unjust toward others, but also just and also unjust within one-self – one part of oneself can be unjust toward other parts of oneself. And similarly to the group, injustice within oneself has similar effects to injustice within a group – it makes for inner discord and enmity and thus hinders any common endeavors of the self as a whole, whereas justice within the self makes for inner harmony and self-love and thus makes common endeavors of the whole soul easier and more successful. Inner justice, then, is a great enabling power of the individual – inner injustice a disabling quality.

This argument clearly foreshadows the division of the self in Book IV and the application of the concept of justice to one's soul as structurally similar to the application of the concept to a city state. But the question immediately arises: can one be unjust toward oneself, in the sense that one part of the self is unjust to other parts of the self? We might well concede to Socrates that there is such a thing as inner psychic conflict and inner harmony, and that such conflict makes individual successful conduct more difficult and inner harmony easier and more effective, other things equal. But this still leaves open the question whether justice can apply to the relations among parts of the self within an individual, as Socrates now supposes, or only to relations among individuals, as Thrasymachus and most of us assume.

Having argued that justice is a virtue and that it is something stronger than injustice, Socrates finally argues more directly that the just man is happy, the unjust miserable (352e–354b). To do so, he introduces fundamental new ideas that play a large role in the later constructive parts of the dialogue. Some things have a function, Socrates begins, and defines function (*ergon*) in a twofold way: the function of something is the work *only* it can do, *or* the work it can do *best*. For example, we can see only with the eyes, so seeing is the function of the eyes; we can hear only with the ears, so hearing is the function of the ears. Let us call these *exclusive* functions. On the other hand, we can prune vine branches with a saw or a dirk and with many other instruments, but with none so well as with a pruning knife made for that work, so pruning vines is the function of that kind of knife. Let us call such functions *optimal*.

Next, Socrates illuminates the concept of virtue (*arête*). He asks whether things with function don't also have virtues (or vices), gives the same organs as examples, and proceeds to characterize virtue and vice in general: a thing performs its function well by the virtue(s) appropriate to that kind of thing, and badly by the vice(s) appropriate to it. Thus, the virtue(s) of the eyes will be qualities that enables eyes to see well, of ears the quality that enables ears to hear well; and similarly with vices. Socrates is speaking abstractly, without committing himself to what the virtues of the eyes are; presumably, an ophthalmologist could tell us what in the structure and composition of eyes enables eyes to see well and what causes them to see badly. Thrasymachus agrees to this abstract theory without any show of reluctance.[18]

The theory does indeed illuminate the concept of virtue: if, for example, justice is a virtue, then according to this theory, we can suppose that it is a virtue of something with function(s), and a quality of that thing that enables it to perform its function well. The earlier dispute between Thrasymachus and Socrates, whether justice is a virtue, is now cast in a new light and it might have a new resolution.

The theory also might be helpful in discovering what, say, courage is: if we believe that courage is a virtue, first, we find out what it is a virtue of, say, persons; next we find what are functions of persons; then courage will be a quality of persons that enables persons to perform some of these functions well, and in its absence poorly. In Book IV we shall find that Socrates proceeds in this manner when he defines courage.

But here Socrates hurries along to apply the abstract theory immediately to prove to Thrasymachus that the just live happy lives, the unjust miserable. He assumes that justice is a quality of the souls of persons, not their bodies (353a–354a). He then claims that the soul has the exclusive functions of "living," managing, ruling, and deliberating, because only with the soul can we do these things. From the theory and these premises he concludes that the virtue(s) of the soul will enable the soul to do these things well, the vices poorly. Thrasymachus reluctantly admits that justice is the virtue of the soul, injustice its vice. And from the abstract theory and these premises Socrates concludes that the just soul will manage, deliberate, and live well, the unjust one badly; and the soul that lives well is happy and the one that lives badly unhappy.

4 Thrasymachus Unconvinced, Socrates Dissatisfied. What Has Gone Wrong?

Plato portrays Thrasymachus at first as saying boldly only what he believes and Socrates uses only such admissions as premises in his arguments – thus satisfying a rule of the Socratic method (the part of it called *elenchus*) of examining oneself and others about how we should live (the "say only what you believe" rule). But eventually Plato has Thrasymachus challenge the rule (349a): "What difference does it make to you, he said, whether I believe it or not? Why don't you test the argument [rather than me]? No difference, I said." Thrasymachus challenges the rule again (350e), and though Socrates protests, he gives answers "to please" Socrates and counter to his own beliefs. And when Socrates finally concludes that injustice cannot be more beneficial than justice, Thrasymachus says to him sarcastically: "Let this complete your entertainment, Socrates, at the festival of Bendis" (354a). Since Thrasymachus does not believe some of the replies he gives to Socrates, and since Socrates uses these replies as premises in the arguments against him, we can understand why Thrasymachus remains unconvinced. Whether Plato is thus indicating that rational discussion with Thrasymachus about justice and its benefits has broken down and come to an end is more controversial.[19]

But, as it turns out, Plato portrays Socrates himself as being dissatisfied with his own performance (at least some of the arguments), though for different reasons. He says that, like a glutton, he rushed to discuss whether justice is a virtue, and whether it is better than injustice, before finding out "the first object of the inquiry, what justice is." "So that for me," he continues, "the present outcome of the discussion is that I know nothing; for if I don't know what justice is, I can hardly know whether it is a virtue or not, and whether its possessor is or is not happy" (354bc).

This is just what happened earlier: Socrates remarked (347e) that he still disagrees with Thrasymachus on what justice is, but he will leave that for another occasion and take up the issue whether the life of the unjust man is better than that of the just (as well as whether justice is a virtue). Now Socrates says that he was mistaken to take up these other issues before "the first object of the inquiry" – what justice is – was completed. We notice at once that this fault lies not with Thrasymachus: *he* did things in the right order of investigation: first he gave an account of what justice is and then proceeded to argue that injustice is better for (some of) us. But Socrates failed to proceed similarly: to first give his own account of what justice is and then argue the issues of the benefits of justice. Socrates is dissatisfied with his own procedure, and we can see that he is correct, by reflecting on his last argument for the conclusion that the life of the just is happier than the lives of the unjust. What is the life of justice that Socrates is arguing about here? Socrates himself has so far given no account of what justice is. We cannot suppose that Socrates was arguing that justice *according to* Thrasymachus (i.e. the advantage of the rulers) is a virtue and that it makes its possessor happy, since Socrates does not think that this is what justice is (nor can we attribute to Socrates the accounts of what justice is by Cephalus or Polemarchus, since he disagrees with them as well). As far as a reader is concerned, it looks as if Socrates has been arguing that justice, *whatever it is*, is a virtue and makes its possessor happy. But how could anyone possibly show or know *that*?

Socrates' last argument has been criticized also for using the notion of "living well" ambiguously: it can mean living successfully – attaining one's ends – or living according to the virtues; happiness is more likely the former, but the argument needs to show the latter. This is an important point, and it may signal different concepts of happiness at play. But it is not what Socrates is complaining about; and his complaint is more fundamental.

Further, Socrates' own dissatisfaction here is not unfamiliar to readers of Plato. In the opening lines of the *Meno*, for example, Socrates implies that we cannot know whether virtue can be taught without first knowing what virtue is. What virtue is, is "the first object of the inquiry" about virtue. Similarly, what justice is, is "the first object of the inquiry" about justice. We shall find that in the next major theory of justice, Glaucon follows this rule of the order of investigation; and when Socrates starts his own constructive efforts, he too follows the rule: what justice is takes up Books II, III, and IV, before the next question of the benefits of justice is argued.

We must notice, however, that Socrates' dissatisfaction does not extend to his arguments against Thrasymachus on what justice is, or to the abstract theory itself of function and virtue, or the ideal embedded in that theory, of a well-functioning living thing. We shall find that this abstract theory is employed later, in a more successful application, to find out what justice and the other virtues are.

Notes

1 The classical example of a normative theory by a list of rules is found in Ross (1930). The theories of justice of Thrasymachus, Glaucon, and Plato provide for such greater generality. For an interesting parallel see Rawls (1971: chapter I, section 7 on Intuitionism and section 8 on The Priority Problem).

2 See Plato's later choices of subject matter for justice, and Rawls (1971: chapter I, section 2).

3 See Glaucon's theory for the role of justice, and Rawls (1971: chapter I, section 1).

4 Aside from Socrates' criticisms, Polemarchus' theory of justice is grossly incomplete: there are many people in my society, and beyond that in the world, who are neither my friends nor enemies; clearly I can treat such people justly or unjustly, but Polemarchus' theory is completely silent on this point.

5   See Allen (2006: ix–xv) for an excellent discussion of the political problem of faction, how Plato's Thrasymachus poses it, how the American Federalists accepted Plato's analysis of the problem, but rejected Plato's solution of eliminating the causes of faction, and how they opted instead for controlling its effects.

6   Cephalus gave no argument for his view; it may have been simply a generalization from his experience. Similarly, his son Polemarchus gave no argument, but simply cited a poet in support of his view.

7   See Allen (2006: ix) who thinks that Justice O.W. Homes adopted legal positivism from Plato's Thrasymachus

8   Ancient participatory democracies are very different from modern representative democracies. We cannot say, for example, that in modern representative democracies the poor rule, as Aristotle could plausibly say of ancient participatory democracies. See, for example, Miller (2007).

9   See Aristotle, *Politics* (Book III, chapter 6), and Barker (1946: xxxiii).

10   It may be instructive to reflect how different regimes, especially democracies, try to deal with such uncertainties, especially in the case of civil disobedience and conscientious objection. Socrates' own case of disobedience in the *Apology* and obedience in the *Crito* are a case in point.

11   This problem is elegantly pointed out by Allen (2006).

12   There are in fact several versions of this question debated in the book. First, there is the abstract question – is justice good for me? But this question needs interpretation, since several accounts of what justice is are being debated – what justice is at issue when we ask this question? There may be one answer for the justice of Thrasymachus, another for Glaucon's justice by rational agreement, another for the theory of what justice is that Plato puts in the mouth of Socrates. For a different view, that this question is always the same – is what justice really is good for me? – see Penner (2004) and Santas (2003).

13   This passage shows quite clearly that Thrasymachus is speaking of the advantages or disadvantages of his own justice.

14   The importance of this question was brought to my attention by David Keyt. See also Allen (2006: xv–xviii) for another reading that Thrasymachus changes his view, to injustice now being the advantage of the stronger.

15   In the *Euthyphro* (7b6–7d11) Socrates implies that unlike many things, such as size and weight, the good, the just and the beautiful cannot be measured, and disputes about them cannot be resolved by counting, measuring, or weighing. In the *Protagoras* (356b–357a) he says that if the good is identical with pleasure the good can be measured. But Plato is not a hedonist, certainly not in the *Republic*. So counting, measuring, and weighing are not available, he thinks, to resolve the dispute about the goods and evils of justice and injustice. For more discussion of this see Santas (2006a).

16   As he does in *Gorgias*, 474d–475e against Polus; see Santas, *Socrates* (1979: 233–40) for a detailed discussion. The arguments from the admiration of

justice are also disputed by Callicles; and Adeimantus provides a different explanation for this admiration, in his own speech right after Glaucon's speech.

17 In *A Theory of Justice* (1971) Rawls presents a theory of domestic justice, in *The Law of Peoples* (1999) a theory of justice among nation states. See also Barry's *Theories of Justice* (1989: 3–9). There are some passages discussing relations among states in the *Republic* but the theory of social justice put forward is clearly a theory of what a just state is, not a theory of international justice.

18 For more detailed discussion of the functional theory, see Santas (2006a).

19 See J. Lear (2006).

3

Justice by Agreement. Is It Good Enough?
The Challenge of Plato's Brothers

The speeches of Plato's brothers, Glaucon and Adeimantus, enrich the *Republic* remarkably. Glaucon reopens the debate on what justice is, and gives a major new answer different from Thrasymachus: the fundamental principle of justice is a rational agreement not to harm others in exchange for not being harmed by them. He also sharpens the question, whether justice is better for us than injustice, with a new classification of goods, and supports a negative answer with thought experiments. Adeimantus rounds out the theory by explaining the high reputation of justice in a new way that seems compatible with the alleged advantages of injustice. Plato thus uses his brothers to introduce new ideas and methods into philosophy and to give major alternative answers to the views his Socrates will put forward. But Plato's brothers are presented as reluctant advocates of injustice; they want to believe that justice is something we have good reason to want and to prefer to injustice, and they challenge Socrates to show them that this is so. When Socrates builds his own theory of justice they become friendly interlocutors. But they are not afraid to raise important objections and play devil's advocate – Plato's own devices for dealing with readers' anticipated objections.

1 What is Justice? Glaucon's Theory of a Social Contract

Social contract theories of justice had hardly been born when Plato wrote the book. In one short paragraph Aristotle attributes one to the sophist Lycophon (*Politics*, Book III: 9, 1280) and its significance seems to escape him. It took some twenty centuries for such theories to make a significant re-appearance, but then they had a most fruitful run from Hobbes to Rawls.

It is not easy to say how far Plato appreciated the theory he puts in the mouth of Glaucon. The brothers' speeches take up some eleven pages (357–68), but only two paragraphs are devoted to the question of what justice is; the rest take up the second great issue, whether one is better off or happier being just rather than unjust, and the vast majority of the philosophical scholarship on these speeches is devoted to this second issue. Whether from ignorance, choice or art, Plato's statement of the origin of justice by social contract is very elliptical. The reader can see that for herself if she compares it to ch. III of John Rawls' *A Theory of Justice* (1971), which we can fairly say is a state of the art account of a contractarian theory of justice; on all the gaps in Plato's account noted below Rawls is quite explicit.

Of course Plato was a pioneer; he did not have the benefit of subsequent philosophy as Rawls and others did. But Plato's account is well worth our attention, not only because of its subsequent influence, but also because in the *Republic* it represents the major reasonable alternative to Socrates' theory of justice and the most plausible theoretical foundation for the democratic justice discussed in Book VIII. The Socrates of the *Crito* appeals to his agreement with the laws of democratic Athens to justify his refusal to escape from jail.

A contractarian theory of justice claims that justice is the object and the product of a voluntary and rational choice and/or agreement in a certain situation (later called a state of nature); and it usually supposes that before there is such an agreement there is no such thing as justice. Contractarian theories must have at least two main parts: the conditions under which the agreement or choice is made, usually called the circumstances of justice, and the content of the agreement (or the alternative chosen) that is reached voluntarily and rationally in the circumstances described. The conditions under which the agreement is made and the reasoning used to reach some agreement may be called the contractarian method.

Glaucon's account of justice is contractarian and it is usually so taken. He tells us explicitly that the first thing he is going to do is to give "the nature and origin of justice," and he starts with the origin:

> by nature, they say, to do injury is good for one, to suffer injury bad, but the bad of being injured exceeds the good obtained from injuring others. So that when men injure and are injured by one another and had a taste of both, those who lack the power to avoid one and do the other determine that it is in their interest to agree with one another neither to injure nor to

be injured; and this is the beginning of legislation and covenants among men, and they name what the law commands the legal and the just, and that is the origin and the nature of justice. It is a compromise between the best, which is to injure with impunity, and the worst, which is to be injured without the power to retaliate. (Republic: 359 (Shorey 1935))

Here we find the two main parts of a contractarian theory. Glaucon describes a state of affairs in which men presumably had no justice and they were injuring and harming each other and suffering injuries and harm. Glaucon seems to say (358a) that in that stateless condition men did do injustice to each other; but to avoid inconsistency we have to correct him, by supposing that he means harm or injury rather than injustice, something that can exist and be understood independently of justice;[1] or that men did what would later be called injustice. Glaucon also tells of the contract they made: each agrees not to injure others in return for a similar agreement by others not to injure him. The first part gives us the circumstances in which justice was created by agreement, and the second part gives us the content of this fundamental agreement. Though we can see here these two parts of a contractarian theory of justice in outline, many pertinent questions are not answered in our texts, and we can only try to make educated guesses about answers Plato would have given.

In the lawless state of nature, what was the environment like? Since it seems that men found it necessary to injure and harm each other, presumably as a means to getting the things they wanted (and not for its own sake, as the text might be read), we can infer that these things were not in abundance – that it was a state of moderate scarcity in the things men usually need and want. Perhaps it was a state represented by a zero-sum game: if we sum up all the transactions among men, voluntary or not, the gains and losses sum up to zero, and normally one man's gain is another man's loss. Some have suggested that it might even be a negative-sum game (since Glaucon says that "the bad of being injured exceeds the good obtained by injuring others," (359)).

And what were the human beings like in this state? Apparently they were self-seeking, whether completely or predominantly so (359c): each seeks the things which presumably he thinks he needs or wants or regards as good for him; including apparently injuring or harming others, at least as a means to getting what he wants, and apparently in the hope he will not be retaliated against, or that he can successfully repel retaliation and come out ahead.

So much for their circumstances and their motivation. But what of their capacities? Apparently, they were roughly equal; though some were stronger than others, the stronger were not so superior as to impose their will on the rest and establish ruling over them by force. Apparently, they were also minimally rational: at least able to learn from their experience in the state of nature (358e), and presumably were able to figure out effective means to their own ends and their overall good. Thus, moderate scarcity in the things they want, their self-seeking nature, rough equality, and minimal rationality, seem the minimum assumptions necessary to account for the conflicts among them and their stateless condition.

And what do they agree on? Glaucon says, "neither to injure nor to suffer injury." Apparently this means at least that each agrees not to injure others (to give up his freedom to do that) provided that others agree not to injure him (others give up their freedom to injure him).

Presumably they all give up the same freedom (to harm others) equally, in exchange for the same security (from being harmed by others) equally. Why would anyone agree to give up more freedom than others do, or receive less security? This equality of freedom and security is built into the fundamental agreement, and must be the equality Glaucon is referring to (359c) when he says that such equality is contrary to human nature who "seeks more."

Once men set up laws in accord with this fundamental original agreement, just conduct will be determined by such laws; and sanctions for disobeying them presumably can be expected to give to each the security of not being injured by others in return for the freedom each has given up.

And why would men make this agreement? Because they do not have the power to do whatever they please, including injuring others and avoiding retaliation; in such exchanges they too often lose more than they gain (358e). They have the freedom (in the complete absence of laws and their enforcement) but not the power. Once they experience this, they reason that they would be better off if they exchanged their freedom to harm others in exchange for security from being harmed by others. Relative to their circumstances, motivations, and experience, their decision seems rational.

This interpretation of Glaucon's account of the origin and nature of justice, though minimal, is still full of inferences from our texts. We inferred moderate scarcity, we supposed at least predominant psychological egoism, and suggested a zero-sum game. We assumed instrumental practical rationality – taking effective means to one's own ends and rationality about one's overall good. Further, we suggested that the equality referred to by Glaucon (359c) applies to the content of the agreement: the parties to the agreement all give up equally the same freedom in exchange equally for the same security. We softened the extreme emphasis on injuring or harming others – we described it as a perceived means to one's perceived good, not as something pursued for itself.

Even so, several important questions remain unanswered. In the state of nature, what alternatives did men have to choose from? Only the state of nature and what they ended up agreeing on? Why so? Social contract theory is open on what the alternatives are in front of the choosing parties. Even within the limited philosophical space of the *Republic*, we can imagine different principles of justice as alternatives, or different constitutions and forms of government: the parties could have considered Thrasymachus' principle of justice, Plato's own principle of social justice, as well as the one they actually agreed on. More concretely, they could have considered a choice among democratic, plutocratic, timocratic, even tyrannical constitutions. And if they had all these alternatives, they might have to use more complex reasoning to make a choice, and perhaps take into account odds as well as outcomes.

Was the agreement unanimous? This is an important question, since contract theories use rational choice or agreement (or both) in the circumstances of justice to explain why we should obey laws in civil society, at least just laws – laws consistent with the agreement. Thus Socrates in the *Crito* explains his obligation to obey the law of Athens (that the verdicts of the courts should be obeyed by the citizens) by appeal to his basic agreement, explicit or implicit, with the laws of democratic Athens. Unless the agreement were unanimous, those who did not agree would have no obligation to obey the laws made on the basis of the agreement; for them the theory would provide no answer to the question, why should I obey laws and be just?

Our texts say nothing of unanimity, though conceivably they imply it. One problem is that Glaucon says: "those who lack the power to do the one [injure or harm others] and avoid the other [being injured or harmed by them to even a greater extent] ... agree with one another " (359). This suggests that not everyone was in that situation of weakness: perhaps there were some who had the power to injure or harm others and get away with it. Why would they agree? Indeed, Glaucon considers this possibility: "anyone who had the power to do it [harm or injury and avoid retaliation] and was in reality a man would never make a contract neither to injure nor be injured; he would be mad" (359b). The difference between the strong and the weak in the state of nature does not seem to be reflected in their agreement of equality. We may have to suppose a two stage agreement: first, those individually weak agree among themselves for the reasons given; once they band together, being perhaps a considerable majority, they are collectively stronger than the few individually strong men, and then the latter find themselves in the weak position and also come to agree for similar reasons.

Glaucon's theory is incomplete in another important respect: the agreement provides terms only for non-aggression against one another. It says nothing about the distribution of other benefits and burdens of social cooperation. Are there to be any laws for the distribution of property and wealth, or are these to be left outside the reach of justice? What about the distribution of burdens, such as defense? And how is government to be arranged and political power distributed? Glaucon is silent on all these important issues; his theory is very minimalist, at least explicitly.

2 Glaucon and Thrasymachus on what Justice is: Results and Methods

Glaucon has given a very different account of the origin and nature of justice from Thrasymachus. In origin, Thrasymachus' justice can be created by force, but Glaucon's justice is created only by voluntary and rational agreement. Further, in Glaucon's theory, the fundamental agreement the parties make contains an important equality: they all give up equally the same freedom to injure others in exchange for equal security from being injured by others. Glaucon's justice is impartial, at least with respect to the freedom to harm others and the security from being harmed. On the other hand, Thrasymachus' justice, no matter what its origin, favors the rulers systematically – his justice is partial to the rulers and that partiality is built into the laws. These are enormous differences between these two conceptions of justice.

Moreover, while Glaucon says that just conduct is determined by laws made in accordance with this fundamental agreement of equal treatment with respect to freedom and security, his theory clearly leaves room for unjust laws: namely, laws not consistent with the agreement. Laws forbidding theft, property damage, bodily injury, and homicide – the standard kinds of harming others that the agreement presumably would forbid – would have to be written so as to apply to all the citizens, including whoever are rulers, without exception, and they would have to be administered accordingly, or else they would be inconsistent with the fundamental agreement and therefore unjust. Unlike the theory of Thrasymachus, there is no legal positivism in Glaucon's theory.

We can see how different the two theories are on the nature of justice by using Glaucon's contractarian method to test Thrasymachus' principle of justice. Suppose that in Glaucon's state of nature the parties have not only the two alternatives Glaucon gives them but also Thrasymachus' principle: their options are to continue in a state of nature, or to agree to give up equally the freedom to harm others in exchange for equal security from being harmed by others, or to agree to the principle that justice is the advantage of the ruling party. Which of these three options would it be rational for each of them to choose?

Clearly there is an obvious question that each party would need to ask about the third option, Thrasymachus' principle: in the ensuing society would I be a member of the ruling party or a subject? In a Thrasymachean society a member of the ruling party would be better off than a subject would be. Justice would favor him; whereas for a subject justice would be, as Thrasymachus says, "the other person's good," the other person being a member of the ruling party (343c); and this would be true for all three constitutions – aristocracy, democracy, tyranny – as Thrasymachus conceives them (even in a participatory democracy, presumably he would argue, there are permanent majorities (of the poor?) who rule for their own advantage).

Now, if a choosing party could not reasonably answer this question – either because of a veil of ignorance or because of too much uncertainty even without a veil – he could well reason that he would run the risk of being on the losing side of Thrasymachus' justice. If he ends up as a subject, he still might be better off in Thrasymachus' society than in a state of nature: for in that society there would be law and order, and so he would be protected from being harmed by some other men. However, he would still be prey to the stronger rulers: he would have to obey laws which systematically favor the rulers. But if he opted for Glaucon's justice, he would run no such risk: at least with respect to freedom and security, the laws would protect him as much as anyone else, no matter who he turned out to be (if making a choice behind a veil of ignorance), and no matter whether he ended up ruler or subject (if making a choice under normal uncertainty). Thus, under either uncertainty, a person would be better off choosing Thrasymachus' principle over the state of nature and Glaucon's principle over that of Thrasymachus.

On the other hand, if a person in the state of nature did know whether he would be member of the ruling party or be a subject, he would opt for Thrasymachus' principle in the former case and for Glaucon's in the latter; in such a case, unanimity on Thrasymachus' option would not be rationally possible – indeed probably only a minority of the stronger would go for it. With these three options – behind a veil, or ignorance, or under normal uncertainty – the rational choice would be Glaucon's justice; and with complete knowledge, there would be no unanimity on Thrasymachus' justice.

How far Plato considered this question – whether Thrasymachus' view on what justice is can be reached using the contractarian method – we can only conjecture. It is one of Plato's silences. But if we are correct in thinking that the answer is negative, we have one more reason not to attribute to Glaucon a defense of Thrasymachus on the nature of justice. On both content and method, the nature of justice is significantly different.

We can reach a similar conclusion by considering whether Glaucon would have reached his view of what justice is by using Thrasymachus' method. When Thrasymachus used that method, it will be recalled, he assumed that the actual positive laws of each city state determine completely what justice is in that state – the assumption of legal positivism; this assumption is what made his big empirical generalization – that in all societies rulers make laws to their own advantage – relevant to the nature of justice. Since laws in all societies have this in common, and the laws in each society determine completely what justice is in that society, justice is everywhere the same, the advantage of the ruling party.

Now if Glaucon had proceeded in Thrasymachus' way he could not very well dispute the positivist assumption, for that is integral to the method. Whether he would reach his own view of what justice is – that its fundamental principle is to restrict equally everyone's freedom to harm others and to protect all equally from harming each other – would depend on what the empirical investigation into actual positive laws of society discovered. If Glaucon conducted the empirical investigation – à la Aristotle – and found that Thrasymachus' empirical generalization is true in all states, then of course he would not reach his own view; even if he found Thrasymachus' generalization false in some cases, he still might not have found his own view true. Whether Glaucon would reach his own view of what justice is by using Thrasymachus' method is clearly a contingent matter: he might or he might not.

In sum, we can see that if we apply Glaucon's contractarian method to answer the question of what justice is, we would not reach Thrasymachus' result, and that if we apply Thrasymachus' method we might or might not reach Glaucon's result. This shows clearly that in this comparison at least, methods make a difference to the results, and that the results are indeed fundamentally different.

However, while there are these differences in methods and results on what justice is, Glaucon does agree with Thrasymachus on the other major issue: the benefits of injustice. Thrasymachus and Glaucon have the same conception of the human good embedded in their different theories of what justice is (freedom and power to do as one pleases, property and wealth, pleasure (343–4, 360–2)), and they share the view that injustice is a greater good to the unjust man than justice in circumstances of secrecy and deception favorable to the unjust man. This, in fact, broadens the targets that Plato sets up for refutation in the rest of the *Republic*: not only in the many systems of Thrasymachus' justice (Thrasymachean aristocracy, oligarchy, or democracy), but also, in the more egalitarian and seemingly fairer system of Glaucon, a citizen would be better off being unjust if he could place himself in such favorable circumstances. On the reasonable assumption that it would take high intelligence and courage to place oneself in such circumstances and carry out significantly profitable acts of injustice, Plato would be suggesting that in such systems the brightest and best would be only too tempted to lead a secret life of injustice (secret in Glaucon's story, secret or successfully violent in Thrasymachus'). Perhaps Plato thought that only by going to extremes, in his radical proposals on the institutions of his just city, could justice overcome such temptations.

3   Why should I be Just?

Thrasymachus, Plato's brothers, and Socrates might agree that I should pursue justice if justice is a greater good for me; and that I should pursue injustice if that is a greater good for me – these would be rational choices. It is hard to disagree with the idea that pursuing one's own good is rational. Whether justice falls under such a choice may be disputed by Kantians. But the ancients took it for granted. What the characters in the *Republic* disagree about (besides the nature of justice) is whether justice is a greater good than injustice. Socrates thinks it is and will argue repeatedly for justice in the rest of the work. Thrasymachus is convinced that injustice is the greater good if one can get away with it. And Plato's brothers think that most people will side with Thrasymachus on this issue, even in Glaucon's more egalitarian justice.

But what kind of good do these disputants have in mind? Do Thrasymachus, Socrates, and Plato's brothers agree on what are the good things of life and on their order of importance, and disagree only on whether the life of justice or the life of injustice has most of them? Or do they disagree also on what is good, on what are the major goods, or their order of importance?

Thrasymachus and Plato's brothers have different theories of what justice is, but similar views on the good things of life, and similar views on the relation of justice to these goods. Socrates, on the other hand, will argue for a very different theory of what justice is, but also for very different theories of what is good, on what are the good things of life, and their order of importance.

The *Republic* is a great pioneering work because Plato explores fundamental questions not only on what justice is and its relation to our good, but also on what our good is. Plato realizes that one cannot have a theory of what justice is without some assumptions or theory about what is good for human beings. This is already implicit in the theories of Thrasymachus and Glaucon: for both theories the need for justice arises from conflicts among men in pursuit of certain seemingly important goods, such as power, property and wealth, freedom and security; and their accounts of what justice is differ because they contain different solutions to the problem of the division and distribution of these goods. The good belongs in the dialogues of the *Republic* not only because of the debate about the benefits of justice, but also because justice itself cannot be understood without some view of what the good is. The good is sovereign.

The *Republic* is an important book also because, by a succession of deeper dialogues between Socrates and the other characters in opposition, Plato tries to show that these fundamental disagreements are amenable to human reason. We can disagree about fundamental ethical principles, about justice and the human good, but we can have rational dialogues about them and the possibility of discovering the truth or at least reaching rational agreement (see J. Lear (2006) for a different view on the disagreement, at least between Socrates and Thrasymachus).

Plato does not explicitly present his own view of the good till later. In Book II he has Glaucon open his challenge with a threefold classification of goods that Socrates accepts (357–358b). First, there is "a kind of good which we would choose to possess not for its results, but welcoming it for its own sake," for example, enjoyment and pleasures that are harmless and nothing results from them afterwards other than enjoyment. Then, there is a kind of good "that we love for its own sake and for the things that result from it," for example, understanding and seeing and being healthy. Finally, there are goods, such as exercise and being healed and the arts of healing and making money, which we would say are laborious or painful "but also benefit us," and which "we would not choose to have for themselves but for the sake of rewards and other things that result from them" (357cd). Glaucon's examples, especially the first two classes, are only illustrations of the kinds of good he characterizes; they are not necessarily the goods he uses in his theory of justice by agreement. Indeed these particular goods are Platonic – they are about human faculties or capabilities and their uses – and do not figure significantly in the rest of the brothers' speeches.[2]

Glaucon uses this classification to sharpen the dispute about the benefits of justice: "In which of these classes [of goods] do you place justice?" In the "most admirable," replies Socrates, "that which a man who is to be happy must love for itself and for the things that result from it." And Glaucon shows how the issue is now joined: "the many," he says, do not think so, but place justice under the laborious kind of good, "which is to be practiced for the sake of rewards and good reputation, but for itself to be avoided as being disagreeable" (358a).

Glaucon opens this issue with the remarkable statement that the justice that is created by rational choice and agreement is a compromise between "the best, to injure with impunity, and the worst, to be injured without the power to retaliate" (359a). The worst is easily understandable. But why is the best to injure with impunity? Glaucon's theory need not suppose that generally men injure others for its own sake or because they enjoy it – that men are evil or sadists. They are self-interested, in pursuit of relatively scarce resources, and, more likely, they injure others as a (perceived necessary) means to get more of the scarce goods they want. The parties to the agreement think that the best state of affairs for each is to have the freedom to do whatever he pleases, including injuring others with impunity if necessary to get what he wants. They prize freedom to do as one pleases without any restriction – complete freedom as it were – as their greatest good, provided that it is accompanied by the power to avoid retaliation, and more generally the power to avoid being injured by others. Thus freedom, power, and security (from being injured) are the greatest goods they prize. And it is the lack of power, and consequently of security, in their lawless state of nature that motivates them to choose rationally and to agree to exchange some of their freedom in the state of nature for security in civil society.

What kind of goods these are within his own classification, Glaucon does not say. They have the look of major instrumental goods. He does, however, claim again and again that justice is regarded as only an instrumental good, which "all who practice do so with reluctance, as something necessary and not as a good"[3] (358c, 359b); and famously offers the story of the ring of Gyges and a thought experiment to prove it.

A shepherd, an ancestor of Gyges, the story goes, found a ring which made him invisible when the turned the collet inside. After he confirmed this power of the ring, he managed to be sent to the court, and there "he seduced the queen and with her aid set upon the king and slew him and possessed his kingdom" (360a). And the thought experiment:

> If now there should be two such rings, and the just man should put one on and the unjust the other, no one would be found, it would seem, of such diamond-like strength as to persevere in justice and endure to refrain his hands from the possessions of others and not touch them, though he might with impunity take what he wished even from the market place, and enter into houses and lie with whom he pleased, and slay and loose from bonds whomever he would, and in all other things conduct himself among mankind as the equal of a god. And in so acting he would be no different from the other man, but both would pursue the same course. This is a great proof, one might argue, that no one is just willingly, but only from constraint, in the belief that justice is not a good to him; because every man, when he believes he has the power to do what is unjust [with impunity], does what is unjust. (360bc)

Now, in reality, there are no such rings, and so no such experiment has been performed or is forthcoming. What Glaucon gives us is a thought experiment, an experiment in "the laboratory of the mind," as Shields (2006) puts it. So how can it be a "great proof" that justice is only an instrumental good, or that men practice it not for its own sake but reluctantly to avoid punishment? Several *actual* experiments with the ring or its equivalent, in which a variety of both just and unjust men did in fact behave as Glaucon's thought experiment predicts, *would* be a great proof that men regarded justice as an instrumental good, not desirable for itself, and necessary only because they lacked the power to do whatever they wanted. But Glaucon's thought experiment is just that, an item of imagination, which might or might not be true of reality, or might be true of some men and not others – true of Thrasymachus, not true of Socrates, perhaps not true of Plato's brothers. Who knows?

Still, the thought experiment does touch hands with reality. Invisibility stands for undetectability, and the power of the ring to make one invisible stands for the ability to do something without being found out. And men do have the ability to do some things without being detected, at least some of the time, and some men have it more than others. So, though the ring is pure magic and the story perhaps wishful thinking, there is in reality something like the ring: men in reality can and do, at least on occasion, behave with the knowledge or at least probable belief that they might do something unjust and not be found out. The story and the thought experiment differ from reality in taking the possibility of doing injustice with impunity to its logical limit, as it were, being able to do it always and at will.

And this is some of their relevance. Unlike real cases, in which the risk of detection can be high and never completely absent, the thought experiment completely separates acts of injustice from detection and punishment. By separating these two circumstances it allows us to separate two motives that are never completely separated in reality, the desire for justice and the fear of punishment (Shields 2006). If there were no possibility whatsoever that my injustices would be detected and punished, would I still desire to do what is just and be a just man? Why would I? Why would I want to be just in such circumstances?

This is Glaucon's challenge to Socrates, and Socrates has to meet it since he claims that justice is to be desired also for itself, and not only as a means to security (from being injured, retaliated, or punished). But it is also Plato's challenge to us, the readers, to search our souls to see how we stand with justice. Do we stand with her even when there is no possibility of punishment for deserting her?

But Glaucon goes further. In a final thought experiment, the choice of lives, Glaucon portrays and compares two extremes: a man who *is* just but *seems* unjust, who is stripped of any rewards of justice or the reputation of being just, but also loaded with all the disapprovals and punishments of his false reputation for injustice; *and* a man who is unjust but seems just, who escapes all the disapprovals and punishments for his injustice but reaps its benefits and even wins the approvals and benefits of his false reputation for justice (360e–362d). Which life is better for us? Which would we choose?

Here Glaucon first separates the just man from the reputation of justice, because unless we do that "we cannot be sure whether he is just for the sake of justice or for the sake of the gifts and the honors [that the reputation for justice can bring]" (361c). So far this is similar to the previous thought experiment, except that it now separates the desire for justice from the desire for the rewards and honors (or offices) that the reputation for justice can bring (rather than the fear of punishment for injustice). And once more this seems a fair challenge for Socrates: do we desire justice for itself at all or only for the rewards of the reputation for justice?

But Glaucon also loads the just man who seems unjust with the most extreme punishments for his false reputation for injustice: "the just man will have to endure the lash, the rack, chains, the brandishing iron in his eyes, and finally, after every extremity of suffering, he will be crucified, and so learn his lesson that not to be but to seem just is what we should desire" (361e). Analogously, Glaucon's unjust but seemingly just man not only escapes punishments for his injustice, but is loaded up with all the possible rewards and honors that a reputation for justice can bring:

> first office and rule in the state, then a wife from any family he chooses, and giving his children in marriage to whomever he pleases, dealings and part-nerships with whom he will ... [he] is rich and benefits his friends and harms his enemies, and dedicates offerings to the gods adequately and magnifi-cently ... far better than the just man, so that he may reasonably expect the favor of heaven also to fall rather to him than to the just. (362c)

Plato has Socrates exclaim: "Bless me, my dear Glaucon ... how vigorously you polish off each of your two men for the competition for the prize as if it were a statue!" (361d). The people who defend injustice, Glaucon responds, would point to these extreme lives as evidence that the life of "perfect injustice" is better than the life of "perfect justice" and to be chosen over it. Can Socrates show otherwise?

Is this new challenge reasonable to someone who believes, like Socrates, that justice is good for itself and for its results? One would think that separating the just man from the fear of punishment (first experiment) and from the rewards of a just reputation (second experiment) would be enough to show that justice is desirable for itself if the man would still act justly.

But the very last experiment or hypothesis also loads up the just man with the most horrid tortures, punishments and death due to his false reputation for injustice. Even Socrates, a just man who seemed to the Athenian Jury unjust, did not have to suffer all that. Glaucon's last experiment portrays the most successful unjust man similarly; it separates the unjust man from the fear of punishment, but also loads him up with all the possible rewards of his false reputation for justice. But would this show that the life of injustice is *generally* better than the life of justice?

Glaucon's extreme unjust life would not be a possible life for most men. It would take extraordinary intelligence, great daring, and lots of luck to commit profitably large injustices and get away with it over a lifetime in one's society. On the terms of Glaucon's own view of justice by agreement, most (even all) men are better off in civil society than they would be in a state of nature, and most men are better off being just in their society. Glaucon's choice of the two extreme lives is limited by lack of generality. It seems unreasonable for me to prefer a life of injustice to a life of justice generally because in very unusual, unlikely, and lucky circumstances I might profit greatly by injustices and get away with it. At least it seems unreasonable if I am *any* man.

Glaucon might concede that the unjust life is not for the many, but might still claim that it is the best life for the few who have the societal equivalent of the ring, the ability to carry out secretly profitably large injustices, and the intelligence to successfully cultivate the deception of a just reputation. By being a successful combination of free rider and hypocrite, these few can reap the rewards of Glaucon's just society, security from being harmed, *and* the rewards of doing whatever they please beyond the limits of the justice they agreed to – they have the security of a just society and almost the freedom and power they had in the state of nature.

Plato, who does not have his Socrates cross examine his own brothers, may have cleverly hidden here a criticism of Glaucon's contractarian justice: in the city state which would result from Glauconian agreements, the best and brightest individuals would be dissatisfied and tempted to try to escape the bounds of the agreed upon justice; they would represent the strong in the state of nature and the least benefited by the original agreement. Glaucon's just city might be unstable. A justice that tempted the best and the brightest under it to act unjustly leaves something to be desired. But this implied criticism may be tempered somewhat by the minimalist character of Glaucon's contract: it restricts equally only the freedom to harm others, and says nothing explicitly about the distribution of political power, property and wealth, or the burdens of social cooperation such as defense and taxes. Aren't the brightest and best left free to acquire and secure more of these goods and bear fewer of these burdens?

In any case, the demand placed on Socrates by the choice of lives seems excessive for another reason. Socrates' view is that justice is good for itself *and* good for its consequences: this does not imply that the good of justice by itself outweighs the bad of all possible consequences of seeming unjust. Socrates need not show that one is better off being just no matter what the consequences, in order to show that justice is good in itself; he needs to show only that we would do what is just even in the absence of rewards and the fear of punishment. In a choice of lives the good of justice itself and the good of its consequences is to be compared to the good or bad of injustice itself and the good or bad of the consequences of injustice – this is the rational comparison. But Glaucon portrays a man who is just without any of the good consequences of justice (which even in his view justice has, namely security) and with all the bad consequences of injustice. He seems to challenge Socrates to show that *that* life is better.

Of course, to win the competition and give the prize to justice Socrates must explain what the good of justice in itself is, the good in the soul of the just man, aside from social rewards and punishments; in Glaucon's view there is none. Socrates will do that later, in the health analogy (Book IV) and in the theory of pure and genuine pleasures (Book IX). But he need not fear Glaucon's "great proofs" that injustice is better for us. Glaucon has no proofs. He has only thought experiments, hypotheses, and challenges for Socrates.

Plato's brothers' speeches serve Plato's purposes in another way. Plato is using the speeches to introduce a special case of a fundamental distinction he will use repeatedly in the *Republic*, between appearance and reality. The special case is the distinction between being just in one's soul and appearing just to others, and being unjust in one's soul and appearing unjust to others. This distinction makes it possible to attach social admiration and social rewards not to justice itself in one's soul but to the reputation for justice; and social disapprovals and punishments not to injustice itself in one's soul but to the reputation for injustice. Perhaps the admirations and disapprovals attach to the appearances to begin with, since we witness what can be thought of as appearances, speech and actions, not the souls themselves and the motives of the just and the unjust, their desires and thoughts; and we reasonably presume that the reputation and the reality usually go together. The distinction allows Glaucon to construct his thought experiments, to attach punishments and rewards to false reputations, and to portray his extreme lives.

The speech of the other brother, Adeimantus, takes up two questions or objections that can be made to Glaucon's praises of injustice, and answers them by using the distinction between the appearance and the reality of justice. First, if the life of injustice can be as wonderful as Glaucon's thought experiment and the perfectly unjust life make out, why is justice praised and injustice censured? "We must set forth the reasoning and the language of the opposite party, of those who praise justice and condemn injustice, if Glaucon [his praise of injustice] is to be made clearer" (362e). After citing poets and other writers on both sides of the question, Adeimantus argues that those who praise justice are really praising the reputation of justice, and those who condemn injustice are condemning the reputation of injustice.[4] Clever young men understand this and calculate accordingly that a life of injustice with a reputation for justice promises a "godlike life," and that it is "the seeming, as the wise men show me, that masters the reality and is lord of happiness" (365b).

But, the second objection goes, even the most successful of unjust arch-deceivers, one who manages to be most unjust and seem the most just among men, cannot similarly deceive the gods; the gods will know what he did and what he is and they will punish him accordingly. Adeimantus replies that there may not be any gods or they may not take any interest in human affairs. Even if there are and they do, the poets – the authorities on gods, Homer himself – tell us that the gods can be brought around by prayers and sacrifices (364e, 365e). So, "if we are just, we shall, it is true, be unscathed by the gods, but we shall be putting away from us the profits of injustice; but if we are unjust, we shall win those profits, and, by the importunity of our prayers, when we transgress and err we shall persuade them and escape scot-free" (366a).

The distinction between the appearance and the reality of justice (and injustice) has enabled Glaucon to work up his thought experiments and his extreme lives, and it has enabled his brother to explain the social praise of justice and the social censure of injustice. And while deception could not escape detection from the popular gods of the poets, the unjust man could still escape punishment by the human weaknesses of these same gods – their vanity, their need for worship and adoration. Here we see one reason why Plato re-conceptualized the Greek gods in his new canons of theology in Book II: Plato's god would not allow the unjust to escape punishment or reap the rewards of injustice, at least not in the afterlife.[5]

The distinction also serves Plato's purpose of drawing attention to the differences between just conduct, something that seems public and observable, and justice in one's own soul, which seems more fundamental than the conduct, providing the causes and motives of the conduct, and providing some assurance of just conduct in difficult circumstances. Cleverly, Plato puts in the mouth of his brothers the demand to show "what each of them [justice and injustice] is and what power it by itself has in the soul" (358b); "what each of them is by its own power in the soul of the one who has it ... no one has adequately set forth in poetry or prose – the proof that one is the greatest of all evils that the soul contains within itself, while justice is the greatest good [that the soul contains within itself]" (366e).

Some readers have thought that this is a most formidable demand, and wondered how Plato thought he could meet it. And it is. But it also serves Plato's belief in the *Republic*, that justice pertains to more than legal structures and conduct, perhaps primarily to the human soul itself. So his investigation into the nature and benefits of justice must and will go beyond civic constitutions; beyond just conduct, which can be deceptive; beyond rules of conduct, which can have exceptions; to psychic constitutions, the structures and the functions of the human soul.

Finally, the challenge of Plato's brothers serves to introduce, sharpen, and highlight Socrates' sustained dispute throughout the *Republic* with Thrasymachus' view of the human good, essentially the same view assumed by Glaucon's contractarian theory. Are power, freedom, security, wealth, and pleasure the chief human goods? Are these the goods of which possession would make us happy?

In the theories of Thrasymachus and Plato's brothers, it is conflicts in the pursuit of these goods that give rise to the need for justice, and it is in the pursuit of these goods that men commit injustice.

Some of the goods that Socrates will later explain and recommend to us make their first appearance as examples of Glaucon's threefold classification of goods. But it is remarkable that they are not at all featured in the rest of his story – they are conspicuously absent in the myth of Gyges and the thought experiment. Apparently nobody fights for knowledge in the state of nature or guides his life by it in Glaucon's society. Nor does being healthy, physically and psychologically, play a role in significant choices. And the pleasures of men with magic rings are anything but harmless. A significant theory of the human good – a list of major instrumental goods, or hedonism, or the satisfaction of desire – seems to underlie Glaucon's story. It is a theory that Plato attacks in several places (e.g., 421–2, 557–61, 575–87) in the rest of the *Republic*.

Notes

1   Some notion of good and harm must be independent of justice, since social distributive justice itself is concerned with the benefits and burdens of social cooperation. In any case, this is clear enough in Polemarchus' definition of justice as benefiting friends and harming enemies, and in Socrates' own view that it is never just to harm anyone.

2   For discussions of the threefold classification of goods see White (1984), Irwin (1995), and Shields (2006).

3   Presumably Glaucon does not mean to deny that justice is not good at all; only that it is not good in itself, since in his own theory men are better off in a just society than in a state of nature.

4   Interestingly, this neutralizes the way Socrates seems to prove the benefits of justice in his round with Polus in the *Gorgias* – namely, to infer the benefits of justice from societies' admiration of justice.

5   See McPherran's discussion of Plato's gods in the *Republic* (Santas 2006).

4

What is a Just Society?
Plato's own Social Ideal

We have seen Plato discuss two major theories of justice, which he thinks are mistaken alternatives to the view his Socrates will now develop – mistaken on what justice is and mistaken on the benefits of justice. We can read the *Republic* as an opportunity to understand three major theories of justice and an invitation to make a reasoned choice among them.

Plato's discussion of the theories of Thrasymachus and Glaucon makes an excellent introduction to his own view. We are now aware that there are several important answers to the question what justice is, and different constitutions and systems of justice that can embody different answers. We had a chance to consider different methods for answering this question, which might give us different results. We have learned that there are serious disagreements whether being just is good for us even when we can get away with apparently profitable injustice. We have discerned that there are deep disagreements about what is good for us and what our happiness is; and yet that to construct a theory of justice or defend it one needs some assumptions about human happiness and what is good for human beings. In his discussion of the first two theories Plato already has opened for us wide and exciting vistas of justice and the human good and has educated us in questions and problems we might encounter in understanding his own theory.

1   What is Justice? Socrates Divides the Question

Socrates is willing to make a new start into "the nature of each [justice and injustice] and the truth about their respective advantages," but cautions that "the inquiry we are undertaking is no easy one but calls for keen vision" (*Republic*: 368cd). Since we are not clever, he continues, "we should employ the method of search we should use if we, with not very keen vision, were bidden to read small letters from a distance, and then someone had observed that these same letters exist elsewhere larger and on a larger surface" (368d). Similarly, Socrates claims, justice is something that can be found in a city-state and also in an individual; the city is larger than the individual and justice in the city writ in larger letters than justice in the individual. So, as in the case of the inscription they would try to read the larger first and then inspect the smaller, so in this case they should try to find out what justice is "in states, and then only also examine it in the individual, looking for the likeness of the greater in the form of the less" (369a).

The analogy between justice in city-states and justice in individual persons is one of the fundamental building blocks of Plato's theory of justice. We shall discuss it here and also in the next chapter, as Plato does here, in Book II and again in Book IV.

The analogy is both suggestive and problematic. It suggests that the final goal of the inquiry is to find out what a just person is, but since justice exists in society as well, it would be easier to discover justice in the society and then in the individual. But why would it be easier? Perhaps because society and justice in it are more public and observable than the soul and justice in the soul. Only the individual herself can look into her own soul and observe justice in it, others cannot see into her soul; they can observe at most the individual's behavior which, as Thrasymachus and Glaucon made abundantly clear, can be deceptive. But presumably any and all can observe a society, its constitution and other institutions, and see whether it has justice in it. Society is larger and justice in it writ larger, though not literally (as in the case of the inscription), but in the sense of being public and observable and so more perspicuous to all. We shall find that Socrates was quite correct in this: parts of the soul, for example, are ghostly entities compared to parts of the city-state.

But reading the larger inscription, in a larger surface with larger letters, is relevant and helpful to the goal of reading the smaller one only if the larger is the same as the smaller. In the analogy itself we are told that someone "observed that these same letters [the letters of the small inscription] exist elsewhere larger and in a larger surface." But in the case of justice, how do we know that justice in the city is the same as the justice in the individual? Who observed that they are the same? Perhaps for the present the inscription analogy is only a guiding hypothesis, to be reconsidered and argue for later (Book IV).

But we have another fundamental question: in what way is justice in the city "the same" as justice in the individual? The analogy says that the letters in the larger inscription are the same. But if the larger inscription is to be relevant and helpful for reading the smaller one, not only the letters have to be the same, but the relations among the same letters have to be the same. A large page of large letters may contain exactly the same letters as a smaller page with smaller letters, but if the letters are arranged differently, the pages can have different – indeed very different – contents. So, the larger inscription has to have the same letters arranged in the same way as the smaller, or the smaller as the larger. Similarly, the analogy suggests, justice in the city and justice in the individual will have to have the same "parts" and the parts arranged in the same way. Let us say that, according to this analogy, a just individual and a just city are *isomorphic to each other* (structurally the same): they have at least similar parts arranged in the same way.[1]

Now Thrasymachus and Glaucon had talked about both just and unjust persons and just and unjust societies. They did not explicitly say how they thought of the relation between a just person and a just society. But it seems that in Thrasymachus' view a just person is one who obeys the laws of the stronger or the ruler in his society (an unjust person is one who disobeys the same laws (*Republic*: 338e)); in Glaucon's view, a just person is also one who obeys the laws of his society (359a), at least the laws that are consistent with the social contract. There is no hint of isomorphism here. In both of these views the concept of justice is applied first to society, defined for this case, and then a just person is thought of as one who obeys the laws of the just society as defined. This is one way to conceive of the relation between just society and just individual; and it is the dominant tradition in moral and political philosophy after Plato, especially the modern tradition from Hobbes to Mill to Rawls, whether the theory of justice is teleological or contractarian.[2]

Another way to relate a just person and a just society is to apply the concept of justice first to a person, define it for this case, and then conceive of a just society as a society composed of just persons as defined. Such a conception of a just society would be like a conception of a divine city as a city of angels: we define angels first then think of a divine city as a city composed of angels. It is hard to find significant writers who thought of the relation between just society and just persons in this way. And again there is no hint of isomorphism here.

But the way Socrates thinks of the relation between a just city and a just person – that the two are isomorphic to each other, like the two inscriptions – is different from these two. In Socrates' view neither just society nor just person is defined in terms of the other (by causal relations or the relation of composition): the isomorphism by itself does not imply that a just person is a person who has a strong and normally effective desire to obey the laws of a just society, nor that a just society is one composed of just persons (even though both might in fact obtain in a Platonic ideal society).

Plato's way of relating the two is in fact highly unusual, and may turn out to be highly problematic. In the other views there is only one standard of justice: in Thrasymachus' and Glaucon's views the one and only standard is a just society; in the other view, the one and only standard is a just person. But in Plato's view, there seems to be two standards of justice, a just society and a just person. And the isomorphism between the two does not seem to guarantee that the two standards will always coincide. Would a person who satisfied Plato's standard of a just person also satisfy his own standard of the just society s/he lives in? And conversely?

The inscription analogy, however, is suggestive in another way, which might help us with this problem. If we found two pages or two inscriptions, one larger with larger letters, the other smaller with smaller letters, but with the same letters arranged in the same way (and so with the same content or information), we would think it unlikely that it was a coincidence. We would consider it more likely that someone made a copy of one from the other, or both were copies in different sizes of the same master, or that both were written by the same person. Similarly, if we found a just society and just individuals in it, which were mirror images of each other with respect to justice, we would think unlikely that it was a coincidence. We would consider it more likely that the just society brought up and educated the individuals in it to be like itself in justice, or that the just individuals in it fashioned the society to be like themselves in justice. The isomorphic relation Socrates specifies does not by itself imply such causal relations, but they are compatible with it. A society might try to educate its young individuals to exemplify its ideals, and individuals might try to fashion their society, through constitutions and laws, to mirror the ideals in their souls. So the isomorphism together with the activities of educating and legislating might well solve the problem Socrates created by constructing two standards of justice. I believe that this is Plato's solution of the problem within his ideal city. Indeed, his program of early education in the ideal city (Books II and III) is designed to inculcate the virtues of cities and persons he later defines; and the program of higher education (Book VII) is designed to educate reason and the future rulers of the ideal city.

2   What is a Just Society? The Problem of Justice, and How Socrates Tries to Solve It

The analogy between just city and just person might guide Socrates and his friends later to discover what a just person is, but it is no help with what they have decided to start with, to discover first what a just city (society) is. How are they going to do that?

Plato does not tell us what method his Socrates will use. If we track his actual investigation from its starting point (367) all the way to his account of a just city-state (432), we can plainly see that there is no trace of Thrasymachus' empirical method, nor of Glaucon's contractarian method. There is also not a trace of a Socratic method we might extract from the earlier dialogues of definition: collecting some clear examples of just city-states or just persons, generalizing from them, and testing the generalization by further examples and by consistency with other firmly held beliefs.[3]

Yet we can hardly suppose that Plato reaches his specific results randomly or by sheer good fortune. Can we discover a method from what he actually does between his starting point and his definition of justice in a city state? Let us first follow what Socrates actually does in outline, and then try to figure out why he thinks what he did resulted in the discovery of justice in the city.

Socrates proposes that they begin by considering the origin of the city-state: "if we should observe a city-state coming into being in speech [discourse, imagination] we might also see justice or injustice coming into being in it" (369a). He then suggests that a city-state comes into being because each one of us is not self-sufficient but lacks many things.

> As a result of this, then, one man calling in another for one service and another for another, we, being in need of many things, gather many into one place of abode as associates and helpers, and to this dwelling together we give the name of city-state, do we not? By all means. And between one man and another there is an interchange of giving ... and taking, because each supposes this is better for himself? Certainly. Come, then, let us create a city from the beginning in speech. Its real creator, as it seems, will be our needs. (369c)

Glaucon agrees here that this and no other is the origin of the city-state. But there appears to be a deep contrast between his story of the origin of justice and Socrates' view.[4] Unlike the earlier Glaucon, who supposed the origin of justice to be found in individuals' *desires*, the scarcity of resources for satisfying them, and the consequent conflicts among individuals, Socrates suggests that the origin of the city-state is to be found in human *needs*, the fact that each individual is not self-sufficient to satisfy them, and in the resulting cooperation between them. In Glaucon's view, the need for justice is set up by human desires, scarce resources, and the consequent conflicts among individuals over these resources. This is the dominant tradition in modern times.[5]

But Socrates focuses on needs, which are not the same as desires: we may desire things we do not need, and we may have needs for things for which we have no desires. Need seems to be a more objective concept than desire, especially bodily appetite: a subject may be the best authority about what his appetites are, but medicine and biochemistry are far better authorities on what one's body needs. Needs, individual insufficiency to satisfy these needs, and the consequent rational desire for cooperation – these are Socrates' rational basis for creating city-states; and since Socrates thinks that he can discover the origin of justice by looking at the origin of the city-state, we can infer that he sees the problem of justice differently from Glaucon.

For Glaucon, the first question of justice is how best to resolve the conflicts that arise from desires and scarcity of resources desired, and his answer is: by each limiting equally his/her freedom to harm others (in the pursuit of resources) in exchange for equal security from being harmed by others. This is his fair solution to the problem of conflicts created by human desires and scarce resources. These conflicts, the scarcity of resources and the presumption of justice as equality[6] guide the solution.

But for Socrates the first question of justice may be: what is the best way to cooperate in order to satisfy human needs best, given what these needs are and the insufficiency of individuals to satisfy them each by himself? Given Plato's frequent analogies to medicine, he may think that desires, especially appetites, are not an objective enough basis for formulating the need for justice or for a solution to the problem of just distribution. And there is no presumption of equality to direct his solution.

It seems as if each approach is one-sided. We have both needs and desires, resources are not abundant for satisfying either, and in societies we both cooperate and compete for the satisfaction of needs and desires. It is noteworthy that John Rawls seems to take both sides into account.

Then, although a society is a cooperative venture for mutual advantage, it is typically marked by a conflict as well as by an identity of interest. There is an identity of interests since social cooperation makes possible a better life for all than any would have if he were to live solely by his own efforts. There is a conflict of interests since persons are not indifferent as to how the greater benefits produced by their collaboration are distributed, for in order to pursue their ends they each prefer a larger to a lesser share. A set of principles is required for choosing among the various social arrangements which determine the division of advantages and for underwriting an agreement on the proper distributive shares. These principles are the principles of social justice: they provide a way of assigning rights and duties in the basic institutions of society and they define the appropriate distribution of the benefits and burdens of social cooperation. (Rawls, 1971: 4)

In Rawls, the circumstances in which the problem of justice appears are the same as in Glaucon and Hume (Rawls 1971: 109–12); human desires and moderate scarcity of resources for satisfying them – we can satisfy them better by cooperation in societies, but then we need principles of justice to determine the distribution of the "greater benefits" and burdens of social cooperation. And for Rawls the problem of distribution is solved by the contractarian method of selection of distribution principles behind a veil of ignorance in the fair situation he calls the original position. But Plato does not use such a method in his own solution and certainly does not get the same results.

The view of justice Glaucon articulated earlier appears incomplete on the problem of distribution since it is silent on cooperation and the distribution of the greater benefits (and burdens) of social cooperation (such as property and wealth, political power, and other rights and freedoms besides the freedom to harm others). The view of Plato's Socrates so far also appears incomplete as a theory of justice, since it appears to be silent so far about human conflicts and competition and the distribution of the greater benefits of social cooperation. Glaucon's view of justice is not completed in the *Republic*. We will see that Plato's theory of social justice handles directly the problem of the distribution of political power; while the problem of the distribution of property and wealth is handled indirectly by what Plato thinks is required for the rulers, the defenders, and the providers to function well.

In rapid order Socrates (1) proceeds to list the economic needs for food, shelter and clothing, (2) proposes a division of labor for producing these goods, (3) supposes that human beings are born with different abilities for different kinds of occupations (what I call the "natural lottery assumption")[7], and concludes that "more things are produced, and better and more easily when one man performs one task according to his nature, at the right moment, and at leisure from other occupations" (370c). This general conclusion puts together two things: division of labor *and* matching labors to different inborn talents or abilities.

Socrates does not claim that each person can practice only one kind of occupation (as some readers have supposed and objected), but only that one cannot practice *well* more than one, given that different inborn abilities, education, leisure and timing are necessary for doing such things well. We see this point again (374), and again (394e): given that inborn ability, education, and time are required, "it is impossible that one can practice well many arts."

In these passages it is also clear that it is not minute division of labor that is at issue, as in Adam Smith's masterful discussion of the advantages of division of labor (1937: *The Wealth of Nations*, chs. 1–3), but division into the productive arts and sciences. In minute division of labor,[8] as in assembly lines of modern factories, inborn talent or ability may not be important (and Smith downplays it), since it is usually a single small task that each worker is required to do over and over; nor do these tasks usually require a lot of training or education. But Socrates is clearly talking about division of labor along trades, occupations, and professions. Here the natural lottery assumption gains in importance, especially for such occupations as music, mathematics, defending, governing, agriculture, architecture, building and even trading or business. Moreover far greater education or training is required to reach competence in these occupations and professions than what learning is required to do assembly line work well. Thus Socrates seems justified in the crucial roles he attributes to the natural lottery assumption and to education.

In successive passages Socrates expands the needs of citizens of his imaginary city, beyond provisioning themselves, to defending and governing themselves (373d–374e); tries to figure out what inborn abilities are best suited for doing each of these social tasks well (374e–376e); suggests a system for educating these several abilities (376e–415cd); proposes institutions of (no private) property and (no private) family for the citizens whose inborn abilities and education suit them to defend and govern (415–27); proposes functional ceilings and floors for wealth and poverty, and ends up by claiming that the city they have imagined, if they made no mistakes, is "completely good"(427e)[9].

He immediately infers from the city's complete goodness, that it is "wise, brave, temperate, and just" (427e). Finally, he proceeds to give an account of each of these four city virtues in the order just given, trying to catch in each case the particular good that each virtue contributes to the city. He ends up with the claim that the justice of the city is to be found in the principle of organization they started the city with. "For what we laid down in the beginning as a universal requirement when we were founding our city, this, I think, or some form of this, is justice ... that each man must perform the one social service in the state for which his nature was best adapted" (433a). The universal requirement clearly refers to the general conclusion he drew (370c), that the needs of the citizens would be satisfied best by each citizen doing that for which he is best suited by nature (and appropriate education).

3   The Functional Theory of Good and Virtue

Now why should Plato suppose that by proceeding as his Socrates did he would discover what justice in the city is? Why did he think the origin of the city was relevant to finding out what justice is? Why did he suppose that by organizing the city by division of labor and matching labors to inborn talents and appropriate education he would end up with a "completely good city"? Why could he infer from its complete goodness that the city had these virtues? And why did he think he could thereby discover the nature of each virtue?

I think we can find convincing answers to these questions in a procedure suggested by a theory Plato has Socrates expound and use at the end of the first book (352e–354c). We looked at it briefly at the end of chapter 2, and now need to discuss it more fully. It is fundamental to the main ethical and political ideas of the *Republic*.

The theory first gives an account of two kinds of functions: "the work (function, *ergon*) of a horse or anything else [is] that which one can do only with it or best with it"; and again, " when I asked whether that is not the work (*ergon*) of a thing which it only or it better than anything else can perform." (Shorey 1935: 353a). I call the first kind of functions exclusive and the second optimal. Socrates gives seeing as the exclusive function of eyes (since only with the eyes can we see), and hearing as the exclusive function of the ears (since we can see only with the ears); and he gives pruning as an optimal function of a pruning knife, since, he says, "we can use a dirk to trim vine branches and a knife and many other instruments ... but nothing so well as a pruning knife fashioned for that purpose" (353a).

Second, the theory proposes that there is (an) appropriate virtue(s) for each thing that has a function, and characterizes the appropriate virtue(s) of a thing with a function as that by which it performs its function well, and its vice(s) that by which it performs it poorly (353bc). Here we have a general characterization of the concept of virtue, which presumably would guide us when we try to find out what, for example, courage is. If courage is a virtue, it is a virtue of something with function(s) and it is a quality which enables that thing to perform that function(s) well.

Next, Socrates claims that this theory applies to "all other things" (presumably to all things with functions), and immediately applies the theory to prove to Thrasymachus that a just man is happy and an unjust one unhappy (353d–354a). We saw (ch. 2) that this immediate application proceeds by supposing that the soul has the exclusive functions of managing, ruling, and deliberating, and that justice is the virtue of the soul and injustice its vice; from the theory and these premises Socrates then concludes that the just soul will do these functions well, the unjust one badly, and that the soul that does these things well will live well, the unjust will live badly; and further that the soul that lives well is happy and the one that lives badly unhappy.

During this application Socrates adds to the theory: he says that a soul that has the virtues of a soul will be a good soul (and one that does not have them a bad soul), and that a good soul will perform its functions well, a bad one poorly (353e). Presumably, generalized versions of these two premises can be added to the theory: a thing of a certain kind (with functions) that has the virtues appropriate to that kind will be good of its kind; and a thing good of its kind will perform the functions of that kind well.

Arguably, in this application he also needs the assumption that functioning well is good for the thing that functions well, perhaps its chief good; seeing well, for example, is the good of the eyes, and anything that contributes to seeing well is good for the eyes.

I think we can see from the examples Socrates gives that the theory generalizes from practices, including evaluative practices, in medicine and the productive arts. The medicine of Plato's day had determined that the human body has a natural division of parts (especially organs, but also fluids, tissues, and bones – see the long discussion of the human body in the *Timaeus* (Cooper 1997: 72–9)) and a natural division of labor matched (or assigned by the divine craftsman in Plato's view of creation in the *Timaeus*) to those parts; eyes and ears are natural parts of the human body and each has a unique (exclusive) function matched to it; we can understand the human eye by understanding what that function is and by finding out what qualities, such as structure and composition, enable it to perform that function well. Further, we evaluate the human eye by how well it performs that function, and we can think of the qualities that enable it to perform that function well as its virtues. It is then a truism that an eye that performs its function as well as possible is a completely good eye and that a completely good eye has all the virtues appropriate to eyes (i.e. the virtues relative to that function).

The theory for human artifacts is the same, except that it uses the concept of optimal function: any artifact can be used for many purposes, but usually it is the best instrument (better than others) for the purpose or use it was designed for (rather than other uses); and it is good of its kind and functions well when it has the virtues appropriate to its function.[10]

The theory of function and virtue expresses an ideal: the ideal of a well functioning thing, whether natural or artificial, a living thing, a city, a ship or a house. Such things, the theory says, are best understood if we can discover their natural division into parts, the functions of their parts, the qualities that enable them to perform their functions well, and the things that cause them to malfunction. If we know all these things, then we can also determine when such things are good of their kind and what is good bad or bad for them, since the theory tells us that things with functions are good of their kind when they perform their function well; and also that whatever causes them to perform their function well is good for them, and what poorly, bad for them.

We must not suppose, however, that it is easy to discover what the functions of things are – the essential start of any application of the theory. The examples Socrates uses are obvious, and a deceptive familiarity with such examples may lead us to think that the functions of things are evident. Some things may not have functions at all, and for others their functions are major discoveries: the functions of the heart and the functions of leaves of plants, were both major discoveries in medicine and biochemistry, and are instructive examples. Not to speak of the recent major discoveries in molecular biology, in which structure and function play crucial roles. In all these cases it takes major expertise to discover functions and what enables things to perform their functions well. The same is true for discovering the virtues of things with functions. Even in Socrates' obvious example of the function of the eyes, it took major discoveries in ophthalmology to understand what enables eyes to see well.

It is also noteworthy that while Plato's definition of optimal function makes reference to design and presumably a designer, his definition of exclusive function makes no such reference. We need not know that someone designed the heart, nor with what purpose in mind he designed it, in order to discover the functions of the heart. Even with artifacts we might be able to discover their optimal functions, by experimenting to see what they can do best, without knowing a designer or creator of them and what he or she had in mind.

The functional theory suggests a procedure for discovering the virtues of objects of a given kind, on the assumption that such objects have functions: (1) find out what the functions of such objects are; (2) determine (by observation, experiment, or even thought experiment) cases where objects of such a kind perform their functions well and cases where they perform them poorly; and (3) finally find out the qualities which enable them to perform such functions well (and in the absence of which they perform poorly), and these are their virtues.[11]

And we can now see that this procedure accounts well for Socrates' major moves in trying to determine what justice in a city is. On the assumption that justice can be found in cities (as well as in individuals), he first tries to discover what the functions of such city-states are: to provision, to defend, and to govern themselves. Next he tries to organize an imaginary city-state so as to perform these functions as well as Socrates and his interlocutors can think of; by division of labor matched to a division of citizens by natural ability for these functions and suitable education. Finally, Socrates appropriately claims that if they made no mistakes in the way they divided, structured and educated their imaginary city (so as to perform its functions as well as they can think of), their city is indeed completely good. If it is completely good it has all the virtues appropriate to the city. And since justice is a virtue of city-states, their city will have justice, and now they can try to locate it among the qualities which enable their city to perform its functions well.[12]

We asked earlier why Plato thought that by following the procedure his Socrates actually does follow he would discover what justice is. We answered that he thought so because he had a very general theory, taken from medicine and the productive arts, which suggested a procedure for discovering the virtue(s) of anything with function(s). In turn, we can ask why he thought that this functional theory, whose logical home is the realm of natural organs and of artifacts, would be appropriate for discovering justice, a virtue whose domain is not natural organs and arti-facts but cities-states and souls. A good answer to this question is not easy to find, but its outlines may be partly in the *Phaedo*, partly in the *Republic* and partly in the *Timaeus*. In the *Timaeus* we have the postulation of a cosmic teleology, according to which a non-envious and good divine craftsman formed the existing physical universe to be as good as matter allows, using the Platonic forms as paradigms or patterns. The physical universe is generally the best it can be, and that is why Plato suggests in the *Phaedo* that the finest explanation of why things are as they are, on a cos-mic scale at any rate, is that it is best for them to be that way. When in a particular case they are not the best, as in the case of a defective eye or a rusted pruning knife, the fault is to be found in the nature of body or mat-ter. The physicians of the day had begun to discover, Plato thought, the natural goodness of the body (health) in the natural divisions of the body, the functions the natural parts served, and the structures that enabled those parts to function well; and this is to discover the ways the divine craftsman created the human body as best as it can be. Similarly with the astronomers and the celestial part of the universe; while human craftsman, such as architects and shipbuilders tried to discover and create, perhaps by imitation of the structures of the physical universe, structures that would enable their objects to be as good as possible and perform their functions as well as possible. Similarly perhaps, Plato thinks of legislators and educa-tors as trying to discover and enhance the structures in cities (and souls), which would make such cities (and souls) the best they can be and perform their functions as well as possible.

4 Plato's Definitions of Justice and the other Virtues of his Completely Good City

The three step functional procedure we described earlier is by no means complete. If, for example, a thing has many functions and many virtues, it does not tell us how to differentiate among its several virtues. Plato has indeed told us that the city (and the human soul) has several functions – provisioning, defending, and ruling itself; and so it may have several vir-tues. By Book IV, it has become clear that Socrates' investigation has been broadened beyond justice to all the principal virtues of a society: though he started with the inquiry about what justice is (and what its benefits are),

Socrates ended up with the claim that the city they built up is "completely good." So we have here a whole social ideal, not only the ideal of justice.

But if the city has several functions, which virtue accounts for the performing well of which function, so that the virtue can be characterized accordingly?

Plato takes up the virtues in a certain order: wisdom, courage, temperance, justice, and tries to define them in that order; supposing probably that it is easier to see which social functions wisdom and courage enable the city to perform well; that temperance is more difficult, and that justice is the remaining virtue after the others have been defined.

He has an easy time with social or political wisdom. The city is well counseled or well governed, he tells us, not necessarily if the city flourishes in other arts and sciences, but only if the rulers have knowledge of what is good for the city as a whole in its internal and external relations; given that the city exists and is organized for the benefit of all its members, not only the rulers, as Thrasymachus supposed and Socrates argued against (419e–421c). Thus Plato defines this virtue by three conditions: what it is knowledge of, in what part of the city it resides,[13] and what city function it enables the rulers to perform well (428b–429a).

This definition of social wisdom may seem non-controversial, close to the common sense view that those who govern a country need to know what is the public good or the common interest in order to govern well. Plato, though, tells us later, in Bks. V and VI, that knowledge of the good is very difficult and possible only for very few, very talented, and highly educated individuals. Knowledge of the good of society is far more difficult, he thinks, than is commonly supposed.

Plato proceeds similarly with the definition of social courage, using three corresponding conditions to define it. He takes it for granted that social courage, the courage of the city, must be the quality that enables the city to defend itself well. Further, assuming that not all of the inhabitants of the city defend the city or can defend it equally well, he further specifies that social courage must reside in those citizens who are best suited by inborn ability and appropriate education to defend the city well. Finally he tells us what social courage consists of, a cognitive and a habituated component: true belief taken from the rulers about what the city should fear and not fear, and the power (in the soul) to abide by that belief in all circumstances (429–430d).

This analysis of courage is less controversial than Socrates' definition of courage in the *Laches* and the *Protagoras*, as knowledge of what is to be feared in war or anything else, which accords with the Socratic view that knowledge of good and evil is sufficient for virtue. Knowledge is now replaced by true belief, which presumably can be instilled in the defenders by cognitive learning; and a non-cognitive element is added, a disposition to abide by this belief in all circumstances, something instilled by habituation and tests in dangerous circumstances. Even so, in requiring *true* belief, Plato is imposing a stronger condition than common sense requires for courage. Noteworthy is also the implied control of the military class by the rulers of the city. The courage of the soldiers is directed by the wisdom of the rulers.

Socrates' analysis of temperance (430d–432b) is even more complex. In earlier dialogues, especially the *Charmides*, temperance was considered as a virtue of individuals only, though even so it was highly uncertain about what it is, with no fewer than seven different definitions of it being examined in that work and found wanting. In the *Republic*, to give an analysis of social temperance, Socrates feels more secure to go to temperance as a virtue of individuals first, and then apply the concept similarly to the city, given that the analogy between city and soul is applied to all the virtues.

In individuals, he now thinks, temperance combines self-mastery and inner psychic harmony. Both of these notions presuppose that the human psyche or soul has at least two parts, one of which can be in control of the other. And since temperance is a virtue, he reasons, it must be that one part is better than the other (in some relevant respect), and the better is in control of the worse. Otherwise, why would it be better for one to control the other? Finally, the mastery of one over the other must be harmonious.

Socrates then applies the same concept to the whole city, the isomorphism between city and individual being assumed for all the virtues (432a). So, if temperance can be a virtue of the city at all, one part of the city must control the other(s), that part must be better than the other(s), and the control must be harmonious. The control in question must be the political control of ruling the city; the better part must be the rulers since they have the virtue relevant to ruling well – social wisdom. The worse part (in the relevant respect of ruling) must be the defenders and the artisan classes; and the harmony in question must be agreement among all three classes that those with the inborn talents, appropriate education, and the virtue of social wisdom, are the best citizens for ruling the city. It is noteworthy that social temperance as defined here is not any control and harmony among the three classes, but the control specified by social justice (that the best by nature and education should rule (431c)) and harmony on that control.

Unlike wisdom and courage, which reside in parts of the city, social temperance is a holistic virtue (431e). It applies directly to the whole city, since both ruling and harmony among the social classes relate parts of the city to one another with respect to ruling and being ruled. And it accounts for all the social functions being performed better than they would be without temperance, given that deep disagreements about who should rule can be socially disabling and even lead to civil war.

Notice that common sense might agree that harmony among the citizens within the city would be helpful generally in the citizens' performing their social labors, and conflict among them would generally hinder good performance, as Socrates noted this earlier (*Republic*: 351). But the harmony of Plato's temperance is more specifically agreement that the best "by nature and education" should rule, as Plato's social justice requires; so the good of Platonic social temperance depends specifically on the good of Plato's social justice. His social temperance cannot obtain without his justice, and the good of his temperance depends on the good of his justice.

Finally (432b–434c), Socrates takes up justice, repeats his earlier remark, that justice must be the "remaining" virtue, after the other three have now been defined, and pretends to be "hunting" for this virtue. This procedure has been reasonably criticized: how does Socrates know there are just four virtues in his completely good city, and how is he going to identify the quality that is the remaining virtue?

We must remember, though, that he has help from the functional theory and his construction of his completely good city on the basis of it. On the functional theory a completely good city is one that performs all its functions well, and its virtues are the qualities that enable it to perform one or another or all of its functions well. Socrates has already accounted for the city being ruled well by his analysis of social wisdom; he has accounted for the city being defended well by his analysis of social courage; and he has accounted for some of the city's performing all its functions well by his analysis of social temperance (the performing well due to harmony and the absence of conflict). But there is still some performing of all the city's functions that none of the other virtues have caught: namely, the performing better of all the city's functions due to the organization of the city by the division of social labors and the optimal matching of labors to inborn natural ability and appropriate education. Socrates is quite right to refer us back to the founding of their city by this principle (370c), and his original argument that a city so constituted would perform all its functions better than any city without division of labor or without matching labors to inborn talents. This good the other three virtues have not accounted for, and so this quality – this way of organizing the city – that enables the city to perform all its functions better must be the remaining virtue.

This makes understandable why Socrates proceeds in this way. This quality indeed accounts for the better performance of all the city's functions. Further, it is the foundational virtue: without it the other virtues, as defined by Plato, would not be possible (433b). Further yet, it is a holistic virtue: like temperance, it applies to the whole city and it benefits all the members of the community.

Even so, Plato's conception of social justice is highly unusual. A city-state is just, we are told, when it is so organized that each citizen[14] is required[15] to do "his own task," that is, that social function for which s/he is best suited by nature and education to do; the three main social functions are provisioning the city, defending the city, and ruling the city; those of very high inborn intelligence and advanced education are best suited to rule the city; those of inborn high spirit and appropriate education and training are best suited to defend it; and those of inborn ability for and education in the productive arts to provision the city.

We may concede that this is indeed a well-functioning city-state, and that this particular organization or structure does account for some of its sound functioning, maybe for all the benefits that Plato claims for it. But why is it justice, rather than some other virtue of societies or institutions, such as efficiency, for example? Plato is well aware of this question, and tries to convince us that the quality he has identified is justice. Indeed this is part of his defense of his justice. We shall see that the same important question arises about his definition of justice in a person's soul. We take up both questions in the last chapter.

5 Return to Plato's Methods for Discovering Justice

Conceding for the moment that the quality Plato defined is justice, we can apply another test, to see whether we would rationally choose his justice over other conceptions of justice.

Plato has three characters use three different methods for discovering what justice is, the empirical method of Thrasymachus, the contractarian method of Glaucon, and the functional method of Socrates. These three characters, using three different methods, also obtain three different results – three different conceptions of justice.[16]

We saw (in chapter 2) that Plato rejects the method of Thrasymachus for discovering what justice is, since he rejects the assumption that makes the empirical investigation of justice and its result possible: that justice resides entirely in the positive laws of each society.

However, Plato does not explicitly or implicitly criticize Glaucon's method for discovering the nature of social justice by looking for a contractarian origin of justice. Nor does he consider whether the contractarian method would validate Thrasymachus's justice; we, the readers, discussed that question, and found that if we use the contractarian method, the justice of Thrasymachus would be rejected.

Plato also does not apply Glaucon's method to his own conception of justice. If we think of the contractarian method as an analytic device for testing principles of justice, would Plato's principle pass this test? Would we, if we were in the appropriate circumstances choose Plato's justice over other principles of justice?

The answer is most probably negative. What results are reached by Glaucon's method depends in part on what empirical assumptions are made about men and their circumstances in the state of nature (e.g. moderate scarcity, degree of rationality, motivations and conceptions of the human good), as well as procedural assumptions, such as unanimity, and the reasoning used to make a choice.[17]

Conceivably, Plato thought that if we supply what he thought were true or reasonable assumptions, men in a state of nature would choose his principle of social justice over the state of nature. Certainly, one of his theses in the *Republic*, that men are better off or happier being Platonically just rather than unjust, might have led him to argue that in a state of nature individuals would rationally choose his principle of social justice over the state of nature, each on the basis of his/her happiness. He might also accept the procedural assumption of unanimity of agreement, since his social temperance implies agreement among all the citizens on who should rule and who should be ruled, and unanimity on his principle of social justice would produce temperance in addition to justice.

But would individuals rationally choose Plato's principle of social justice over the less restrictive and minimal principle Glaucon has them choose? In a state of nature, would they rationally agree to give up not only their freedom to harm others, but also the freedom to choose a career or occupation in society, the freedom to own property, or the freedom to choose a mate, all the freedoms lost in Plato's just society (at least for rulers and warriors)?[18]

Here the theory of human good embedded in Glaucon's theory of justice, in which the freedom to do as one pleases is thought to be a great good, stands in the way. If we could replace Glaucon's theory of the human good with Plato's own, and attribute Plato's conception of human goods and happiness to men in a state of nature, such men might well choose Plato's principle of social justice over the state of nature, each making the choice on the basis of his/her own good as Plato conceives it. But Plato's own theory of human good, with its radical downgrading of freedom and the goods and pleasures of ordinary men (e.g. *Republic*: 555–61, 582–7), seems hardly something that we can attribute to men in a state of nature; at least most men as we know them have something closer to Glaucon's conception of the human good rather than Plato's, and closer to Rawls' conception of primary goods. All in all, it seems doubtful that Plato could claim that Glaucon's contractarian method would produce Socrates' result, at least if we make reasonably realistic assumptions about the state of nature and men's capacities, conceptions and desires.

Plato in fact had his characters use three different methods to answer the question, what social justice is, and they plausibly obtained three different results. The different results were obtained by using different substantive assumptions as well as different methods. Plato apparently did not appreciate fully the power of the contractarian method, and he certainly did not use it as an analytic device to test the results reached by Thrasymachus or by his Socrates. But by including a diversity of methods as well as a diversity of accounts of justice in his discussion, Plato broadened and deepened both the accounts of justice he criticizes and the justice he defends.

Notes

1 See Keyt (2006b) for a fine discussion of the inscription analogy and examples of its use in epigraphy. We discuss analogy again in chapter 5.
2 See, for example, Rawls (1971: 24).
3 For a recent discussion of the Socratic Method in ethics and a comparison with Rawls, see Santas (2010).
4 It should be recalled that Glaucon earlier was speaking on behalf of the many or "what people say"; here he is speaking for himself.
5 See, for example, Hume (1955: *Treatise*, Book III, part II, section ii), Rawls (1971), Barry (1989), and even B. Skyrms (1998) on the same issue.
6 Or, the rational unwillingness of the contracting parties to accept anything less than equality, at least with respect to limits of freedom to harm others and with respect to security.

7   The phrase comes from Rawls. Plato indeed supposes that individuals are born with relevantly different abilities and talents for various social occupations, but whether he thinks that this is the result of a natural random lottery is an open question. He may think it is the result of divine design.

8   In Smith's famous "pin factory" each worker performs a small task (e.g. cutting wire into pieces of a certain length) over and over, the result being an enormous increase in productivity over the case where each worker makes a whole pin.

9   Plato's procedure shows that he is doing what Rawls calls "ideal theory" first and "partial compliance theory" after that: first we need to find out what a completely good or just society is, and only then are we in a position to identify and try to remedy injustices in existing societies. See also *Republic* (504c), where Socrates says that "nothing that is imperfect is the measure of anything." Only if we know what a completely just society is do we have a measure of the justice or injustice of existing societies. Plato and Rawls are in agreement on this point: Rawls also proceeds to find out what a completely just society is, what he calls "a well-ordered society," and only after that, he thinks, can we identify and address existing injustices (Rawls 1971: 8–9). Recently, this approach has been challenged by Sen (2006), who apparently thinks we can do well enough if we can compare more or less just institutions – the so called "comparative approach"– and have no need for ideal theory. It is hard to see, though, how he can tell injustices or greater or lesser justice, unless he assumes what justice is, apparently in his case democratic or egalitarian justice in rights and resources. It is possible that Sen's approach narrows the debate about justice too much. Plato and Rawls try to find out what justice is among a broad list of candidates (three theories of what justice is in the *Republic*, and an even wider list in *A Theory of Justice* (1971: section 21, 122–6)).

10 For a more detailed critical discussion of the functional theory, see the author's *Goodness and Justice* (2001: 66–75). For recent discussions of function in biology, see Hull and Ruse, 1998. For a contemporary duality in the concept of function, paralleled in Plato's disjunctive definition of function, one for natural organs and one for artifacts, see Preston (1998).

11 For a systematic procedure, consisting of an ordered series of steps, which Plato calls a *methodos* (method), see *Phaedrus* (270b–271c), *Sophist* (243d–244), and *Republic* (532ff.). For further discussions of theories and methods see Price (2008).

12 Some have thought that the first book is a Socratic dialogue whose theories cannot be relied on to interpret the rest of the work; that this applies to the theory of function and virtue. I disagree with this view. Book I foreshadows many important themes in the rest of the work and it is beautifully integrated with it (e.g. Aune 1997). The textual evidence for the use of the functional theory after Book I is impressive (Santas 2006a and Coumoundouros

and Polanski 2009). Especially notable are passages in which the concept of optimal function is used in the explication of Plato's principle of justice (*Republic*: 369e, 370b, 370c, 374b, 374e, 406c, 421c, 434abc). The concept of optimal function indeed is the best explanation of what Plato means by the formula of social and psychic justice, "doing one's own work," one for the optimal function of each citizen in the just city and one for the optimal function of each part of the just soul.

13 It must be remembered that Plato means by rulers not simply those with de facto political power, but those with that power and the inborn ability and education to rule well, more so than any other citizens.

14 Indeed, each member of the society, we are told at 433d.

15 Plato makes this quite clear: not doing what one is best suited to do, or doing several social functions, is an injustice (*Republic*: 434bc).

16 In considering this question we must keep in mind the distinction between methods and substantive or empirical assumptions made in applying the methods – a distinction that might not be all that sharp. If our question includes differences in such assumptions, then it would not be too surprising if different methods gave us different results, though logically there might still be room for the same result, since the same conclusion can be validly deduced from different premises, something Plato was probably aware of from, say, the different existing proofs of the Pythagorean theorem.

17 Rawls is quite explicit, that if we change the descriptions of the original position we can get different results, and argues strongly for his description of it (Rawls 1971: 146).

18 In Bks III and IV it is already clear that Plato's principle of social justice requires the citizens to do that social work for which they are best suited, on pain of doing injustice – so there is no freedom of choice of profession in Plato's completely good city. Further, the rulers and soldiers are not permitted to have any private property, nor do they have a choice of mate (see chapter 8 below). Presumably, the choosing parties would know these things in the state of nature or in a Rawlsian original position, since they are part of Plato's conception of justice, though possibly the abolition of private property and family are not necessary parts.

5

Plato's Ideal of a Just and Good Person

After Socrates has defined the virtues of the city, he begins his investigation about justice in the human soul by elaborating the analogy he supposed earlier between just city and just soul:

> But now let us work out the inquiry in which we supposed that, if we found some larger thing that contained justice and viewed it there, we should more easily discover its nature in the individual man. And we agreed that this larger thing is the city, and we constructed the best city in our power, well knowing that in the good city it would of course be found. What, then, we thought we saw there we must refer back to the individual and, if it is confirmed, all will be well ... That seems a sound method ... Then, said I, if you call a thing the same whether it is big or little, is it unlike in the respect in which you call it the same or like? Like, he said. Then a just man too will not differ at all from a just city in respect of the very form [kind] justice, but be like it. Yes, like. But now the city was thought to be just because three natural kinds existing in it performed each its own function, and again it was temperate, brave, and wise because of certain other affections and habits of these three kinds. True, he said. Then, my friend, we shall expect the individual also to have these same kinds in his soul, and by reason of identical affections to these with those in the city to deserve correctly the same names.
> (434d–435c, Shorey translation, modified)

To discover justice and the other virtues in the human soul Plato thus proceeds on the assumption that justice in the human soul is "the same" as justice in his completely good city, or that the just soul is isomorphic (the same in structure) to the just city. Accordingly he sees as his new task to find out whether the human soul has in it "the same [three natural] kinds, equal in number" (341c). His pioneering analysis of the human soul, into reason, spirit, and appetite (434–42), is new and independent of his theory of social justice; together with the isomorphism, it makes possible his deduction of the definition of justice (and the other virtues) in the human soul from his previous definition of justice (and the other virtues) in his completely good city (441–45).

The isomorphism between just city and just soul requires that the formula of justice in Book IV, "each [part] is doing its own," has the same interpretation in both cases. If justice in the city obtains when each part of the city does that city function (of the three general city functions of provisioning, defending and ruling the city) which it can do best (i.e. optimally), then a soul is just when each part of it is performing that psychic function (of the corresponding three general psychic functions of providing for, defending and ruling oneself) which it can do best (i.e. optimally).

As we shall see, Plato argues that reason is the psychic part that can best perform the psychic function of ruling oneself, spirit can help best to defend oneself, and appetite functions optimally when it obeys reason on appetite satisfaction. Together with the psychic virtues of wisdom, courage, and temperance, this forms Plato's ideal of a completely good person. It is an ideal of optimal order, rationality, and harmony within the human soul.

1   The Analogy between a Just City and a Just Soul

Plato says that the form or kind justice in the human soul is "the same form" (434d) as justice in a city; and later that the just soul is "like" the just city with respect to justice (435a). What kind of likeness does he have in mind? And why does Plato think a just soul is like a just city?

At first sight it looks as if the basis for it is a linguistic principle of univocality: "if you call a thing the same whether it is big or little, it is like, rather than unlike, in the respect in which you call it the same ... then a just man too will not differ at all from a just city with respect to the very form justice, but will be like it" (435ab). But the principle seems false of natural languages, including English and Greek. There are many counter examples to it in English and Greek: for example, "sharp" as in "sharp knives" and "sharp notes" (and *aischron* in Greek, according to Plato's Callicles, in *Gorgias* 482). Moreover, Plato himself does not apply it to just actions and just persons: Socrates says (*Republic*: 443e) that actions are just in so far as they produce and preserve the agent's just psyche; so just actions are defined by a causal relation to a just soul, not by just actions being similar to a just soul (see Keyt 2006b, "Plato on Justice").

Rather than a linguistic principle of univocality ("that a formula that defines a term in one application defines it in all applications"), Keyt suggests a more subtle principle at work:

> if (i) two systems have the same number of parts, if (ii) the parts of the one system can be paired one to one with parts of the other on the basis of the kinds to which the parts belong, if (iii) these kinds of parts are the seats of certain affections, and if (iv) the one system has a quality in virtue of its parts having such an affection, then (v) the other system has the same quality if its parts have the same affection. (Keyt 2006b: 349)

This is intricate and we must not confuse its various elements: we have two systems, one a city, the other a human soul; parts of the city (social classes) and parts of the human soul, and the parts of the soul are not identical with parts of the city; but we also have kinds, and a part of the city can belong to the same kind as a part of the soul and can be paired accordingly; further, the parts can be seats of "affections"; and finally, each system can have a quality by reason of affections of its parts, which can be identical to a quality the other system has by reason of similar affections of its parts.

The parts of the completely good city are the class of citizens best suited by nature and education to be rulers, or defenders, or providers; from the subsequent argument for the division of the soul, it is clear that the parts of the soul are reason, spirit, and appetite; and the qualities in question are the virtues of justice, temperance, courage, and wisdom.

From the definitions of the social virtues already at hand we can infer what the affections are by which social virtues are present in the city; thus it is by the defenders of the city preserving in action true beliefs from the rulers about what the city should fear, that the city is courageous. From the isomorphic principle and the division of the soul we can similarly infer that a human being is courageous by some part in her soul preserving in action the true beliefs of another part about what she should fear. But this is an incomplete definition of psychic courage: how can we tell which part of the soul corresponds to which part of the city, so that we can define psychic courage similarly to city courage?

We need to know how to pair parts of the soul to parts of the city, and to do that we need to know the similarities between the two, the "kinds" to which social parts and psychic parts can belong.

2   Plato's Analysis of the Human Psyche

The isomorphism of just soul to just city raises some fundamental questions.

Does the human psyche have in it different natural psychic parts, three in number and the same in kind as the three natural social parts of the city?

Does the human psyche have psychic functions that correspond to the general social functions of the city?

Finally, if the psyche has three natural psychic parts and if it does have three general psychic functions, which psychic activity is the optimal function of which psychic part?

Is Plato's answer to this last question based simply on the isomorphism, or are there independent and confirming arguments that it is best for reason to rule and the passions to obey?

One reason Plato has that there are psychic kinds corresponding to city "kinds and dispositions" is that "these could only come from individuals"; therefore, "the same kinds and dispositions [affections] are to be found in each one of us that are in the city" (435c). For example, the city of Thrace is said to be high spirited and this can only come from its citizens being high spirited; similarly with Egypt's being money loving, or Athens being a lover of knowledge.[1]

But this is not enough for dividing the human soul, as Socrates says:

> But the matter begins to be difficult when you ask whether we do all these things with the same thing [the whole soul] or whether there are three things and we do one thing with one and one with another – learn with one part of ourselves, feel anger with another, and with yet a third desire the pleasures of nutrition and generation and their kin, or whether it is with the entire soul that we do these things. (436ab, Shorey translation)

This makes it clear what the psychic activities are – learning, feeling anger, and "desiring"; and the issue is whether the psychic thing that learns is distinct from the thing that feels anger and both distinct from the thing that desires food, drink, and sex.

There is an obvious analog here to bodily activities: we can walk and we can shoot arrows; we might ask whether we do these things with the whole body or there are distinct parts of the body and we walk with one and shoot arrows with another. Here the true answer is easier to see: we walk with our legs and shoot arrows with our hands; again we now locate the bodily source of different psychic activities in different parts of the brain. Perhaps similarly in the soul there may be a natural division of parts and a natural division of psychic labors that match the parts?

Socrates gives a long argument to show that there is indeed such a natural division of the human soul into psychic parts and a division of psychic labors that match the parts uniquely. This argument takes for granted that there are distinct psychic activities: that learning in every human being is distinct from feeling angry and each distinct from desiring food, drink, and sex; all these things exist in every human being and each is distinct from the others. The question is whether we do all these things with the whole soul or each with some different part of the soul.

Plato's division of the psyche into parts or powers is made on the basis of a principle of contrariety,[2] that "the same thing cannot do or suffer opposites in the same respect in relation to the same thing and at the same time" (436b); an unspoken assumption that psychic activities imply psychic powers for such activities; and evidence of psychic conflicts within the following pairs of psychic activities: (1) between desiring food, drink, or sex and refusing to indulge due to reasoning,[3] from which the non-identity of the powers of reasoning and of desiring these things is inferred (439); (2) between desiring something and being angry at one's desiring it (the case of Leontius who desired to see dead bodies and was angry at himself for that (439–41)), from which the non-identity of the powers of desiring and of feeling angry is inferred; (3) between feeling angry at something and calculating that it is best not to act on one's anger (the case of Ulysses who became furious at his betraying servants but was held back from punishing them at once by reasoning about what is better to do (441)), from which the non-identity of the powers of reasoning and of feeling anger is inferred.

The argument thus construed has three stages: first, it assumes that individual psychic activities can be collected and divided naturally into three kinds, "desiring," getting angry, and reasoning;[4] then examples are given of evident conflicts among such activities; and finally, from these conflicts, the principle of contrariety, and the unspoken assumption that psychic activities of a given kind imply psychic powers of that kind, the non-identity of three powers is inferred, each power being named after the kind of activity it uniquely performs: "naming that by which it reasons the reasoning, that by which it (erotically) loves, hungers, thirsts, and feels the flutter and titillation of other appetites, the a-rational and appetitive, companion of various repletions and pleasures … and that by which we feel anger, spirit [literally: angry-kind]" (439de; Shorey 1978)[5]

It should be noted that not every kind of conflict seemingly within our souls forces us to divide the soul. Some conflicts we can explain by appealing to facts in the external world: I want to eat caviar and drink champagne and I cannot have both, but this maybe so only because I cannot afford both. Or, I might both hate and love my car, but this conflict does not force us to divide the soul, if we can explain it by dividing the object of my love and hate: I love its power but hate its gas consumption. Again I might both want to sail and not want to sail, but this does not force us to divide the soul if we can divide the time: I want to sail when the weather is good and not when there is a storm. When we can explain seemingly inner psychic conflicts by appealing to the external world (my finances), or by dividing the object of the conflicting psychic states (different properties of the car), or by dividing time (when the weather is good, when there is a storm), we are not forced to divide the soul. Plato's arguments from inner psychic conflict to a division of the soul are successful only for inner conflicts for which such other explanations are not available.[6] The same holds true for Freud's similar arguments for his famous psycho-analysis.

Contemporary psychologists attribute direction to drives: for example, we try to approach an object when we desire it, avoid it when we fear it; and classify psychological conflicts accordingly: conflicts of approach–approach, conflicts of avoidance–avoidance, and conflicts of approach–avoidance. The first two already divide the object (desiring two things both of which we cannot have because of the state of the external world, or fearing two things both of which we cannot avoid for similar reasons) and give us no reason to divide the self. But a subset of approach–avoidance conflicts, where, say, we desire and fear the same thing and cannot divide the part of the object we desire and the part we fear, or divide the time, presumably might force us to divide the self, as Plato and Freud did.

3 Parts of the Human Psyche: Faculties or Agents?

Now assuming we can divide the soul, how can we tell what each part is? Psyches and psychic parts are not things we can publicly inspect. By comparison to the human body and its parts or the city and its parts, they are much harder to understand. One persistent dispute is worth discussing because of its significance for Plato's moral psychology: is each part of the soul in Plato's analysis a distinctive psychic power with its own exclusive psychic activities, or is each psychic part a psychic agent that can desire, feel anger, and reason?

There is some textual evidence for each interpretation and there have been distinguished commentators on each side. But the agent interpretation presents us with too many paradoxes, and I will argue for the parts of the soul being faculties or capabilities.

We indeed find Plato giving different characterizations of the parts of the soul and parts of the city in different places. We saw that just before he argues for the division of the soul, Socrates says: "Is it not necessary to admit this much, that the same kinds and qualities that exist in the city are to be found in each one of us. They could not get there from any other source. It would be absurd to suppose that the element of [high] spirit was not derived in cities from the citizens … or love of learning … or love of money" (*Republic*: 435e). So perhaps the three kinds are three kinds of love, love of learning, love of honor, and love of money (see also *Republic*: 374d–376c, 544d, 580c–581b). Rulers and reason can be paired because both love learning, defenders and spirit because both love victory and honor, and artisans and appetite because both love money. Of course, to see what this implies we need to understand what Plato thinks this love is: his term in all these passages is *philia* (not the *eros* of the *Republic* which, unlike the *eros* of the *Symposium*, is only sexual, in these passages at least). And if *philia* requires cognition and beliefs, as it seems to do in the *Republic*, then it is natural to think that Plato attributes beliefs to each part of the soul since each part has *philia* for something; and if beliefs then cognitive powers, and if so then each part seems to be an agent.[7]

We have a similar situation with Plato's view that any part of the soul can rule the individual: in the just man reason rules, in the timocratic character spirit rules, while the oligarchic, democratic and tyrannical characters are ruled by appetite (Book VIII). Since ruling surely requires reasoning, it seems that the appetitive part and spirit must be capable of reasoning, and if so they are psychic agents, each capable of desiring, reasoning, and even being angry. As in the case of each part of the soul loving, so in the case of each part of the soul ruling, a ruling part of the soul looks like an agent.[8]

However, in Plato's initial division of the soul, the hypothesis that Plato's parts of the soul are agents becomes problematic. The Ulysses example, Plato's last example in the long argument for the division of the soul in Book IV (441bc), would be useless in showing that spirit and reason are distinct, if spirit can reason; and notice that the reasoning here has nothing to do with forms since Ulysses' reasoning is entirely about sensible objects. It is reasoning about the past and future that spirit cannot do, and if it also cannot reason about forms, as every one grants, it cannot reason at all.

Similarly, if appetite can reason, then Plato's first example, of a man thirsting and refusing to drink on the basis of reasoning, would be equally useless in showing that appetite and reason are distinct parts of the soul. And here too the reasoning that holds back the person from drinking is about sensible objects.

Further, Socrates calling the appetitive part a-rational, in the very sentence where he is naming reason and appetite after what they do (*Republic*: 439d), is strong evidence that he is using the concept of exclusive functions, and that the appetitive part cannot reason. He makes a similar move in his last example of the division, the Ulysses example, when he calls Ulysses' feeling anger unreasoning (*alogistos thumoumeno*) (*Republic*: 441c): he is using the example to isolate feeling anger (or perhaps getting angry) itself before there is any reasoning mixed with it. The whole point of the example is that feeling anger itself is not identical (or similar enough) with reasoning, and so the capability to do one and the capability to do the other are not identical capabilities.

The agent interpretation seems also excluded in the way Socrates sets up the issue of division to begin with: "whether we do all these things with the same thing, or whether there are three things and we do one thing with one and one with another – learn with one part of ourselves, feel anger with another, and with yet a third, desire the pleasures of nutrition and generation and their kind, or whether it is with the entire soul that we do each of them" (*Republic*: 436ab).

It is this question that the argument for the division is meant to answer. This question poses two alternatives and asks which is the case:

1   We learn, feel anger, and desire the pleasures of food and sex with our whole soul. Or:
2   We learn with one part of our soul, feel anger with another, and desire the pleasures of food and sex with a third.

But the agent interpretation opts for a third alternative not posed by the question:

3   We learn, feel anger, and desire (food and sex?) with one part of the soul, we learn, feel anger, desire with a second part of the soul, and learn, feel anger, and desire with a third part of the soul.[9]

Is this coherent? It is certainly not coherent as an answer to Socrates' question. But is it even coherent apart from that, by itself? How could we or Plato, distinguish the three parts, if they can all perform the same kind of activities – desiring reasoning, and even feeling anger?[10]

Further, how could we or Plato distinguish what reasons in one part from what reasons in another? Perhaps by what they reason about? Appetite and spirit can reason only about what is good for them, not about what is good for the whole soul as reason's reason can (Irwin 1995); and they cannot reason about the forms either or the form of the good (Bobonich 2002). However, we just saw that in the initial argument for the division, Socrates distinguishes between reason and appetite (first example of conflict) by distinguishing between reasoning about the good of the sensible things that appetite wants and appetite; but if appetite also can reason about the good of the sensible things it wants, the example is useless distinguishing reason from appetite. A similar problem exists for the Ulysses example.

Further yet, since each of the three psychic agents can reason, desire, and even feel anger, it looks as if in each agent these activities could be related to each other and ordered in different Platonic ways, so that *each* of the three agents within a person can have Plato's psychic virtues or vices; each person might have three just agents in her soul, or one just agent and another unjust, and so on with similar absurdities.

Indeed, the difficulties and paradoxes of the agent interpretation are best brought out by Bobonich (2002: 254–8) and by Keyt (2006b: 350), though they and others are strongly inclined to adopt the agent interpretation, not unreasonably since Plato's language often suggests it.[11]

I take Plato's initial question and his initial division of the soul to be giving us what he thinks are the kinds to which the parts of the soul essentially belong, the kinds that tell us what they are, what they always are, and what they are by *nature*. I take him to think that he is discovering a natural division of the psyche, a division into innate or inborn (natural in *that* sense) psychic capabilities: reason is that psychic part by which we reason. When he asks a few lines later (*Republic*: 439e) whether "spirit" is a third part, he repeats the phrase for spirit when he introduced the whole issue (*Republic*: 436ab): "that by which we feel anger" and invents a name for it, literally "the anger-kind" (a name of the psychic power as distinct from the psychic activity which is its exclusive function), usually translated spirit. "That by which we feel anger" is what spirit is by nature; what we feel anger at is contingent and depends on our learning and experience; just as drink is the object of thirst by nature; what we like to drink (hot, cold, sweet, good or bad drink) is contingent and depends on learning (*Republic*: 437–439a);[12] as "that by which we reason" is what reason is by nature.

It is mainly in subsequent passages, when Plato is mostly speaking of the educated and experienced psychic powers of adults, that we find some evidence that he thinks of the parts as agents; in his image, for example, of the embodied soul as a man, lion, and many headed beast (*Republic*, Book IX: 588–9, Keyt 2006b: 350); or in his attributing desires and pleasures to all three parts; or in supposing that a man who is ruled by a dominant desire for wealth is ruled by the appetitive part of the soul.[13]

Whenever Plato speaks of parts of the soul we need to consider whether he is speaking of the faculties as already educated (not always by his educational program, of course), as mixed with learning and experience (as he does most of the time because he is speaking of adults or children of some experience), or as what they are by nature (as he does in the initial division of the soul). It is essential to remember that Plato allows for the development of the inborn parts of the soul and interaction among these parts to produce conduct. Plato's psychology is not static, but developmental and interactive. His educational programs show that he fully realizes, as Freud did, that the adult "human soul is an achievement," the result of experience of the world, education, and interaction among its parts.[14]

The oligarch's ruling desire to produce and maintain wealth above all is an educated desire and the result of appetite and reason working together. This desire has been placed by some commentators in the appetitive part of the soul (Irwin 1995; Bobonich 2002), inferring that appetite can reason, if not about the forms, then about means and ends and overall sensible goods, since the oligarch, along with the democrat and the tyrant, is said by Plato to be ruled by the appetitive part.

But the appetitive part ruling can be accounted by the person taking the satisfaction of appetites as his ultimate end, and using reason to find out the most efficient, effective, and general means of satisfying appetites; the oligarchic man's reason finds that wealth is that means; the democratic man reasons that it is freedom and equality; the tyrant reasons that it is power. The resulting dominant and ruling desire for wealth or freedom and equality or power is a mixture of appetite and learning. The various psychic rulings are done by developed, experienced, and interacting psychic parts. It is not necessary to suppose that each part of the soul by itself and as it is by nature produces action, since they can interact with each other to do so.[15]

In Plato's portraits of characters, such as the timocratic and the oligarchic men, reason and spirit or reason and appetites already work together, but these two characters use reason "as a slave," to figure out ways and means to victory or wealth and even to discipline the appetites (*Republic*: 553e). Their conduct is the result of developed and experienced faculties interacting with each other. In order for the timocratic man to reason about ways and means to victory and honor, it is not necessary that his spirit has reason in it – a second reason in addition to reason he has to begin with! Or that the oligarchic man's appetite has reason in it, in addition to the reason he already has, like everyone else. Even for Plato this seems like a prolific and futile proliferation.

Plato's language does indeed sometimes suggest agents. The educated and experienced parts of an adult can look like agents, because they are developed and can be the result of that development and interaction. And it is certainly tempting to think of the interaction among the psychic parts on the model of linguistic interaction among persons: "one part can persuade another and they all can agree," as Bobonich puts it; and, like persons, "each [part of the soul] can, without the cooperation of the others, move the agent to act" (Bobonich 2006: 220). It seems easier to understand the parts of the human psyche if they are like persons who can love, rule or be ruled, agree or not with each other and act without the others. But as Bobonich himself has argued, the price is very high in paradoxes. If each part is complex and can desire and reason, we have further divisions within each part; and we still have the problem of understanding interaction between reason and desire within each part. And with all these divisions, unity of the self becomes more problematic (Bobonich 2006: 247–58; Keyt 2006b).

Each inborn part of the soul is complex, but it is complexity in each of the original inborn or natural psychic faculties, not to be confused with agent complexity that is the result of development and interaction. We can see this complexity within a psychic part in the trouble Plato has from the beginning finding a unified principle for appetite; there is a multiplicity of psychic functions and natural objects that he is grouping together: erotically loving (i.e. lusting, with sex as the object), hungering for (solid) food, and thirsting for drink, and even "other similar appetites" (*Republic*: 439d). Later in Book IX (580d), he calls the appetitive part "multiformed," and apparently for convenience of reference proposes to call it the "lover of money," since money is the major means for satisfying all these appetites. But this way of referring to it is actually misleading – it has led readers into thinking that appetite is an agent who can think. The invention of money was a recent development in Plato's time, and it is implausible to have Plato think that *Homo sapiens* is born with an appetite for money; the desire for money is clearly a cultural construct involving much learning, only a tiny bit older in biological time than the desire for a Cadillac. Plato would have been better off seeking some reference to the body as a unifying principle for the appetitive part; for example, that appetite, as distinct from the other parts and as distinct from the desires of other parts, always has some bodily source (organs, for example) and its object is related to a bodily need or a bodily satisfaction.

There is a passage in Book V that reveals how Plato goes at understanding psychic parts:

> Shall we say that powers belong to that kind of existing things by which we ... can do what we can do ... In a faculty (power) I cannot see any color or shape or similar mark such as those on which in many other cases I can fix my eyes in discriminating in my thought one thing from another. But in the case of a faculty I look to that only – that to which it is related and what it effects, and it is in this way that I come to call each one of them a faculty, and that which is related to the same thing and accomplishes the same thing I call the same faculty, and that to another I call other. (477cd)

He gives as obvious examples the powers of sight and hearing: sight is the power by which we see colors and shapes in objects (the power itself has no color or shape), and seeing is what it accomplishes; hearing is a different power because it is related to different objects, sounds, and it accomplishes a different thing, hearing. Socrates then applies this principle to distinguish knowledge and opinion as different faculties or powers: the former relates to forms as its objects and accomplishes knowing (cognitive states that are always true); the latter relates to sensible things and accomplishes opining or believing (states sometimes true, sometimes false). This has to be a distinction within the faculty or psychic part of reason (since, among other things, the states have truth values in either case); and it shows that Plato tries to understand psychic powers by the objects they are related to (presumably characteristically or by nature, as thirst is for drink) and by what they accomplish when the faculties work on those objects (presumably their exclusive functions). In this principle we again see the functional theory at work, this time relying on exclusive natural psychic functioning, in conjunction with the natural objects of these functioning, to understand psychic powers.[16]

Can we go back and see if this principle is at work in the division of the soul in Book IV? I think so, but of course we must distinguish the role of this principle from the role of the principle of contrariety. The latter, in conjunction with psychic conflicts, can lead us to divide the self or soul, in cases where we cannot account for the conflict by reference to the state of the external world, or by dividing the object or aspects of it, or by dividing time.

But once we do divide the self into parts, we still need to understand the nature of each part. The principle of contrariety is not sufficient for individuating the parts. And here is where the principle of identifying a psychic power by its characteristic objects and exclusive functions comes into play. In the case of reason, Socrates characterizes it by its exclusive activity, reasoning or calculating, and eventually by its natural object – truth; in the case of thirst by its natural object, drink and the psychic activity of moving towards the object. Even so, it can still be difficult to characterize the nature of each part; the appetitive power has, after all, three different kinds of objects – liquids, solids, and sex. We can group the first two as food or nutrients, but how do we group together nutrients and sex, especially when different physical systems are involved?[17]

The paradoxes of the agent interpretation together with the ambiguity of the evidence suggest strongly Plato's parts of the soul to be faculties, especially if this is coherent and does not have similar difficulties. Plato's initial division of the soul suggests distinctive psychic powers.

When we also take the functional theory as a premise for understanding the nature of the psychic parts as innate psychic powers with characteristic functions and objects, we can have a coherent and consistent interpretation of Keyt's principle of isomorphism. The division of the city is based on inborn capabilities of citizens for the three general functions of cities – provisioning, defense, and ruling the city; and the division of the soul is also based on inborn capabilities of souls for the three general functions of souls – provisioning, defending, and ruling oneself; these general social and psychic functions are similar enough to be of the same kind, and so are the social and psychic parts required for the optimal performance of these functions. Given these similarities, parts of the city and parts of the soul can be matched, and the virtues can be similarly defined: for example, reason and persons of inborn high intelligence can be matched because they are better suited, with appropriate educations, to rule the city and the soul, respectively, than the other (relevant) parts of city and soul – and similarly with the other parts and functions of city and soul.

4   Just, Temperate, Brave, and Wise Human Souls

At the end of the argument by which Socrates distinguished three parts in the human soul – reason, spirit, and appetite – he reminds us of the analogy with the city: " we are fairly agreed that the same kinds equal in number are to be found in the state and in the soul of each one of us" (*Republic*: 441c). From the argument and the analogy, then, he proceeds at once to deduce the virtues in the human soul from his analysis of the virtues of the city already at hand. We must of course remember that Plato seeks to find *virtues* of both cities and souls, and that these are qualities that enable cities or souls to perform their functions *well*. That is why Socrates searches for optimal matching of parts to functions.

> Is it not necessary that as and whereby the state was wise so and thereby is the individual wise? Surely. And so whereby and as the individual is brave, thereby and is the state brave, and that both should have all the other constituents of virtue in the same way? Necessarily. Just too, then, Glaucon, I presume we shall say a man is in the same way in which a city was just. That too necessarily. But ... the state was just by reason of each of the three classes found in it fulfilling its own function ... We must remember, then, that each of us in whom the several parts within him perform each their own task – he will be a just man and own who does his own. (Republic: 441cd)

Notice that these are general statements about the psychic virtues; they must still be made appropriately specific. Yes, if we assume the analogy between a just city and a just soul, justice in the soul obtains when each of the three parts – reason, spirit, and appetite – is performing its own optimal psychic function. But what are the relevant psychic functions? And which psychic function is optimal for which psychic part?

For justice, Socrates proceeds to specify at once: "Does it not belong to the rational part to rule, being wise and exercising forethought on behalf of the whole soul, and to spirit to be subject and its ally ... and these two to preside over the appetitive part?" (441e–442a). It is best for reason to rule, better for the functioning of the whole soul, with spirit as its subject and ally, and for appetite to obey because reason, and presumably only reason, can have wisdom and forethought for the whole soul. Justice in the soul obtains when reason rules, spirit helps reason execute its commands, and appetite obeys. Justice is a holistic virtue – it pertains to the functioning well of the whole soul, as justice in the city is a holistic virtue.

We can set out a full schematic account of Platonic justice in the city (from the last chapter) and the isomorphic justice in the soul.

Justice in the city

1   A city is just when each of the natural kinds of people in it performs its own (its optimal) social function. This is the abstract or formal principle of social justice (433, 435b).
2   The city has three main functions: to rule, to defend, and provision itself (369bff., 374ff., 428dff.).
3   There are three natural kinds of persons in the city, persons of inborn high intelligence, persons of inborn high spirit, and those of inborn abilities for arts and trades (415, 435).
4   The optimal social function of persons of high intelligence is to rule the city; those of high spirit to defend it; and those of abilities in arts and crafts to provision the city (434).
5   Therefore, a city is just when it is so organized that those of high intelligence (and appropriate education) are assigned to rule, those of high spirit (and appropriate education) to defend, and those of artisan abilities (and appropriate education) to provision the city. This is the full definition of the just city; it puts together the formal principle and relevant information (from premises 1 to 4, 433).

Justice in the human soul

1   A person is just when each of the natural psychic kinds (parts) in his/her psyche performs its own (its optimal) psychic function. This is the abstract or formal principle of psychic justice, fully parallel to the abstract principle of social justice (435ac, 441e).
2   The human soul has three main functions, to rule oneself, to defend oneself, and to provide for one's bodily needs (441e, 442).
3   There are three natural psychic kinds (parts) in the human soul: reason, spirit, and appetite (by an independent argument, 436–41).
4   The optimal function of reason is to rule the person, of spirit to defend, and of appetite to provide for bodily needs (441e).
5   Therefore, a soul is just when it is so organized that reason is assigned to rule the person, spirit to defend it, and appetite to provide for one's bodily needs. This is the full definition of psychic justice (441e–442a).[18]

We can see clearly in the case of justice that the analyses of the psychic virtues assume three general functions of the soul that correspond to the three general functions of the city: ruling oneself to ruling the city, defending oneself to defending the city, and providing for oneself to providing for the city. They also assume the correspondence of parts – reason to rulers, spirit to defenders, and appetite to providers – because of corresponding optimal matching of part to function. The virtues then are defined by the corresponding "affections" or actions of the psychic parts. Thus for bravery:

> Would not these two [reason and spirit], then, best keep guard against enemies from without also on behalf of the entire soul and body, the one [reason] taking counsel, the other [spirit] giving battle, attending upon the ruler and by its courage executing the ruler's design? That is so. Brave, too, then, I take it, we call each individual by virtue of this part in him, when, namely, his spirit [the angry-kind] preserves in the midst of pains and pleasures the rule handed down by reason as to what is or is not to be feared. (*Republic*: 442c)

Here the function of defending oneself is specified and attributed to the psyche, and its correspondence to the function of the city to defend itself is assumed as evident.[19] The correspondence of spirit to the city defenders and of rulers to reason is also assumed, and the structure of psychic courage is then specified as analogous to the structure of city courage.

As certain men in the city are best suited to defend it – by their inborn high spirit and education to follow the true counsel of the rulers – so a matching part of the soul (spirit) is best suited to defend itself by its ability to feel anger and its education to follow the true counsel of reason.

Notice that Socrates' conception of courage is richer than mere daring, "guts," or mere bravado. Common sense is willing to call an action an act of courage even when the person was mistaken about danger and risk, at least if the person's beliefs were rational. Not so Plato or Socrates: not only must spirit enable the individual to act according to the counsel of reason; reason must also be correct or true in its counsel. Virtue, it seems, requires more than rationality of beliefs; it requires truth.

Notice also that courage is not a holistic virtue. For the city, it is a virtue of a part of the city, its defenders; for the soul also, it is a virtue of a psychic part, spirit; though a whole person can be said to be courageous, s/he is so by spirit preserving in action the counsel of reason.

Socrates next defines wisdom, another non-holistic virtue, one that reason and only reason can have: "But wise by that small part that ruled in him and handed down these commands, by its possession in turn within it of the knowledge of what is beneficial for each [psychic part] and for the whole, the community of the three" (442c). Wisdom, as a virtue of an individual, is knowledge that only reason can have about what is beneficial for each part of the soul and the whole soul.

Can every citizen in Plato's ideal city have such knowledge? Common sense and democratic societies suppose that individual persons and citizens can have knowledge about what is good for themselves; indeed that the individual person is the best judge of what is good for him/her, though not necessarily because s/he knows best – witness how far more a physician or biochemist knows about what is good for the human body. But Plato's view, revealed in Book VI, that no one can know what is beneficial unless one knows the form of the good, makes his wisdom a very controversial virtue, in ethics and politics, since in his view only very few highly talented and highly educated persons can attain knowledge of the form of the good (we return to the elitism of the ideal city in chapter 7).

The analysis of temperance in our souls, a holistic virtue like justice, follows a similar path: "And again is he [a person] not temperate by the friendship and symphony of these same parts, when they are one in the belief that reason must rule and not raise faction against it? Temperance, he said, is nothing else than this, whether in city or individual" (442d). For the whole soul to perform well, it is necessary that the three parts are in agreement on the order that is justice in the soul – agreement that reason is to rule, spirit to help carry out its commands, and appetite to obey reason on appetite satisfaction.

Temperance may seem to be the least controversial of Plato's virtues, since it seems evident that internal psychic conflict (psychic civil war) makes choice difficult and hinders optimal performance, while psychic harmony among the parts makes choice and performance easier and perhaps even better. But it must be remembered that Plato's temperance is harmony about the psychic order he calls justice; it is not harmony about any order. It is possible that an oligarchic character, a person whose ultimate end is appetite satisfaction and whose soul is ordered and disciplined by the desire for wealth as the necessary and best means to appetite satisfaction, has harmony about this order in his soul, an order in which reason is a slave to appetite. But this is not Platonic temperance. Platonic temperance can obtain only when a soul is Platonically just.

But what kind of psychic agreement among the psychic parts does Plato have in mind? In the case of social temperance, this does not seem problematic: the citizens of the completely good city might have the same beliefs, or not, that persons of inborn high intelligence and appropriate education should rule the city, persons of inborn high sprit and appropriate education should defend it, and persons of inborn ability and appropriate education for production and trade should provision the city. Here agreement seems to be having the same beliefs on this issue. But what is it for parts of the soul to agree to a similar psychic order?

In fact, Plato tells us explicitly that the agreement is not purely cognitive, that education for such harmony has a division of labor in it: "Then is it not, as we said, the blending of music and gymnastics that will render them [parts of the soul] concordant [literally, 'one in voice'], intensifying and fostering the one [reason] with fair words and teachings and relaxing and soothing and making the other [spirit] by harmony and rhythm?" (441e–442a). Here Socrates refers us back to 411–12, the longer discussion of this issue. Reason is educated and strengthened by words and lessons; spirit is tamed by harmony and rhythm. Thus, the parts of the soul need not be agents that communicate cognitively as whole persons do. Plato's saying that in temperance the parts of the soul are of "one opinion" is probably a metaphor; as his saying that reason and spirit are "one in voice" is also a metaphor and surely does not imply that parts of the soul can literally speak or sing.

5　Plato's Ideal of Rationality

It is essential not to confuse facts and ideals, nor to confuse what Plato thinks is natural and what is a human creation. The division of the city into persons of high intelligence, high spirit and productive talent is natural for Plato because it is division by inborn, and so natural abilities and talents; it is a division made by the "natural lottery," in Rawls' phrase. Similarly, his division of the soul is natural because it based on the inborn, and so natural capabilities of the psychic parts. On the other hand, the virtues themselves, both social and psychic, are not natural in this sense; we are not born with the psychic virtues, nor do Platonically just cities come into being as seasons do or as plants grow. These virtues are human constructions, the result of legislation and education. They are not completely determined by the natural lottery, since we can have different legislative constructions with the same distributions of the natural lottery, as with timocratic or democratic states. As Rawls remarks, the distributions of the natural lottery are neither just nor unjust; what society does with them, can be; witness what societies can do with the natural distributions of gender or color. Or what Plato himself did with the natural distribution of gender.

Similarly, Plato uses the natural divisions of the psyche as a base for the construction of the psychic virtues; but the virtues themselves are human constructions, the result of education, and are not completely determined by the natural lottery. And Plato is clearly aware of this, since he knows that education can shape a soul so as to be Platonically just or oligarchic or timocratic. His virtues are ideals, not just the product of nature without human intervention.

Thus Plato needs strong reasons for the central claims he makes in Book IV about justice and social and individual good. For social justice, we saw that he makes two central claims: the justice of a city consists in the optimal matching of innate talents and abilities to the three important functions of a city; and this matching, together with the other social virtues, is the best way to organize a city, best for the parts and best for the whole city.

Similarly, according to the isomorphism, the justice of a person consists in the optimal matching of the natural parts of her psyche to the three important functions of one's psyche; and this way of organizing a psyche is best for the parts of a psyche and for the psyche as a whole.

Plato can use his central claims about social justice and the isomorphism to justify his central claims about psychic justice. But the isomorphism is a much disputed way to relate social and individual justice. And, anyway, it is doubtful that the isomorphism can work out as neatly as Plato seems to suppose.

For these reasons Plato needs grounds independent of the isomorphism for the central claims he makes about his psychic virtues; and especially justice, since the other psychic virtues are more easily recognized. He needs such independent reasons, for example, for the anti-Humean claim that reason ought to rule the other parts of the soul, or that a person is just only when reason rules; and that it is best for a person when reason so rules. Plato cannot take his anti-Humean view of reason and passion for granted. His discussion of Callicles' view in *Gorgias* (Cooper 1997) and his discussion in *Republic* (Book VIII) show clearly enough that he was aware a person's psyche can be so organized that spirit or appetite can dominate, and reason is used purely instrumentally and in that sense is a slave; and that some think that this is virtue and this psychic organization best for one.

I think perhaps we can see some of the central reasons for Plato's claims, if we think of the functional theory of good as applying to the psyche as well as to the city; and if we ourselves use the isomorphism as a heuristic device; not as Plato uses it to define the psychic virtues, but as our guide to Plato's deeper reasons for his claims. Proceeding in this way, we can see at least two strong arguments for Plato's claims, one proceeding from his conception of appetite, and another from his conception of reason.

Let us start with a well-known difficulty about the function of appetite. The optimal function of the citizens with talents for production and trade is to provision the city, to provide it with the economic goods of food, shelter, clothing, etc. According to the isomorphism, the part of the soul that corresponds to the artisans is appetite; accordingly, the optimal function of appetite is to provision the person – presumably provide for his/ her bodily needs. But surely appetite cannot do that at all – appetite for food cannot provide me with food! Here the isomorphism seems to break down.

I think we have to be satisfied with a more limited correspondence between the optimal social function of the artisans to provision the city and the psychic optimal function of the appetitive part to provide for the individual. And we have to go back to the nature of appetite as Plato thinks of it in the division of the soul.

We need to remember that in the original division of the soul Plato thinks of appetites as separated and in abstraction from learning about objects; thirst, for example, he considers as simply the appetite for drink, not cold or hot, sweet or bitter, good or bad drink; the latter would be mixed with learning, a cognitive function and a function of reason. For "drink" is necessary for identifying the appetite as thirst and so identified, the appetite is not mixed with learning.[20] Most appetites we are acquainted with are of course mixed with learning. But if we want to find out what appetite by itself is and what it does, we must abstract from such learning. And this is how Plato thinks of it, I submit, when he comes to think of what is the optimal psychic function of appetite: its optimal function, given what it is, pure and unmixed with other parts of the soul.

He may be thinking of appetite, simply as such, as a kind of psychic signal system for bodily needs, or a system which brings to consciousness signs of the kinds of things the body needs and motivates seeking them: thirst for drink, hunger for food, sexual impulse for sexual release, and other such. Appetite by itself cannot *provide* for bodily needs, but it can *signal* such needs and *motivate* providing for them. However, simply as such a psychic signal system, without the help of learning, appetite is not accurate or specific enough about what particular objects the body needs, or what quantities of them, or how frequently. With respect to these questions, therefore, it should be guided by learning or wisdom or at least true belief, all of which are cognitive functions or virtues of reason.

A person needs reason's learning to tell her what and how much to drink when thirsty, how much and what to eat when hungry, what would keep the body warm, and so on.[21] The exclusive function of appetite as such is to signal bodily needs and to motivate the activities required for their satisfaction. This is all it *can* do toward providing for the body's needs; this is its exclusive function. But because of its essential lack of accuracy, appetite cannot by itself do even these things *well* (i.e. signal and motivate correctly) unless it is guided by learning and reason. Appetite may keep wanting sweets long after the body's need for sweets has been satisfied; and on the daily need for vitamin C appetite is almost totally blind.

We can appreciate the force of this argument by imagining beings like us but with a completely accurate appetitive signal system, a pre-established harmony between what our body needs or what is good for us, and what we have appetites for: what substances, in what amounts, with what frequency. In such beings appetite would not need to be ruled by learning and reason, and some branches of ancient medicine, such as dietetics, would not be necessary. But, of course, we are not such beings. So we can see from below, as it were, from the nature of our appetites, in abstraction from learning, that the optimal function of appetite is to be ruled by reason on all questions of what will satisfy bodily needs.[22]

This argument, that reason, not appetite, should be our ruler, *is* independent of the isomorphism; it proceeds from the nature of appetite, what it can do and what it cannot do by itself, and what it does best for the person given what appetite cannot do. It can signal and motivate bodily needs; but it is not by itself, by the intensities and durations of appetites, the best measure for their satisfaction. It becomes the best instrument when obedient to reason and its discoveries, such as the sciences of medicine and biochemistry. Therefore, the psyche is best organized, best for the parts and for the whole psyche, only when appetite is obedient to reason on what will satisfy bodily needs, how much and in what frequencies.

And if, as teleological ethical theories suppose, the right is what produces the most good, for persons as well as for societies,[23] appetite being obedient to reason will be part of the virtue of a person.

In this argument we can see why Plato uses analogies with medicine again and again. The patient tells the physician what s/he feels, his pains and pleasures, his fears and cravings. But as a patient, s/he does not know their causes or what her body needs or what would be good for it. It is medicine and the physician, as a physician who knows what are the needs of the human body, what appetite satisfaction will satisfy or not the needs of the body, what appetite is excessive (as in gluttony), what appetites defective (as in anorexia). The analogies are relevant to Plato's psychic virtues, because the discoveries of medicine and nowadays of biochemistry are indisputably the discoveries of reason. In the analogy, the patient as a patient corresponds to appetite and spirit, the physician as a physician corresponds to reason.

The argument from above, from the nature of reason, as to why reason should rule, might be somewhat different: it begins with the nature of reason, but it also uses Plato's theories of good and his view that goodness is the object of reason, not of sentiment. The argument is based on the exclusive functions of the three psychic powers, as conceived in the partition argument, *and* what is required for assigning optimally to the various parts of the soul the psychic functions of ruling, defending, and provisioning. The argument might run as follows for assigning ruling to reason.

To rule oneself, one needs to make decisions about what to do; to do that, one needs to reason and calculate about alternative courses of action and their comparative good.[24] But only reason can do these things – appetite and spirit cannot do them at all. Therefore, ruling oneself is the optimal function of reason, not of appetite or spirit.[25] Here such psychic activities as thinking about possibilities, about causal connections, and making judgments about good, are said to be necessary for ruling oneself, and from this and the premise that such thinking is an exclusive function of reason, it is inferred that ruling oneself is the optimal function of reason. We know from Book VIII that Plato thinks spirit and appetite *can* rule a person, for example, in the timocratic person spirit rules; in the oligarchic person desire for wealth rules; so ruling is not an exclusive function of reason. The argument gives grounds why spirit and appetite cannot rule *as well as* reason can, because of what is required for ruling oneself; so ruling is assigned to reason as *its* optimal function. Of course reason will rule *well* only if it has attained the virtue of reason, wisdom, knowledge of the good, or at least true belief about it; and this too is something that only reason can have.

This argument is strong, but it does have some controversial premises, which David Hume would dispute and thus dispute the conclusion. In a well-known passage of the *Treatise* Hume sets himself in explicit opposition to moral theories, "ancient and modern," which maintain that reason and the passions can conflict and that in such conflicts the person should follow the counsel of reason, right conduct being conduct prescribed by reason. Hume appears to accept some of the terms of the debate which Plato set: of several "elements" or at least activities in the soul, the idea that some of them might conflict with each other, and the idea that one or another of these might rule or be ruled. But he disputes that reason and the passions can conflict with each other, and that reason should rule. Reason cannot oppose preferring "the destruction of the whole world to the scratching of my finger;" it cannot even oppose a preference for "my own acknowledged lesser good to my greater." And Hume certainly disputes that reason is or ought to be our ruler; "reason is and ought to be the slave of the passions."[26]

In support of these striking propositions, Hume argues that reason by itself cannot move us to action, that some passion must always be part of the motive. Reason does play a role in motivation, but it is only to judge whether the objects of our passions exist, to discover necessary or efficient *means* to the satisfaction of our passions and the consequences of satisfying them. Reason's operations are value neutral, except purely instrumentally; reason cannot set ultimate ends of human action; only the passions, perhaps the calm passions, can do that. Plato's appetites and spirit are passions and these, contrary to what Plato says, are and ought to be the rulers and reason their "slave," that is, their instrument. Calculating possibilities and their causal networks *are* things that only reason can do; but setting ultimate ends or what is ultimately good only the passions can do. To secure their satisfactions, the passions need and can allow the logical and purely instrumental powers of reason; but they and only they set the ultimate ends of life, and in that sense they are the ultimate rulers. Plato's timocratic, oligarchic, democratic, and even tyrannic personalities of Book VIII are anti-Platonic, Humean personalities, though they might not be ideal, even for Hume, since they might not be using instrumental reason well enough, or they may be giving precedence to the violent over the calm passions.

This disagreement between Plato and Hume is not easy to understand, let alone adjudicate. For one thing, Hume does not appear to think of the passions, such as desires and preferences, in isolation from or in abstraction from learning about objects. He seems to separate the cognitive psychic functions, the functions of learning and reasoning and judging, from "the sentiments" and "the passions;" indeed his views of the relations between "reason" and the "passions" presupposes some sort of separation of the two. But his examples seem to confuse them. He talks as if, for example, the desire or preference to destroy the whole world is a desire with no reason mixed into it; reason might come in only to do such things as judge whether it is possible to destroy the whole world, what might be means to it and what the consequences. But, as Plato and the rest of us might ask, what on earth does desire by itself know about the whole world? It takes an enormous amount of learning about the world to have such a desire, not to speak of having the *concept* of "the whole world." The same goes for preferring, another learned passion. Hume's examples of passions are all mixtures of learning and passions. But all these striking propositions of his presuppose some separation of reason and the passions: somehow, we are to think of reason without the passions and the passions without reason. And the same holds for Plato in his original division of the psyche in Book IV and his talk of what part of the soul should rule what.

But it is hard to know what separation Hume had in mind, since he was neither a logical realist like Plato or Aristotle nor a conceptualist like Locke, and presumably did not believe in "abstract ideas." Whatever separating Hume may have done was still "armchair separating" or "armchair psychology." For the psychology part we can go to someone like Freud. We need not suppose that Hume was Freudian or pre-Freudian. Freud is a good example here because he also, like Plato and Hume, divided the psyche; *but* the separation was not by abstraction in thought experiments, as in Plato or Locke, but a real separation reached by going back to earlier and earlier periods in an individual's life when there was less and less learning present. In analysis, by the techniques of hypnosis, free association, and the interpretation of dreams, Freud was trying to uncover (memories of) earlier and earlier experiences, desires and impulses, all the way to the infantile. The source or seat of such infantile desires and impulses he called the id, and said that the id knows of no time, contradiction, or rationality. So here we have another notion of desire without reason: inborn impulse, uninformed and a-rational. Perhaps this is close to the kind of separation Hume had in mind.

But even supposing we could separate the passions from reason, either in the Platonic way or the Humean or the Freudian way, we have a fundamental question for Hume: why should we trust our "immaculate passions" more than learning to tell us what to do? This is similar to the question we asked of Plato earlier: why should we trust learning more than our immaculate passions to tell us what to do?

Hume's answer appears to be that reason *cannot* judge what is ultimately or intrinsically good or what should be the ultimate ends of life. Here he is denying one of the fundamental propositions of Plato's *Republic*, one of the crucial premises in Plato's argument for the conclusion that reason should be the master, not the slave, of the passions.

But was this a disagreement between Plato and Hume? It might be a disagreement in their estimates about the scope or the powers of human reason.[27] Reason is capable of discovering causal connections and doing logic and mathematics, but it is not capable of discovering what is good intrinsically or as an ultimate end. Or it might instead be a disagreement about goodness (they have different theories of good. If Hume is correct in his view that value judgments and moral distinctions are the objects of sentiment, not reason except purely instrumentally, then he is correct about what element of the soul ought to rule, assuming we accept a psychic division and the metaphor of ruling by setting ultimate ends.

If Plato is correct either in his functional theory of good or his later metaphysical theory of the form of the good, it follows that reason ought to rule: because on either of Plato's two theories of good, reason and only reason can judge what is good or bad, either instrumentally or ultimately. Only reason can find out what the exclusive or optimal function of something is, whether it performs that function well, and what enables it to do so; as, *in fact*, reason performs these tasks in biology, medicine, and the productive arts. Hume might agree that reason can do these things, but he might claim that the functional theory tells us only what is good instrumentally. Plato would further say that only reason can know what forms are and can determine how far something approximates forms. Here Hume might dispute that we can know these things at all, but, in any case, he would dispute that knowing them would tell us what is good intrinsically or ultimately.

6   The Virtues and Vices of the City-soul Analogy

There is no doubt that Plato chose to investigate two most important applications of the concept of justice, to city-states and persons. But, as we have seen, the isomorphism is not the only way to understand the relation between just persons and just cities (societies); they may be related non-accidentally in at least two other ways.

One way is to suppose that a just city is a city composed of just persons; this gives explanatory primacy to the concept of a just person: we first define just persons and then give an account of a just city, not as Plato does, but as a city composed of just persons as already defined. It is difficult to see how this can be a correct or fruitful way to understand a just city or a just society, since it would seem to render the nature of its institutions, its constitution or its economic system, for example, irrelevant to its justice. It seems to imply that if a city is composed of just persons it is a just city no matter what its institutions are.[28]

The other non-Platonic way of relating the justice of society to the justice of individuals in it is to suppose that a just individual is one who subscribes to the principles by which a society is just. Here the justice of society is given explanatory primacy over the justice of individuals: we first define a just society and then give an account of a just individual as one who has a strong and normally effective desire to act in accordance with the principles which make a society just. This is the way Rawls proceeds,[29] going back to an anti-Platonic tradition that begins perhaps with Aristotle;[30] in fact it goes back to the *Republic* since this is the way the justice of persons is related to the justice of society in Thrasymachus' and Glaucon's theories.[31] This seems to be the dominant tradition, that justice is primarily and essentially a social virtue; unlike perhaps such other virtues as wisdom, courage (and even temperance), which may be more plausibly thought of to be primarily and essentially virtues of individuals.

Perhaps the greatest advantage of the Aristotelian–Rawlsian way of relating the justice of persons to the justice of societies is that it assures us of a coherent and unified theory of justice; there is only one standard of justice, the justice of society, and a just person is one who subscribes to that standard. But in Plato's theory there are two standards of justice: one of cities and one of persons. And the isomorphism by itself does not imply that a person who has Platonic justice in her soul will also obey or subscribe to the constitutions and laws that make a city Platonically just, or conversely. There seems to be a gap between a just citizen and a just person even in Plato's completely good city: a just citizen is one who performs that social function for which s/he is best suited by nature and education, that is, one who subscribes and obeys Plato's principle of social justice; but a just person is one in whose soul each part is doing that psychic functions for which it is best suited by nature and education. From the definitions alone at least, there is no built assurance that a just citizen in Plato's ideal city will be also a just person, or conversely. There is a gap between Plato's just society and his just person.

This is a gap like the one that David Sachs pointed out: between Platonic psychic justice and common standards of just and unjust behavior. But it is an even more radical problem than the Sachs problem, since it arises within Plato's own ideal theory, that is to say, within the completely good and so completely just city. In Aristotle's theory of justice or in Rawls theory of justice there would be no gaps between the justice of society and the justice of a just person. In these theories Sachs-like problems do not exist!

So what advantages did Plato see in defining a just person as an image of a just society (his actual order of exposition), or a just society as an image of a just person (possibly his real view)?

One advantage perhaps is that his actual procedure enabled Plato to project a publicly observable social structure onto the mystery of the human soul: if the justice of the city consists in division of social labors which matches optimally inborn abilities of citizens to the city's functions, perhaps the justice of the person will consist in division of psychic labors which matches optimally natural psychic parts to the person's functions. Here the isomorphism can be viewed at least as a heuristic device, to help us understand the structures and functioning of the human soul and discover its virtues.

A second advantage is that the isomorphism provides a strategy for the defense of justice. Plato's defense of his *social* justice is that it promotes *most*[32] the good or happiness of the city as a whole; that particular social ordering is best and so rational and just. This is a recognizable version of a fundamental principle of teleological ethical theories, that the right is what maximizes the good: the social structure which Plato calls just promotes mostly the good of the city as a whole, and so it is rational and just. Now, if the same functional theory of good and the isomorphism are used to construct psychic justice, then we can have a corresponding defense of *psychic* justice: this psychic order promotes most the good of the person as a whole, and so it is rational and just. Thus, the isomorphism, the common functional theory of good, and the proceeding from social to psychic justice, give Plato a heuristic device for understanding justice in our souls, and some leverage in the defense of psychic justice: the same theory of functional good and the same teleological principle are applied to cities and persons. And a reasonable and recognizable defense of a conception of social justice, that it promotes most the good of the society as a whole, is used as leverage for a similar defense of an analogous conception of psychic justice.

We discuss this defense and its merits further in the last chapter.

Notes

1   Some have claimed that in this passage Socrates commits the fallacy of division, that if an entity has a property its individual parts also have it. But Socrates is talking here about only psychological properties, which are primarily the properties of individual human beings and only derivatively of cities composed of such beings. From a basketball team being balanced we cannot validly infer that each of the players is balanced; but from its being aggressive we can infer validly that at least some of its players are aggressive (see Lear 1997: 66–71).

2   For discussion of this principle and its application see Irwin (1995), Bobonich (2002), and Lorenz (2006).

3   Plato says that the conflict is between desiring, wanting, wishing, and not desiring, not wanting, and not wishing, respectively; and that the rejections and repulsions are from reason (439d). And from the latter and the principle of contrariety, he infers that the conflict is between desire and reason. Freud too supposes that inhibitions are the work of the ego.

4   For classic discussions of the three parts see Cooper (1999) and Bobonich (2002). For a fine, more recent and broadly based discussion of the spirited element see Weinstein (2005).

5   Two small changes in Shorey's translation: "other appetites" for his "other desires," to keep the naming each power after the name of the activities; and "arational" for Shorey's "irrational," because Plato need not argue that all appetites are always contrary to reason, which "irrational" implies; it is sufficient to consider appetite in abstraction from any learning or reason.

6   Plato's argument for the division of the soul has been discussed extensively by many authors. See, for example, Bobonich (2002), Price (1995), Lorenz (2006), and Weinstein (2004).

7   For my view of Plato's treatment of *philia* in the *Republic*, especially Book V, see Santas (1988: 89–97). But this holds for persons – whether it can be applied without alteration to parts of the soul is an open question.

8   Bobonich (2002) has made by far the best case, probably as good as can ever be made, for the agent interpretation; see, for example, pages 219–23. His discussion deserves far more attention than can be given here.

9   For the characteristics of the three parts according to the agent interpretation, see Bobonich (2002: 220). Interestingly enough, spirit seems to be entirely left out. There are differences between Bobonich's characterizations and the third

alternative I set out in the text, but they do not affect the paradoxes created by the agent interpretation.

10   Presumably by their objects? Appetite desires food and sex and cannot reason about forms; reason does not desire food and sex and can reason about the forms, and so on.

11   Even Aristotle, certainly a faculty psychologist, uses anthropomorphic language for parts of the soul at times, as in *Nicomachean Ethics* (1102b25–1102b35), where he tells us that appetites and desires "listen" to reason in temperate persons.

12   This long passage is usually explained by commentators as trying to avoid a Socratic objection (to the partitioning), that what we desire is always something good (apparent or real). But while Plato is indeed trying to avoid this objection, the passage tries to isolate thirsting not only from goodness but also from many other (indeed an indefinite list) attributes of an object such as hot or cold, sweet or bitter; we are better off with the supposition that he is trying to isolate thirsting from any learning about the object of thirst: thirsting is just for drink (liquid nutrition); that is its natural object.

13   The only direct textual evidence I know of for the agent interpretation in Book IV (*Republic*: 442d) is in Plato's account of psychic temperance, that all three parts have "common opinion" that reason should rule. And though this evidence cannot be completely neutralized, context should be kept in mind: in his previous account of how a guardian can be so educated as to have the holistic virtue of temperance agreement or harmony among the three parts of the soul that reason should rule. That education is in part cognitive, directed at reason, and in part habituation directed at spirit and appetite. For this division of labor in educating, see *Republic* (441e–442a). Harmony among the parts need not be purely cognitive, any more than harmony among musical notes is. For a recent discussion of some of these points see Modrak (2008).

14   For this part of Freud, see Lear (2005: 173).

15   For a plausible account of the oligarchic personality that does not imply that appetite can reason, see Lorenz (2006: 158–9).

16   See *Republic* (581b) for the natural object or aim of reason: "to know where the truth lies." And Lorenz's fine discussion of the functions of reason (2006: 154–7).

17   Freud too had a hard time with this, first supposing that hunger and libido are two different basic instincts in *Three Essays on the Theory of Sexuality*, and later, beginning with *Beyond the Pleasure Principle*, trying to group them together under the heading of self-preservative instincts – lumping together preservation of the individual and preservation of the species (Freud 1953).

18   The isomorphism between just city and just person, as expounded here, does not specify fully the relation between a just city and a just person. The full definition of a just city together with the isomorphism certainly does not

entail that a just city is made up of just persons. We might then ask the more modest question: what is the relation between a person being socially just and individually just? To answer we have to go to the passage where Plato tells us that a person who has justice in his soul will pronounce those actions just which tend to produce and preserve that just state of soul, and unjust those which destroy it. We can then say clearly that internal consistency of Plato's theory of justice, social and individual, demands at least that the kinds of behavior which social justice requires (namely performing one's own optimal social function) does not conflict with the kinds of actions individual justice requires (actions that preserve psychic justice) – the two "justices" cannot have conflicting requirements with respect to conduct.

19   At the start of his construction of the just city (369–70), Socrates begins with the needs of individuals; their lack of self-sufficiency bring them together to cooperatively satisfy these needs; but they are still needs of individuals for providing for themselves, defending themselves, and ruling themselves. The social functions of satisfying these needs collectively parallel the individual needs, indeed are derived from individual needs and lack of individual self-sufficiency.

20   When we so abstract desire from learning we reach the modern psychologists' distinctions between primary and secondary drives or "unlearned" and "learned" drives; or biological and cultural desires.

21   Plato also says that the object of appetites is pleasure (see Lorenz 2006). The argument here would be very similar: there is not enough correlation between the things that give us bodily pleasures and what is good for out bodies (e.g. sweets). So, once more, appetites need regulation by learning and reason.

22   Of course we must remember the distinction between needs and appetites that Plato had going already at the very beginning of the construction of the ideal city. See chapter 4.

23   See Rawls' fine discussion of teleological ethical theories, and how some of them apply the principle that the right is what maximizes the good to individual persons as well as to societies (Rawls 1971: 22–7).

24   The concept of reason ruling is ambiguous between a value model or a strength model. Reason might be ruling in a person, in that it is the faculty that reasons what is the best thing to do in any choice situation (the value model of human action); but it might or might not be effective in enforcing its decision (the strength model). Plato seems to think that the two go together sometimes, as in a just person who is also courageous, with spirit helping reason to carry out its decisions (see Irwin 1995).

25   There is another ambiguity in ruling: setting ends or only discovering means to ends. Spirit and appetite *can* set ends in that the person is brought up to have or will come to have the satisfaction of appetite or the aims of spirit (victory and honor) as the end of his life; reason here is confined to calculating

the means to such ends. In Hume the calm passions set ends, reason finds means to them, and in that sense they rule and reason is their "slave."

26   Hume (1955), *Treatise of Human Nature*, Book II, part iii, section 3. See Rawls' subtle discussion of Hume's "provocative" propositions about reason and the passions (Rawls 2000: 27–35).

27   This appears to be Frede's view (1996).

28   It is true that a just city with perfect compliance ("a well ordered" society – to use Rawls' phrase for an ideally just society) would be composed of just persons; and it might also be true that one can reasonably doubt that a city is just if it has very low (say, twenty five percent) compliance. Even so, perfect compliance is not a necessary condition of a city being just; while very low compliance would affect its stability and raise questions about the citizens' perception of its justice.

29   Rawls (1971: 1, 7–17, 436).

30   For Aristotle's theory, see Keyt (1991) and Young (2009).

31   Quite explicit in Thrasymachus: persons are just in so far as they (are disposed to and) act according to the laws of their societies; and these laws are just if obedience to them promotes the interests of the ruling party. Similarly, in Glaucon's contractarian theory, a person is just in so far as he obeys just laws – laws that are in accord with the fundamental contract (an agreement by all neither to do nor suffer harm).

32   That is, more than the known alternatives, which are the other models of organization for the city that Plato considered (everyone doing everything to satisfy their needs, or division of labor without regard to natural talent – Adam Smith's model).

6

The Equality of Women
Plato's Blindfold

In the back of many courtrooms there is a statue of justice. She has a sword on her right side, holds an old-fashioned grocer's balance with her left hand, and wears a blindfold.

The sword is the easiest symbol to understand: unlike love, charity, or benevolence, justice demands enforcement. Society has no right to enforce charity, whose statue would have no sword. But it has a right and a duty to enforce what justice requires or forbids.

The grocer's balance is a more intricate symbol: it points to weighing, measuring, and a fair transaction as a result. In a court of law there are always competing claims and interests; and lady justice wants these claims weighed, measured against each other or against some standard in the law, and a fair verdict found. In parliaments and legislatures too, there are competing claims and conflicting interests, evident enough in every tax legislation, and the lawmakers must weigh them, measure them if they can, and enact laws fair to all.

And the blindfold? Why is lady justice wearing a blindfold at all? And what does it hide? It must hide something since she is wearing it; but it can't hide everything, since she would then be completely blind and uninformed and she could not even see enough to weigh and measure anything.

1 The Blindfold of Justice

There is wide agreement that justice must wear a blindfold that hides something or other. Justice must be "colorblind," we are told nowadays, meaning blind to the color of a person's skin when she makes decisions about the rights and interests of peoples of different colors and races: she must not make her decisions on the basis of color differences. Sometimes juries are sequestered, to keep some information from them; or some evidence is "inadmissible" to them, and if they see or hear it by accident or mistake they must ignore it in their deliberations – not at all an easy thing. Wealthy public officials must put their wealth into "blind trusts" upon assuming office, so that they cannot "see" the effects of their public decisions on their private fortunes. And John Rawls tells us that in the "original position," a situation appropriate for choice among competing principles of justice, the parties in that position must make their choice behind "a veil of ignorance," ignorance of at least their particular natural, inborn assets and their particular social and economic advantages or disadvantages. Only behind such a veil of ignorance are they fairly situated for such a choice, all of them – whether in reality rich or poor, very smart or average – making their choice in the same level playing field.[1]

All these cases suggest that justice wears a blindfold so that she can be justice – she can render fair and impartial decisions. If a party in Rawls' original position knew that s/he was born smart or rich s/he would rationally opt for principles that favored smart or rich people – partial principles; similarly, one who knew he was born average or poor would rationally opt for principles that favored average or poor people – more partial principles. And similarly with public officials that have blind trusts and juries that are sequestered. It is no accident that Thrasymachus' justice, a justice that systemically favors the rulers, would fail the blindfold test (chapter 3 above); it is fatally flawed with partiality.[2]

But there is disagreement about what the lady's justice blindfold must hide. Upon publication of *A Theory of Justice*, Thomas Nagel questioned the thickness of Rawls' veil of ignorance, particularly its hiding the parties' own conceptions of the good.[3] Rawls himself allows that in different choice situations – from the abstract original position to constitutional conventions, parliaments and legislatures, and the very specific applications of law in courts – the veil may hide different things, ranging from a very thick veil to no veil at all.[4] But even within the very specific rules of evidence in courts of law, there can be disagreements about what evidence is "admissible."

Deep disagreements about the thickness of the veil may mark important different theories of justice and can produce wide or deeply different results about what is just and unjust. One important disagreement is whether the veil should hide some or all *natural* differences, whether advantages or disadvantages or seemingly value-neutral differences; differences people are *born with* and over which they may have little or no control, not even control in their development. Differences in color are obvious examples of seemingly value-neutral natural differences over whose distribution at birth individuals and societies have no control. There are also inborn differences in intelligence, and other human abilities and talents, over whose development individuals and societies have some control.

All these are quite distinct from *social, political* and *economic* advantages or disadvantages people are born with – of educated parents or not, poor or rich.[5] The distributions at birth of social, political, and economic advantages, of course, depend on the particular institutions of particular societies, and these are certainly under society's control, and can be just or unjust. Nobody would be born homeless in a society that allowed no homelessness. Nobody would be born very poor or very rich in a society that did not allow extremes of wealth and poverty.

The *natural* differences are distributed by the "natural lottery," and as Rawls remarks, what the natural lottery distributes is neither just nor unjust. What society does with such natural distributions, however, can be very much just or unjust. The life prospects of people born with different natural characteristics depend on what social, political, and economic institutions make of such natural differences. Witness what societies have done with the color of a person's skin: if a society's justice blindfolds this difference then people of different colors are not treated differently by that society's political, economic, and educational institutions. But if a society's lady justice does not blindfold color, then that society's institutions are allowed – possibly even required – to treat persons of different color differently and their life prospects can be radically different; in this case, let us say that justice institutionalizes (instead of blindfolding) color differences, even allowing persons to be bought, sold, or bequeathed, as if they are property.

For this reason alone, justice has to take a stand on different natural distributions at birth. Should lady justice leave them alone, blindfold none, and allow any natural difference at birth to influence or even determine different life prospects? Or should she blindfold all of them and declare that no natural difference whatsoever is a reason for different treatment and different life prospects? Or should she blindfold some, and allow others to determine life prospects, and if so, which?

2 Does Plato's Justice wear a Blindfold?

We know that Plato's social justice takes a stand on some natural, inborn differences among people at the very start of constructing in discourse the "completely good city." Right after Adeimantus said that a city with division of labor would more easily meet the needs of its people, Socrates declares: "it occurs to me, to start with, that each of us is not naturally all alike another, one naturally fitted for one function, another for another" (369cd). And he soon concludes that "more things are produced and better and more easily when each person performs one task according to his nature, at the right moment, and at leisure from other occupations" (370c). This is the first version of what later is declared to be the principle of social justice (433ab), which requires not only division of social labors but also matching occupations to inborn abilities and talents, appropriately educated – inborn differences in intelligence, spirit, and ability for productive arts and trades (433–4).

So Plato's principle of social justice does not blindfold inborn (natural in that sense) differences in intelligence, spirit, and productive and trade abilities. On the contrary, Plato's lady justice looks keenly to discern these differences, and she makes them the basis for different educations and different careers. She *requires* that those born with the highest intelligence receive the highest education and become rulers of the city; those born with high spirit are to be defenders of the city and are to receive lesser but appropriate educations; and those born with abilities for productive arts and crafts are to receive lesser yet but appropriate educations and appointed to those tasks. And when she declares multitasking and naturally unfit careers unjust (434c), she touches her sword.

Does Plato's lady justice blindfold *any* natural characteristics? Perhaps she wears no blindfold at all. This would be a hasty and false conclusion. Socrates tells us explicitly that the natural difference between bald and long-haired men would be an absurd basis for assigning them to different occupations – his principle of social justice does not have this absurd implication (454c). And we can reasonably suppose that differences in, say, height or eye color would also be blindfolded in the choice of educations and occupations. So Plato's lady justice blindfolds some natural differences among persons, and she institutionalizes others, making them the basis for the distribution of educations and careers.

But how does his justice choose to blindfold some natural differences and not others?

3   The Gender Blindfold of Plato's Justice

In Book V of the *Republic* Socrates faces the question whether men and women should have similar educations and pursuits: "whether female human nature is capable of sharing with the male all tasks or none at all, or some but not others" (453a). The issue of education is to be based on the decision about pursuits: Socrates proposes the sound principle that persons should have similar educations if they have similar pursuits in life and different educations if different pursuits. This need not be understood except in the sense in which it is true: architects, say, should have similar education, physicians and architects different, because architecture and medicine are different pursuits and so require different knowledge.[6] Thus the question of education depends on the question of pursuits.

Should then men and women have the same or different pursuits? The pursuits in question are the social tasks and occupations, and in particular, in Book V, the tasks of defending and ruling the city; *the* tasks which in Plato's time were then practiced exclusively by men, a practice sanctioned by all existing constitutions and laws.

In his first argument against Thrasymachus, Socrates tried to refute the equation of positive law in a society and justice in that society. The implication of this equation for the role of gender is clear. If the political institutions of all known ancient societies did not legally allow women to vote or to hold office, as indeed they did not, Thrasymachus would have to say, on the basis of his theory of justice, that these legal practices were just for these societies; and if just in *all* societies then just, period. But given his argument against Thrasymachus, Plato refuses to draw this inference and leaves open and investigates the possibility that these universal legal practices were unjust.

Aside from legal positivism, the view of Plato's contemporaries was that men and women should have different pursuits, as in fact they did: men's responsibilities were the affairs of the city, women's the affairs of the home. We can see this in Plato's *Meno* (Cooper 1997: 71e): Meno defines different virtues for men and women on the assumption of different pursuits; the virtue of a woman is what qualities enables her to conduct the household well, the virtue of a man the qualities that enables him to manage the city well. In that dialogue Socrates resisted the idea that there was one virtue for men and another for women, though this resistance was based on the (implicit) theory of forms rather than considerations of fairness or equality.

But in his discussion of the place of women in society in the *Republic*, Plato makes the issue a matter of justice: he appeals to his principle of social justice, to reach results contrary to every existing law. It is important to see that for him the issue of the equality of women in education and careers is an issue his justice must face. Plato's justice refused to blindfold some natural differences (e.g. intelligence) between persons, and was willing to blindfold others (e.g. baldness), so she can be challenged to take a stand on natural gender differences.[7]

And this is what happens when Socrates starts the debate with a challenge from the opposition:

> There is no need, Socrates and Glaucon, of others disputing against you, for you yourselves at the beginning of the foundation of your city agreed that each one ought to mind as his own business the one thing for which he was fitted by nature … Can it be denied then that there is by nature a great difference between men and women? … Is it not fitting, then, that a different function [*ergon*] should be appointed for each corresponding to this difference in nature? (453b)

In response Socrates tries to give a criterion for distinguishing between the natural differences that his lady justice institutionalized and those that she blindfolded:

> we did not then [when we began our city] posit likeness and difference of nature in every respect, but paid heed to that kind of difference and similarity that was pertinent to the pursuits [the main social occupations] themselves. We meant, for example, that a man and a woman who have a physician's soul have the same nature … But that a man physician and a man carpenter have different natures. (454d)

So, if we can tell what natural differences are pertinent, and what not pertinent, to the performance of the main social pursuits, and if we find that the natural gender differences are not pertinent, then these differences Plato's justice will blindfold and will not make them a basis for assigning different occupations to different genders, and consequently not a basis for different educations either.[8]

Plato finds that there are only two natural differences between men and women, considered as groups: first, men beget and women bear children[9] and second, men are *by and large, not always,* physically stronger than women.

These are not the differences on the basis of which persons are assigned different pursuits: they are not differences in natural ability or aptitude for the different social tasks, differences shown in learning how to do these tasks. The differences between a man who is naturally gifted for something, say, architecture, and another who is not, are that the one learns that thing easily, the other with difficulty; the one with slight instruction can discover much for himself, the other after much instruction and drill could at most only remember what he learned (455b).

The two natural differences conceded between men and women are not of this kind, except possibly that the differences in physical strength will indeed be relevant to pursuits requiring great physical strength and stamina. But this difference, unlike the first one, is not universal between the sexes: some women are physically stronger than some men.

At the same time, Socrates points out, the three main natural differences on which Plato relied all along to assign ruling, defense, and provisioning the city, namely, high intelligence, high spirit, and abilities for production and trade, are not distributed in any consistent way between men and women. Some women are more intelligent than some men, some are braver than some men, and some are better producers and traders; while other men are better than some women in one or another of these ways.

> Then there is no pursuit of the administrators of a state that belongs to a woman because she is a woman or to a man because he is a man. But the natural capacities are distributed alike among both creatures, and women naturally share in all pursuits and men in all. (455de)

Therefore, given Plato's principle of social justice, and given *these facts*, it follows that in a Platonically just society men and women will be assigned to the same social tasks and pursuits on exactly the same basis. It will be just that some men and some women be rulers, some men and some women be soldiers, and some men and some women be producers and traders.

And since those who share the same pursuits should share the same education, men and women of the same pursuits should have the same education, and men and women of different pursuits should have different educations; just as men who have different pursuits should have different educations, and women who share the same pursuits should have the same educations.

This is Plato's argument for the equality of women in society. It is a deduction constructed with his *principle* of social justice and his perception of *relevant facts* about men and women. The principle itself picks out what facts are relevant, certain natural abilities and talents that make a difference in the performance of the main social labors. The beauty of this deduction is that it shows cleanly what Plato's principle of social justice can do when put together with what we now know are true propositions about the world.

One of the most remarkable things about this argument is that Plato was actually "stretching the facts" in favor of women. Since women in all the societies he knew were not actually pursuing careers outside the home, it could only be a matter of speculation how well they would do, especially compared to men, if they did venture into ruling, soldiering, and producing goods and services. Women had no opportunities to develop talents and abilities in these pursuits; consequently there was not much evidence how they would do compared to men, and it could only be guessed that they had talents for these pursuits. And Plato was guessing absolutely contrary to what everyone else believed.

4   Was Plato an Advocate of Women's Rights? Was He a Feminist?

There has been a lively debates on these questions for some time.[10] Let us look briefly at Vlastos' answers.

In "Was Plato a Feminist?," Vlastos gives a balanced and judicious answer to this question. He defines feminism by reference to a proposed constitutional amendment (which did not in fact pass): "Equality of rights under the law shall not be denied or abridged by the U.S. or any State on account of sex."[11] He then poses the question whether such equality of rights is consonant with Plato's "ideas, sentiments, and proposals for social policy." After reviewing the relevant evidence he concludes that in *Republic*, Book V, Plato was "unambiguously feminist"; that elsewhere the story is at best mixed; and that "in his personal attitudes to women Plato is virulently anti-feminist."

Our construction of Plato's argument for the equality of women in the ideal city supports Vlastos' general conclusions, but with a rather important qualification concerning rights.

The qualification is that Plato's theory of social justice in the *Republic* does not seem to be a *rights based* theory at all, or a theory that *generates rights*. Plato's principle of social justice is not justified or grounded on any other principle about rights of persons, as, say, Locke's theory of civil government is based on a principle attributing rights to human beings in a state of nature. When we look at Plato's *justification* of his principle, we find him talking about human *needs*, how they can be best satisfied, and about satisfying or promoting the good of the city as a whole rather than some part of it.[12] These appear to be teleological justifications of the principle of social justice, like those of, say, Mill, but not like those of Locke or Rawls. Further, Plato's principle of social justice itself makes no reference, explicit or implicit, to any rights of persons; in the *content* of the principle nothing is said or implied about rights;[13] it is all about social tasks and natural human abilities and talents. How then, in view of all this, are we to decide whether Plato was for *equal rights* for women?

As one might well expect if this is true, the questions about women's pursuits and education in Book V are not posed in terms of rights, any more than questions about careers and education for men are ever posed in terms of rights. We might tease rights, or perhaps freedoms, out of Glaucon's theory (in Book II) or the theory of democracy Plato expounds (in Book VIII). Glaucon's contract theory of justice might generate rights, and Athenian democracy seemed to guarantee equal political rights to citizens, such as participation in the Assembly, and equal freedoms such as the freedom of speech. But these theories Plato criticizes. And his criticism of democracy is precisely that it allows for the freedom to do as one pleases, including the freedom of choice of career, in utter disregard to his own principle of social justice.[14] The freedom to choose a career, a social task in the ideal city, is a freedom his principle of justice denies. Again, there is a fundamental contrast here between Rawls' principle of "formal equality of opportunity," as careers *legally open* to talents,[15] and Plato's principle of justice: the former creates freedom of choice of career, by prohibiting laws which would exclude any persons or groups of persons from pursuing any career they wish.

So, it may be too much to say that "political rights" would be "the same for women as for men among Plato's Guardians." It may be more accurate to say that no one has political rights in Plato's ideal city, at least not "liberty rights," since no one has a right to *refuse* doing that for which s/he is best suited, or a right to do something other than what s/he is best suited for.[16]

However, if we lay aside the question of rights, and look at what Plato actually does when he faces the issue of the place of women in the ideal city, we see clearly that his theory of social justice does not *discriminate* between men and women; that is, it does not differentiate on the basis of gender when assignments of offices and other social tasks are made. On these issues Plato's justice blindfolds gender. And this *was* revolutionary for Plato's time.

How can we explain Plato's revolutionary proposals? We need a two-part answer: one part relates to the formal part of Plato's conception of social justice, the other to his unusual perception of the pertinent facts, men's and women's abilities.

We saw that in the *Meno* Plato argued that virtue is the same for all human beings; he has Socrates explicitly deny that there is one virtue for men and another for women, as Meno had explicitly stated in *his* definition of various virtues. And since justice is one of the virtues, this has to apply to justice: there is one and the same justice for men and women. And we know that this is true in the *Republic*: in Book IV Plato tells us explicitly that justice is one and the same for all (435). This seems supported by his theory of forms, which holds that there is exactly one form justice. So, if cities and citizens can be just, they are so by participation in the same form; similarly, if men and women are just, they are so by participation in the same form. And since women can be just or unjust, the same principle of justice must apply to them as to men.

This explanation is partial because it does not cover the factual part of the argument; it does not account for the fact that Plato stretched the evidence in favor of women. How did he know, or why did he think, that women had talents for producing goods, for soldiering, and for ruling, when hardly any women were doing any of these things in any existing society? Why did he think that a woman can have a "physician's soul" some twenty-three centuries before the Johns Hopkins Medical School admitted its first woman?

Here his metaphysical views about the human soul may have been an advantage. According to him, human souls can exist disembodied and can occupy several human bodies successively;[17] and this would naturally incline him to the view that human souls are not gendered. Gender is an attribute of human (and other animal) bodies, not of human souls. And the inborn abilities or talents, which his theory of justice matches to social labors, are attributes of souls, not of bodies.[18] If souls are not gendered, there is no reason to believe that their attributes, such as intelligence, spirit, and talents and abilities for arts and science, are distributed on the basis of gender. So, when Plato applies his principle of social justice, which matches inborn intelligence, spirit, and talents and abilities with social labors, to women, he supplies factual premises according to which high intelligence, spirit, and various talents are distributed without regard to gender. With respect to such attributes the "natural lottery" is gender neutral. And since these are the attributes Plato's justice uses for distributing careers and education, his justice blindfolds gender.

Similar results may be expected in the case of individual justice, Platonic justice in our souls. If human souls are not gendered, the tripartite analysis of the human soul is not gendered, it is gender neutral. And psychic justice, which requires the matching of psychic labors to parts of the soul on the basis of what these parts can do best, is consequently not gender sensitive; it is gender neutral.

Finally, side by side with the evidence that Vlastos cites for his verdict that Plato, in his less theoretical moments, was also "virulently anti-feminist," we have evidence that goes along with the theoretical explanation we have provided. Plato, we are told, allowed women to enter the Academy, the first institution of higher learning to do so, thousands of years ahead of the universities of Europe. And in the *Symposium* we have striking evidence that Plato thought women could have the highest human intelligence. He has a woman, Diotima, instruct Socrates in the theory of Platonic *eros*. What is remarkable here is not so much that a woman tells Socrates about *eros*, but that Plato has a woman instruct Socrates in the theory of forms, in which his own theory of *eros* is embedded. Indeed, one of the most remarkable statements about Platonic forms in the whole corpus is put in the mouth of Diotima, with Socrates listening to her mystified but with open-mouthed admiration. The form beauty, *she* says, is the highest object of love. And unlike the beauties of the eyes and the ears, it is not beautiful in one respect and ugly in another, or beautiful in comparison to one thing and not beautiful in comparison to another, or beautiful at one time or for some people but not at another or for others. The form beauty, existing alone by itself, is beautiful in all ways for all eternity.

So Plato must have thought that at least one woman could be a philosopher and understand the theory of forms, a mark of the highest intelligence in the *Republic*. And if he thought one women can be that intelligent, why not others? Even a singly contrary token is enough to break down the prejudice of a stereotype.

Plato was no rights feminist, or a rights advocate at all. But he was a revolutionary about gender all the same. If Plato were living today and he had access to our facts, which are far more favorable to the pertinent abilities of women, he would be even a greater supporter of the equality of women. His justice would blindfold gender everywhere that justice reaches.

Notes

1   "The veil of ignorance is so natural a condition that something like it must have occurred to many" (Rawls 1971: 137n11).

2   It is important to note that though Rawls uses a veil of ignorance, of which the blindfold is the symbol, as essential to his social contract methodology, the blindfold is not limited to such methodologies, as the presence of the blindfolded lady in courts and blind trusts for public officials and other such devices indicate. The blindfold is a symbol for what is not a just basis for different and unequal treatment and as such it is a universal symbol of justice.

3   Nagel's review of Rawls (1975).

4   Rawls, The Four Stage Sequence (1971, chapter IV, section 31).

5   Rawls marks the difference by his distinction between *natural* and *social* primary goods; the former are distributed by the natural lottery, while the distribution of social goods is regulated by the institutions of the basic structure of a society (1971: 62, 92).

6.   For Plato, mathematics and architecture, say, are different *technai*, with different subject matters and different goals, and the practice of each would require appropriately different higher educations, as it does for us (*Republic*: 441–2).

7   We may also note that Plato's principle of *social* justice has no part that would exclude women from its scope. This is equally true of his principle of individual justice, which according to him is isomorphic with social justice: an individual is just when reason rules his\her soul, spirit helps to carry out the commands of reason, and appetite obeys. There is no hint of gender, either in the tripartite analysis of the psyche (*Republic*: 434–40), or in the normative assignments of psychic labor to the three parts of the psyche, which is individual justice.

8   Plato's examples of a woman with a "physician's soul" or a man with a carpenter's soul shows clearly enough the equality of women is meant to apply to all three classes of Plato's completely good city, a point also implied by the scope of his principle of social justice – it applies to all the citizens.

9   Plato may have had a false micro-biology, but I do not think it matters here, as there is a biological division of labor in human reproduction and women have to bear children while men do not (*Republic*: 454e).

10   See Kraut (1992: 44–5, 507–8), Smith's judicious discussion and bibliography (1983), Reeve (1997) and Saxonhouse (1997).

11   He abbreviates this into: "Equality in the rights of persons shall not be denied or abridged on account of sex" (Vlastos 1994)

12   See for example, *Republic*, Book II (370), the justification of the principle of social justice when it is first proposed; and Socrates' response, in the opening paragraphs of Book IV, to Adeimantus' objection that Socrates is making the guardians unhappy.

13   In considerable contrast, the equality of rights and liberties is built into Rawls' first principle of justice: "Each person is to have an equal right to the most extensive basic liberty compatible with a similar liberty for others," with a list of basic liberties (Rawls 1971: 60, 61). As Rawls points out, in teleological ethical theories, equality has to be deduced from a first principle and factual premises; and so indeed Plato proceeds.

14   *Republic*, Book VIII, and chapter 8.

15   Rawls 1971, pp. 83–4.

16   See *Republic* (434ac) for an explicit statement that interchanges of social functions would be unjust. In this book I leave aside the question whether Plato or the ancient Greeks even had a *concept of rights*. This question is well discussed by Miller (1995). His chapter 4 contains an illuminating discussion of various kinds of rights, including "liberty rights."

17   In the *Phaedo* and the *Phaedrus*, souls can exist disembodied and can migrate from body to body and even transmigrate to animal bodies. Disembodied souls are also assumed by the theory of recollection in the *Meno*. How could disembodied souls be gendered? David Keyt brought this point initially to my attention. See also Smith's illuminating discussion on this point (1983); the different treatments of women by Plato and Aristotle correlate significantly with their different theories of soul. See also a related discussion in Sorabji (1996).

18   We see this clearly in a passage quoted earlier: "We meant, for example, that a man and a woman who had a physician's soul have the same nature" (*Republic*: 454d).

7

Knowledge and Governing Well
Opinions and Knowledge, Forms and the Good

One main thought in moral and political philosophy is that it can be done independently of other disciplines that discover what the universe is and what man is; ethics is about what is good and bad, right and wrong, and these things can be known relatively independently of the sciences. Plato was aware of this idea, as we can see in *Republic* (493), where he says that right and wrong, good and bad are sometimes defined by the approval or disapproval of the public, and beautiful things by the admiration of the crowd. Plato opposed this view: he started the other main thought: that we cannot know what is good or bad, right or wrong, without knowing what knowledge is, what the universe is like, what human beings are and their place in the universe. Hence, the structure of the *Republic*: ethical and political ideals in Books I to V; some of their grounds in epistemology and metaphysics in Books V, VI, and VII; and back to ethics and political philosophy and even aesthetics in Books VIII, IX, and X. In this chapter we discuss his epistemology and metaphysics and their implications for ethics and politics.

1   Ideals as Standards and their Approximations

In Book V Glaucon raises two new questions about justice: Can the Platonically just and virtuous city-state, the completely good city-state, be realized? And, if so, how? (*Republic*: 471–2). This is an example of more general questions about any ideal of justice: can such justice be realized? If so how? And how far?

Glaucon's questions can also be raised about Plato's ideal of a completely good, virtuous person. Can such a person ever come into being? And if so, how?

Socrates' reply falls into two parts: first, he draws a distinction between perfection and a high approximation of perfection (what Sidgwick (1981) calls excellence) and points out that perfection is not useless even if it is never realized:

> If we do discover what justice is, are we to demand that the just man shall differ from it in no respect, but shall conform in every way to the ideal? Or will it suffice us if he approximates to it as nearly as possible and partake of it more than others? – That will content us, he said. A pattern [paradigm], then, I said, was what we wanted when we were inquiring into the nature of perfect justice. (472a; Shorey 1935, modified)

A painting of a completely beautiful human is not useless if such a being does not exist; even if such beauty can never be completely realized, it can be approximated, and the painting can function as a standard for judging how good the approximations are. Similarly, our paradigm (described in words) of a good city-state, may never exist, never completely realized; but it can be approximated, and if we know what such an ideal is, we can use it as a standard for judging approximations. Plato puts his ideal to use not only in determining its highest approximation (in Books II–VII), but also in defining and judging less just states in (Book VIII).

Similarly, a completely good, completely virtuous human being may never exist, but it can be approximated; and if we know what such an ideal is, we can use it as a standard for determining and judging approximations. And Plato puts his ideal to use to determine its highest approximation (by the higher education program in Book VII) and to define and judge less just persons (in Book VIII).[1]

How are we to understand approximations of the ideal? As we shall see, Plato's metaphysics suggests that one way of realizing an ideal is by its embodiment. The ideal is immaterial, it is purely structural, it is form; its embodiments are materials with that structure. The best material copy is the best that the nature of matter allows – a well-educated Socrates perhaps; persons with more dominant bodily appetites are lesser approximations – Alcibiades perhaps. Further, the immaterial structure does not change, but any embodiment of that structure changes and indeed deteriorates over time – that is the nature of matter. An actual house may be the best copy of an architect's plan that the builder's best materials allow – it is an excellent copy. If it is built with materials that deteriorate faster it is not as good a house; if it is built with mistakes from the plan, it is not as good a house. The lesser copies of an ideal, built with mistakes or inferior materials or both, can go all the way to bad things of that kind; the same architectural plan can be embodied with different materials and different accuracies and the results can vary from an excellent to a bad house (assuming in this analogy that the plan is the standard, though plans, too, can be evaluated). When we soon consider the Platonic imperfections of the material world, we will discuss approximations again.

2   The Paradox of the Philosopher-king: Knowledge and Political Power

The second part of Socrates' answer is that the Platonic ideal of a completely good city can be highly approximated only if there is a union of political power and philosophy. This is the paradox of the philosopher-king; a paradox in the sense of being contrary to common belief; as Plato elaborates, common belief was that philosophers could hardly manage their own affairs – their heads too far up in the clouds to manage the ship of state (*Republic*: 480–96)[2] Plato addresses this problem with his program of higher education and years of experience for future rulers – the experience of the cave, the higher education out of it, and the experience of ruling back in it (*Republic*: 502–41).

What the paradox means depends on what Plato means by philosophy, not necessarily what it is many centuries later. Plato's philosopher here is not only one who loves knowledge and truth, but one who also has knowledge of the sciences, above all knowledge of the good and what is good for societies and for individuals (*Republic*: 474–87, 502–41). The union of political power and philosophy is the union of political power and knowledge of the sciences, including knowledge of the good. And what Plato means by this union is that political power is to be based on knowledge. We know this to be his view also from the role of the virtue of social wisdom in the ideal city, knowledge of the good of the whole city: it is this knowledge of the rulers that entitles them, above all else, to rule the city, because it is the virtue that enables them to rule it well. We may call this the Rule of Knowledge, and a city-state so ruled an epistocracy, as democracy is the Rule of the People.

Of course, we must remember that for Plato knowledge is not enough for ruling well. Rulers can be corrupted to pursue their own good, as well as be incompetent. By the time Plato dared the paradox of the philosopher-king he had already proposed radical institutional reforms – no private property and no private families for rulers, to ensure that rulers would not pursue their own good at the expense of the good of all the other citizens (ch. 8 below). Now Plato is concentrating on another condition for ruling well, knowledge of the good, a very high degree of competence indeed.

Plato has a parallel answer to the paradox of the philosopher-king, about how to realize his ideal of a completely good individual. The completely good person can only be approximated; and it can be highly approximated only if there is a union *within* a person between ruling oneself and personal wisdom, knowledge (or at least true opinion) of one's own good. We have here a corresponding Rule of Reason; and a corresponding paradox of Reason as everyman's king; the very opposite of David Hume's equally famous paradox that "reason is and ought to be the slave of the passions." Plato would agree that all too often reason *is* the slave of the passions, but he argues that it never *should* to be. Reason is the only faculty in us capable of knowledge (or true opinion) of our good, and therefore it ought to be our ruler. But here Plato had more success and more influence than with his paradox of the philosopher-king; so much so that the rule of reason within the individual has been the received ideal for human conduct, and Hume's view, not Plato's, is thought to be paradoxical.

Here too, we must remember that Plato thought reason within us, like rulers in the city, can be similarly corrupted, to favor the good of part of the individual instead of the good of the whole individual. A person can lose true belief, "by theft, or violence, or bewitchment" he tells us in Book III (413): by theft when one is persuaded out of it or in time forgets it; by violence when one is driven to change his mind by pain or suffering; and one can be bewitched by the allurement of pleasure, or scared out of it by a spell of panic. And in Book VIII he describes how unfortunate family experiences or bad education can turn a young man's reason into a slave for calculating ways and means to victory and honors (thus favoring the good of the spirited part of the soul), or a slave to wealth, or the equal satisfaction of every desire, or a slave to lust and power. Plato's rigid and strictly controlled system of education is intended to avoid the corruption of reason in the individual, by cognitive learning and habituation, instilling true beliefs and taming the wilder parts of the soul.[3]

In Books VIII and IX Plato rejects other unions with political power and other bases for ruling the city: the ability to defend the city as the qualification for ruling it (which can result in timocracy), the ability to create wealth (plutocracy), the consent of the governed (democracy), and brute force (tyranny) which he sets as the polar opposite of his own ideal.[4] All these are different violations of the political structure that defines his ideal city-state.

Similarly, he rejects the claims of the passions – the other parts of the soul besides reason – to rule the individual, whether it is the passion for victory and honors (psychic timocracy), the passion for wealth (psychic plutocracy), the passion for freedom to satisfy equally any passion (democracy within the psyche), or the passion to be the master (psychic tyranny).

3 Knowledge and Opinions

Glaucon's original questions cannot now be answered unless Plato can answer some new questions:

1 What is knowledge, as distinct from other cognitive states such as opinion?
2 Is such knowledge possible for human beings, and if so how?
3 Even if such knowledge is possible in mathematics and other sciences, is knowledge in ethics, knowledge of good and evil, and of right and wrong possible?

Perhaps there is no significant distinction between knowledge and opinion; perhaps Protagoras was right in claiming that what seems to me is true to me and what seems to you is true to you; none of us have false opinions, and there is no important distinction between knowledge and opinion. Even if there is a significant distinction between knowledge and opinion in the sciences, perhaps only opinions are possible when it comes to the good of society or even our own good. Protagoras may have been correct at least about what is good and bad.

None of this can Plato admit. Unless there is some important distinction between knowledge and opinion in general, and unless some can have knowledge of good and not merely opinions about good, his political ideal has to be radically modified. After all, most of us have opinions, some of them in conflict with the opinions of others, about what is good and bad for society and for ourselves; and if we can't have knowledge of good but only such opinions, or if there is no distinction between knowledge of good and opinions about it, then some other political structure – such as democracy – may be the correct ideal, not Plato's.

John Rawls tries to open up possibilities between Protagorean relativism and Platonic absolutism, at least for justice and perhaps for good as well.[5] And so perhaps did Aristotle.[6] We have no knowledge of good, at least no Platonic knowledge of good, but at best reasonable or rational opinions about it. And Rawls thought we can reach rational agreement about justice, even in the face of conflicting reasonable opinions about our comprehensive good.[7]

In his system of higher education for rulers, Plato tries to show how knowledge of the good is possible at least for a few very smart, very talented people. But he must first try to answer the first question about a significant distinction between knowledge and opinion.

In answer to this first question, Plato sets some very high standards for knowledge as distinct from opinion. We may summarize the differences:

1 Knowledge can be only of what is true; opinion can be true or false(*Gorgias*: 454; *Republic*: 477).
2 Knowledge is made stable by a causal account;[8] even true opinion need not be (*Meno*: 98).
3 Knowledge cannot be shaken by persuasion; opinion can (*Timaeus*: 51).
4 Knowledge can be only of what is always the same, unchanging and everlasting; of changing things only opinion is possible (*Republic*: 478e).

The first two conditions are commonly accepted; the third perhaps; but the last is characteristic of Plato and leads to his metaphysics – his view of reality. Can human beings have knowledge so demandingly defined? Especially knowledge of what is good and bad?

The theories of forms and the form of the good are supposed to make possible affirmative answers to these questions. If we grant the existence of forms, Plato thinks he can find answers to these questions.

Here we will see clearly how in the *Republic* Plato bases his ethics and politics on his epistemology and metaphysics. It would seem difficult to make sense of Plato's insistence, in his political philosophy, that only men of knowledge of the good ought to rule the city, without recourse to his epistemology and metaphysics; since the great authority of his philosopher-kings would appear hard to justify without the possibility of exact and certain knowledge.

In any case, Plato clearly thought that his theory of the social or political virtues, which we saw was based on his functional theory, was not secure without the theory of the form of the good and the conception of knowledge and forms it presupposes. He *tells* us so in the opening passages of his theory of the form of the good (*Republic*: 504), as we shall soon see. Plato makes his ethics and politics depend on his epistemology; and in turn his epistemology depends on his metaphysics.

The last move comes when he argues that distinguishing between knowledge and opinion requires distinguishing between two kinds of objects: between forms such as beauty itself, justice itself, and good itself; and their sensible (sense perceptible) participants, such as beautiful tones, colors and shapes, actual just cities, and good human beings. He claims that a philosopher is one who approaches and apprehends the forms themselves and never confuses them with their sensible participants, whereas "spectacle-lovers" mistake perceptible resemblances of beauty for beauty itself, or they think the beautiful sensible things are all the beauty there is; similarly with resemblances of justice and justice itself, good things and good itself, and all the rest. It is philosophers who have knowledge, spectacle-lovers only opinion – they are lovers of opinion. When the spectacle-lovers protest, he proposes to convince them by a long, difficult and much-discussed argument (*Republic*: 476–80).

The argument uses three main principles. First, it treats knowledge and opinion not as mental states but as faculties or mental powers which produce mental states. Then using the uncontroversial distinction drawn in *Gorgias* (454), that knowledge never contains error or falsehood whereas opinion sometimes does, Plato concludes that the faculty of knowledge produces only mental states that are free of falsehood (and in that sense knowledge is "infallible" – it does not err), while the faculty of opinion sometimes produces mental states that contain falsehoods. There is a difference in what these faculties accomplish; their results or functions.

A second principle is that faculties or powers are distinguished by their functions and their objects: the powers are the same if they have the same functions and the same objects, and different otherwise. For example, the faculties of sight and hearing have different objects (colors and shapes, and sounds) and produce different results (seeing, hearing), so they are different faculties. Since the faculties of knowledge and opinion have different functions or results (one produces only true mental states, the other some true some false), they are different faculties.

But the question now arises: how is it possible for this marvelous human faculty of knowledge to produce mental states that are always free of falsehood or error? How is it possible for knowledge to be in this sense "infallible"? In response, Plato brings in a third principle – *the* principle which connects his epistemology and metaphysics: that which "entirely is" is "entirely knowable," that which "in no way is" (Parmenides' non-being) is entirely unknowable; and that which "is and is not" is the object of a faculty between knowledge and ignorance, which he claims is opinion (*Republic*: 477ab).

So the objects of knowledge "entirely are," those of opinion "are and are not," and it is this ontological difference which makes the former possible objects of knowledge and the latter only objects of belief.

As is well known, Plato assigns the physical world to the category of what is and is not, and the forms to that which entirely is. Here we face two notoriously difficult questions of metaphysics, epistemology and Platonic scholarship. What is it for some things to "entirely be" and for others to "both be and not be"? And why should Plato suppose that only the former sort of objects, the forms, are knowable, and the latter, the sensible objects that participate in forms, only objects of belief?

Let us first try to understand Plato's view of the "defects" of the physical world that render it unknowable (though it can be the object of "likely" opinion); and then search for the ontological features of forms that render them knowable. We will finally look for a reason for Plato's supposing that the form of the good is responsible for the "being and essence" of the forms which render them knowable.

4   Platonic Forms and Physical Particulars

We are familiar with a distinction between physical objects (e.g. an actual door) and images of physical objects (a picture of a door). And though sometimes we might mistake one for the other, and call a picture of a door a door, when we attend to it we can usually correct the mistake (in class experiments this mistake was made often and easily corrected). We learn and accept the distinction between physical objects and images of them in paintings and photographs, reflections in water and mirrors, shadows, videos, and so on.

Plato wants to draw a new and somewhat parallel but more difficult distinction: between an actual physical object and the form or structure of the object; an actual physical door and the form of a door; an actual physical human being and the form of a human being. We can find a hint of this distinction in the difference between an architect's plan of a house and an actual house built with bricks and stones and wood according to the plan: the plan displays the structure without these materials (though we must note that the plan displays the structure on some other matter, usually paper, and it is really a physical picture of the structure).

The geometry of the day seemed open to this second distinction – figure was structure or form, and geometrical figures have physical embodiments, in diagrams and in physical objects. Consider Socrates' definition of figure in the *Meno* (76a) as the limit of solid: we have, say, a physical cube, a die, whose three dimensional limit is its figure, the geometrical cube. In context it seems correct to say that the physical die is a cube because it has the figure of a cube. And the physical object is named after its figure; it takes its name, "cube," from the name of the geometer's cube. So, the die is a cube because it has the figure of a cube, and it is called a cube because that is the name of its figure. Here we already have some basic elements of Plato's theory of forms. And we can generalize: any set of physical objects that are correctly called cubes are so because they have the figure or structure of cube.

But this distinction also has some basis in the common practice of usually sorting physical objects, artifacts, and plants and animals, for example, largely based on their visible appearance or visible form. We might sort artifacts based on their shape, animals based on their visible appearance that might include shape, size, and colors. The very word that Plato uses for form, *eidos*, originally meant visible form or visible appearance.

Now, it seems that we can make mistakes about this distinction too, and we can correct them, though this might be more difficult since to do so we may have to consult geometry. For example, we do not hesitate usually to call a drawn line (on paper or on the board) a line (in class experiments this was done almost always). But Euclid's definition of line, as length without breadth (the second definition in Euclid's *Elements*), might give us pause, since the drawn line has some breadth and as such is in fact a Euclidian surface rather than a Euclidian line. It seems that a line drawn on paper or on the board "is a line and is not a line": it is a line since it has length and very little breadth (which is not even supposed to be there), but it is also not a line because it has some breadth, no matter how little and no matter how carefully drawn. Similarly, let us say, with drawn circles, drawn triangles, and drawn cubes – indeed any figure – it would appear.

In these geometrical examples we seem to have reached Plato's seemingly contradictory characterization of physical objects as things that "are and are not"; what he might mean in this context is that a drawn line has some but not all the essential features captured in Euclid's definition; and similarly with any other drawn figures. In this sense, a drawn line is not completely or *perfectly* a line. In addition, a drawn line will have all sorts of features, some of which are contrary to being a line, such as some breadth, or irrelevant to its being a line, such as color or location. We might capture this by saying that the drawn line is not *purely* a line.

Given this, it now seems reasonable to think that Euclid's definition of line, since not all of it is true of any drawn line, is about something of which the definition is all true, and drawn lines are merely "approximations" of that object since they have length but also some breadth; and the less length they have the closer they are to Euclid's line. Similarly with circles: a drawn circle, no matter how carefully drawn, will not be completely circular as specified in Euclid's definition (some radius might be longer than others; a straight line touching its periphery might touch it at more than one point, and so on). And this seems to apply to any drawn figure; if nothing else, the problem with line infects all physical or drawn figures!

So, it would seem reasonable to suppose that there are figures of which Euclid's definitions are completely true; this feature of forms is called their perfection. Moreover, the Euclidean objects do not have any contrary or irrelevant features; this feature of forms is called their purity.[9] The forms "entirely are" in that they are perfect and pure.

But there are also physical objects and drawn figures that are recognizable as physical exemplifications of the defined figures: there is the geometrical cube, of which Euclid's definition is all true, there are physical cubes, and there are diagrams of physical cubes. And these three kinds of things cannot be identical with each other: Euclid's line and a drawn line cannot be identical since the first has no breadth whatsoever and the second does have some breadth, no matter carefully drawn, as well as irrelevant features. Similarly with circles and triangles, and cubes – indeed any figure – Euclid's circle is not identical with any drawn circle, nor with a physical wheel, since the last two are not completely circular and they have contrary or irrelevant features: they do not have all the essential features of a circle captured by Euclid's definition and do not satisfy exactly his proven theorems about circles. Here, we have another element of Plato's theory of forms: these forms or structures are never identical with their physical exemplifications, whether diagrams or physical objects.

In the *Phaedo* (74b) Plato seems to use similar reasoning with another example: equality itself and physical equals such as equal sticks or equal stones. Equality is not identical with any two or more physical equals (or with the equality the physical things have with each other). This passage has often been thought puzzling since physical equals are equals to each other – and so there must be at least two of them – whereas equality itself is one. What then is equality itself equal to, if it is equal at all? Equal to itself?[10] But is not everything equal to itself? Perhaps it is simply absurd to suppose that equality itself is equal to anything or that Plato thought so. There might be an interpretation, though, which makes Plato's main point, without any absurdity or triviality: the postulates or axioms or theorems that hold true of equality may fail for physical equals if the latter are only approximately equal. Think of the axiom that if A is equal to B and B is equal to C, then A is equal to C: if the length of a physical rod is approximately equal to that of a second rod, and the length of the second less equal to that of a third, the first may be less equal to the third than it is to the second, so much less that we can reasonably say that the first is *not* equal to the third, and so the axiom might fail for such things as physical lengths. Applied to numbers, though, the problem might seem to be quite different. Transitivity holds for the relation greater-than in numbers. How can it fail for collections of physical things? Approximation does not seem to apply at all to collections that participate in numbers; a set does not have more or less five members; it either has five members or not. But even here Plato argues that we must distinguish the number five from any collection of five sensible things.[11]

The people Plato calls "sight lovers" and "lovers of opinion" make the mistake of not distinguishing between beauty itself, the form of physical beautiful things that make them beautiful, and the physical beautiful things. Or, perhaps they think that the physical beautiful things that exist are all the beauty there is; they deny there is such a thing as beauty itself, rather than confuse one thing for another. They are perhaps nominalists – they deny the need to postulate the existence of abstract entities. For them, the only world there is, as Nelson Goodman says, is "a world of individuals."[12]

Plato thinks that the forms themselves are indeed not identical with the objects which they represent; but also that these forms can exist "separately" from their physical embodiments, whether diagrams or physical objects: the form is not identical with any physical specimen that has that form, and it is also not present in the physical specimens.[13] Some think that separation goes even further: a Platonic form exists even if there are no physical participants.[14] There is such a thing as a Euclidian figure with a thousand sides, even if there is no physical object with a thousand sides in the physical universe; at least the main reason for supposing so, namely that Euclid's definitions, axioms, and theorems require objects to be true, seems to apply just as well when there is no physical exemplification; and Plato's "likely" story of the creation of the physical universe (in the *Timaeus*), modeled after the already existing forms, seems to support the point. Similarly with numbers: it does not seem that the existence of a number requires the existence of at least one collection of physical entities that has that number of members.

Plato may have all these features of the theory of forms in mind when he sets out a central principle of the theory in *Republic* (596): "We are in the habit of postulating a single form for every set of things we call by the same name." This has been called the "one over many principle" – one form over many physical individuals of the same kind – and the "generating principle" – the principle by whose repeated application we generate forms. For the set of physical beautiful things we postulate the form beauty, which is common to all of them, which makes them beautiful, and after which they are named[15] – and accordingly with physical lines and physical triangles, houses and doors, spiders and men, good cities and good citizens, just societies and just men.

We can display some elements of Plato's theory of forms so far:

LANGUAGE	REALITY
The word "cube"	The form CUBE
The word "cubical"	Physical cubes
"Picture of a cube"	Diagrams of physical cubes

Here we have three kinds of entities: the form cube, which is an abstract entity; the physical cubes; and pictures of physical cubes, both of which are concrete entities in space and time. We saw that physical cubes such as dice are cubes because they have the structure or form of a cube, or as Plato says, because they "participate" in the form cube; and they are called cubical because that is the name of their form (the participants are "named after the form," (*Phaedo*: 102bm, 102dm, 103e).[16] In turn, the drawn diagrams are diagrams of cubes because they picture the structure of the physical cubes – they are images of physical cubes, in the broad sense of pictures, reflections, shadows, and so on (some are videos of physical cubes, as we might now say); the images, too, are named after what they picture. So, in the above diagram, we have three types of objects, forms,

The Divided Line

STATES OF MIND		OBJECTS	
		The good	
Intelligence or Knowledge		Forms	
			INTELLIGIBLE WORLD
Thinking		Mathematical objects	
Opinion		Visible things	
			WORLD OF APPEARANCES
Imagining		Images	

physical objects, and pictures of physical objects; and also two relations among them, the relations of participating and picturing. And we also have relations between language and these entities: the relation of naming (Plato's "the cube itself" names the form cube); the relation of naming after ("cubical" names the physical cubes after the name of the form); and the relation of naming after what is pictured ("picture of a cube" names the diagrams after the name of the physical cubes).

Plato himself displays more comprehensively some other elements of theory of forms, especially the correlation between kinds of objects and cognitive states, by means of one of his great similes: The Simile of the Divided Line.

In this simile we have two columns and four rows. In the left column we have cognitive states of mind, in the right column we have objects in the world. In the four rows we have different kinds of objects correlated with different kinds of cognitive states of mind: knowledge takes forms and only forms as its objects; opinion takes physical objects (though we can also have opinions about forms); and sense perception and imagination take images of physical objects as their objects. The correlations between mental states and objects follows Plato's principle that only "what entirely is" is entirely knowable, whereas "what is and is not" can be only an object of opinion (or sense perception) or imagination.

Plato thinks that there are other features of forms that participating physical objects and pictures thereof lack, and so we can have a broader interpretation of "what entirely is" and "what is and is not." Most notable is the addition of temporal features and change (*Republic*: 479–80). The forms always are whatever they are, they do not change in any way; a Euclidean line is always a line, it does not change in any way; whereas a drawn line on paper or on a board might change in all kinds of ways – get less visible, fade, and so on. Further, a Euclidean line always exists (assuming it exists at all), whereas a drawn line can eventually cease to exist – it can come into being and can pass away. And all these points, it seems, we can generalize to all forms and all their physical embodiments, whether physical objects or their pictures. The forms always exist and are always the same in all ways, whereas physical objects and their images change, come into existence and pass away.[17]

To sum up: the form cube (1) is completely or perfectly cube in that it has all the essential features captured by the definition of a cube (and it is cube to the highest possible degree if being a cube admits of degrees); and (2) the form cube is "pure" in that it has no attributes contrary or irrelevant to what the form cube is. Physical cubes or drawn diagrams of cubes do not have all the essential features of cube, they are *either* more or less cubical, *or* they have contrary and irrelevant features. Further (3), the form cube always exists and never changes in any way, whereas physical cubes and their diagrams change in all kinds of ways, and eventually they cease to exist. The form cube "entirely is" in all these ways, whereas physical cubes "are" cubes but also "are not" cubes in one *or* another *or* all of these ways.[18]

Are these features true of all forms? The generality or scope of Plato's theory seems very great; in the *Republic* no limits seem to set to it, as Plato's statement of the "one over many" principle seems to indicate; and he mentions forms of beauty, justice, goodness, city, human being, couch, figures and numbers.[19]

Despite this variety, there is little doubt that Plato holds that all the forms have the third set of features relating to time and change, whether forms of figures, numbers, artifacts, natural objects, and some general value characteristics such as beauty, goodness, justice, and so on. None of these forms come in or go out of existence and none of them change in any way.

But do all forms have the first two sets of features – are they perfect or complete? Are what they are to the highest degree? And are they pure? Indeed, do any forms have them? It might be supposed that all these features require "self-predication": not only are the things that participate in the form *beauty* beautiful, but the form *beauty* itself is beautiful. If the form cube has all the essential characteristics included in the definition of a cube and has them in the highest possible degree (and it has no contrary features), then the form cube must itself be a cube, a perfect cube! But is this not absurd? And if it is not absurd with figure forms, it seems to be with number forms: is the form *five* a collection of five objects? Since there are many such five-numbered collections, which one, if any, is the form? Perhaps the collection of five absolutely indivisible objects? Or is the form the collection of all five-numbered collections, à la Russell?

Self-predication seems absurd with some other forms that Plato allows: is the form large perfectly large?[20] What could this possibly mean? And is the form large the largest object there is, for sure larger than the largest building? Is the form beauty perfectly beautiful, and the most beautiful thing there is or can be? Is the form bed a bed, indeed a perfect bed? Is the form snake a perfect snake?[21]

Trying to avoid the alleged absurdities of self-predication, some writers have suggested that what Plato meant by his seemingly self-predication language is not that, for example, the form line is *a* (perfect) line, but that it is *what it is to be a line*. This seems to mean no more than that the form line is what its definition says it is: to be line is to be length without breadth (since being length without breadth is what it is to be a line).[22] The form line is line, but not *a* line. This is compatible with the form line being an attribute or feature, rather than a self-predicating paradigm or an ideal exemplar: the form line is the attribute of being a line. The definitions are definitions of attributes, and these attributes are not self predicating. But notice that attributes as attributes can still have the third set of features – the form line, as the attribute of being a line (rather than being a perfect line), always exists and is changeless.

Others say by his self-predication language (e.g. that the form line is linear) Plato meant only that necessarily the form line is that by participation in which something is a line.[23] Perhaps this is true, but is it not too opaque? Why should this be so? Why should participating in the form line make something into length without breadth? Surely the answer is to be found in the nature of a line and in the nature of participation. So we are back to that, the nature of a line and how Plato thinks of it.[24] Is it an attribute, the attribute of being a line, and participation is exemplification of an attribute? Or is it a self-predicating paradigm, a perfect line, and participation is resemblance or similarity? Or is it an attribute but can still be a paradigm, an ideal standard?

There is another explanation of Plato's self-predication language. It is to be found in that part of the theory of forms which says that physical objects are "named after" the forms they participate in.[25] As we saw, this part of the theory may have been based on the practice of the geometers who named their diagrams after their geometrical figures: "Let AB be the given finite straight line," Euclid says in the proof of Proposition I, where his "AB" names a physical line on a papyrus roll. But there is also the more common practice of sorting and naming individual physical objects after their usually visible structures (e.g. sometimes we teach children words for animals by pointing to pictures of animals – the pictures depict the visible structures). An individual actual house is named after its structure: it is a house because it has the structure common to houses, Plato thinks, and so it is quite proper that it takes its name from the name of the structure. Its structure, Plato thinks, is named house, and so a physical object that has that structure is named house. But unlike the structure itself, the physical house, because it has the materials that a house is built with, is *a* house, an individual physical house. A biological specimen, a snake, is a snake because it has the visible structure of a snake, and it is named snake because that is the name of the visible form of a certain species, the species named snake (at first the species may be thought of as the visual appearance snakes have in common, eventually its DNA or genome). The species snake is not a snake, anymore than the structure of a house is a house. Notice that we can count species as well as we can count specimens, but that should not mislead us into thinking that species are (higher order, perfect) specimens. The point is that Plato gives names to his forms, and this can look like self-predication, but it need not be: the form line is line, length without breadth, but it is not *a* line.

For Plato, the story here is analogous to pictures being pictures of something and being named after what they picture: a picture of a man is called that because it pictures a man; a picture may be labeled "the most beautiful man" because (we think) it pictures the most beautiful man. But of course the picture of the beautiful man is not a beautiful man – it is not a man to begin with. Images and what they are named after suit Plato's theory quite well in this respect. It is no accident that he often uses the relation of images to physical things they picture as an analogy of the relation the physical objects have to their forms or structures (e.g. in the Divided Line). The picturing relation is analogous to participation, and the naming of a picture after what it pictures is analogous to naming a physical object after the form it participates in. We saw that Plato used, at a crucial point, the picture of the most beautiful man as a model for judging the beauty of physical men and as an analogy to using forms as models for judging their physical participants. The picture of the most beautiful man can be a standard for judging the beauty of actual physical men, even though the picture is of course not a beautiful man! Similarly, Socrates' account of Plato's completely good city can be a model, or at least a standard, for judging actual physical cities.

The example of the painting is appropriate for what Plato is trying to illustrate because pictures abstract from matter (the matter of the thing they picture) and depict form or structure. Similarly, it is the form or structure of the completely good city that is the model, the paradigm to be approximated by actual physical cities and the standard for judging how good actual cities are. Notice, though, that Plato's using of this example to illustrate this point here is truly extraordinary and even ironic: according to his theory of art in Book X, the picture of a beautiful man is "a third removed from reality" – a copy of a copy; a copy of a physical beautiful man who in turn is a "copy" of the form beauty – and the last thing to be a standard. It is the form beauty which is the standard for physical beauties, and they in turn the standard for beauty in pictures. Such is the power of images, analogies, and metaphors that Plato values, and so much can they be misleading!

Still, the point of Plato's example is that it is the form or structure that is the model, the paradigm for judging physical participants in that structure. The image itself, the painting, is not the standard. The lesson is that structure or form can be a standard for its embodiments without it itself being an embodiment; and the species can be a standard for the specimen, without it itself being a specimen.[26]

It is helpful here to remember that Plato tends to think of forms as structures or patterns in abstraction from matter. His geometrical analysis of matter in the *Timaeus* shows how he thought of form or structure as dominant over "stuff." It is forms or patterns, sometimes visible ones, that enable us to sort pieces of matter as one kind of object or another, a snake, a bird, or a fish. And most important, he thinks that at least some faults or imperfections he finds in physical objects, some of the kinds of faults we discussed above, are due to the nature of matter. It is because a physical line is material that it always has some breadth; and it changes and passes away because of its matter. It is because the periphery of a physical circle is a line with some breadth that a straight line touching that periphery will touch it at more than one point. The imperfections here are due to matter, in a similar way that an engineer's "tolerances" may be due to the materials being used; we can have smaller and smaller tolerances (the "fit and finish" in a car's body, for example), but not perfection.

The other major imperfection, the changeability and mortality of all living things and all inanimate material objects, is also due to their matter, not to their structures. The structures themselves that exist in nature do not have such faults (though we can think up faulty structures, as we might define health mistakenly). But the structures themselves are not embodied individuals either; they are countable, but they are not concrete, embodied individuals. The absurdities of self-exemplification may be the result of trying to think of abstract entities, structures, as if they were embodied concrete entities.[27] We know that by self-predication of forms, at least by such language, Plato could not possibly mean that forms are embodied, material individuals.

If we think of the structures as faultless and the faults (in the sense of imperfections or impurities) of embodied structures as due to their matter, we can see how such structures can be standards for judging the comparative faults of their embodiments, even though they are not themselves embodied individuals. Embodied individuals can be models too, the more usual notion of a paradigm, akin to our notion of a "role model." But for Plato an embodied individual can never be as good a paradigm as the structures themselves: the embodied individuals have faults, the structures themselves only are truly faultless.

We shall try to explain Plato's theory of the form of the good without the assumption of *literal* self-predication.[28]

5 Plato's Theory of the Form of the Good

Plato opens his discussion of the form of the good by saying that his philosopher-rulers cannot rule well without knowledge of good, and they would not know that anything is good – that justice or the other virtues are good – unless they know the form of the good. Knowledge of the form of the good, he says, is their "greatest lesson" (*Republic*: 503–4). Once more Plato explicitly connects his politics and ethics with his epistemology and metaphysics.

We notice that in the Divided Line the form of the good is at the very top of the column for objects, of everything that there is. We might well wonder why Plato thinks this. To put it at the top would seem to indicate that the form of the good is something that is "common" to all the things that exist. Indeed, that's what Aristotle supposed of Plato's thought; *good* and *being* were treated by the Platonists as the two greatest genera.[29] *Being* we might well understand to have that top position – if existence is an attribute at all, then it is common to everything that exists. But why should *good* be at the top, common to all that exists?

Further, Plato says that the form of the good "gives" the other forms "their being and essence," though it "surpasses being in dignity and power" (*Republic*: 509b). Why did Plato think that the good in particular, rather than some other form or nothing at all, is something by which the forms have their "being and essence"?

Further yet, in the great simile of the Allegory of the Cave, the form of the good is the very last thing a prisoner sees after he has emerged from the cave (the world of images and physical objects) and studied the objects outside the cave (the forms).[30] And in Plato's theory of higher education, learning the form of the good is the last result of a long and difficult sequential education in the existing sciences and in dialectic.

Why should Plato think that knowledge of the good is the greatest, the hardest, and educationally the last lesson to learn? Why were not geometry, number theory, or astronomy harder to learn? And nowadays, are not physics, mathematics, biochemistry or astronomy a lot harder to learn than how we learn what is good or bad? Aren't courses in these subjects a lot harder than courses in ethics? Indeed, don't human beings learn what is good and bad very early in life?

Plato's statements about the form of the good are simply astonishing, and attempts to water them down are hard to credit. Plato thinks of goodness in a totally different way than his contemporaries, or than we ourselves now think about good and bad. His form of the good is a very special form indeed: ontologically, because the other forms' being and essence is due to it (*Republic*: 509b); epistemologically, because only with knowledge of it can anyone know that anything else is good, including the good of justice and the other virtues; politically, because no one can know what is good for the city and for its citizens and thus be able to rule well, unless s/he knows the form of the good; educationally, because it is the greatest and hardest and last thing to learn; and even anti-democratically, because most people cannot know the form of the good. To understand Plato's view of the form of the good, we have to try to understand how he thought about these things.

The key is Plato's idea that physical objects have faults of many kinds, so that even the best of their kinds are not perfectly good, while the forms themselves are ideals or standards we can use to sort, evaluate and rank the faulty physical objects.

We have seen several ways in which physical objects are faulty: they have some but not all the essential features captured by the definition of their forms or structures; or they do not have them in the highest degree (if their features admit of degrees); or, no matter what features they have, they also have contrary features in some way or another – they are not "purely" what they are; further, they are changeable and they are mortal.

By contrast, the forms themselves do not have any of these faults or defects: they have all the essential features captured by their definitions, they have them to the highest possible degree (if their features admit of degrees), they are pure in not having any contrary features, they do not change in any way, and they always exist. As such, forms can be standards for sorting physical objects into kinds, and for ranking them. Euclid's circle, as defined by Euclid, is the standard for physical objects being sorted and characterized as circular, and for how good circles they are. Though we can use a very well-drawn circle as a model (a paradigm in the sense of a role model) for sorting other physical objects as circular (as we might do when teaching children words using diagrams and pictures) and for ranking them by how circular they are, Euclid's circle as defined is a better model (indeed, the best model), since it does not miss any of the essential features of a circle. It cannot be said to be more or less circular, it is not non-circular in any way (nor does it have any features irrelevant to being a circle), and it does not deteriorate or pass away as drawn circles do. Similarly, though we might use Socrates as a role model for sorting and ranking philosophers (or as a role model for a good person), Plato's definition of a philosopher (if true and accurate), or his definition of a completely good person (if true and accurate), may be better models for similar reasons. Socrates has his flaws as a person and as a philosopher, while the definitions try to capture the flawlessly good person and the flawless philosopher.

We might think that it is sufficient if we can make comparative judgments of goodness among more or less good things of the same kind. Perhaps we cannot define good or best; but maybe we can do well enough if we can define "better than" for any given set of objects of the same kind. But Plato explicitly tells us, at the very beginning of his discussion of the good, that "nothing that is imperfect is the measure of anything" (*Republic*: 504b). The true definition of a philosopher, if such there is and we can know it, is a better standard for judging philosophers than Socrates, or Plato himself.

The "defects" or "flaws" in physical exemplifications of forms make it reasonable to say that the closer a physical object is to a given form, in having more features of its definition or having them to a higher degree or having fewer contrary or irrelevant features, the better an object of that kind it is. The less breadth a drawn line has the better a drawn line it is; the more circular a drawn circle is the better a drawn circle it is. Since the standards for these judgments are objects as captured by Euclid's definitions, it seems reasonable to think of the objects of Euclid's definitions as ideals, as not having the faults of their physical approximations. As such, they can be standards for judging not only what sorts physical objects belong to – are they lines? are they circles? – but also for judging how good they are as objects of that sort, how good they are as drawn lines, drawn circles, physical cubes, existing persons or cities. And this might be extended to living things: biologists sometimes speak of a "nearly perfect specimen" of a species; the species, which is the form common to all the specimens that makes them specimens of that species, seems to function as a standard for judging how good a specimen is, at least if we know what that species is.[31] Artifacts, too, can be so sorted and ranked – at least relative to the plans of their creators. Having more of the essential features captured in their definition, or having them to the highest possible degree (if it can admit of degrees), and even their relative purity, seem to be good making characteristics of objects of a given kind.

It may not seem as clear to suppose that being immune to change and to destruction are good making characteristics. But Plato seems to think they are: "It is universally true, then, that that which is in the best state by nature or art or both admits least of alteration by something else" (*Republic*: 381ab; see Plato's examples from nature and art).[32] And in his theory of *eros* in the *Symposium* Plato makes immortality the final aim of *eros*, obviously assuming that immortality is a great good.[33] Popular thought in his day and in ours seems also to lend some support to this notion. Was not the immortality of the gods envied by mortals and thought to be something that made the gods better than mortals? And do not human beings prize and value living longer and immunity to change? Further, some of these properties clearly admit of degrees, an interesting parallel to goodness which of course admits of degrees: physical objects can last more or less and can be more or less immune to change; some trees are immune to destruction for thousands of years; the specimens of some species are more immune to changes than others. Aristotle was also impressed with the ability of living things to withstand change. He thought that the best of them withstand change the most.[34]

Now if immortality is something good, is not lasting more also good? And if complete immunity to change is good, is not greater immunity also good? Here we must make a distinction: if something is good, its lasting longer is also something good, since we have good extending further temporally (we can add the temporally divided good and get a greater good for the whole lifetime of the object, if nothing else). On the other hand, if a thing is bad or evil, it seems that the longer the thing lasts the more bad there is. Further, if a thing is neither good nor bad, is its lasting longer better? It does not seem obvious. It looks as if lasting longer is only conditionally good; lasting longer is good on condition that the thing is good to begin with. This perhaps applies to immortality itself: an immortal demon (a malevolent and malefi-cent being) is surely a worse thing than the same demon lasting only a thou-sand years; an immortal god (a benevolent and beneficent being) is better than one that lasts a million years. In these respects, the good of existing longer and being immune to change is like the good of stability: stability of democracies is thought to be good by those that think democracy is good, the stability of dictatorships an evil – and heaven save us from a tyranny that would never go out of existence, an everlasting hell.

So it looks very much as if these properties – lasting longer, immunity to change, and immortality – are at most conditional goods. The mere passage of time itself seems neutral with respect to goodness: it can increase good enormously when applied to something good to begin with, but it can also increase bad enormously when applied to something bad to begin with. And this throws doubt on the idea that Platonic forms are good, indeed paradigms of goodness of kind, simply because they are completely immune to change and last forever. But if they are paradigms of goodness of kind to begin with, because of (some of) their other features – they have all the essential features captured by their definitions, have them in the highest degree (if their features admit of degrees), and they are pure – then their immunity to change and to destruction add immensely to their goodness.

In so far as we think of forms as ideal patterns or structures in the sense of being flawless, unchangeable, and always in existence, we can think of them also as the best objects of their kind. The form line is flawless: it has all the features essential to being a line, it is nothing but a line, it never changes, and it always exists. Could there be a better model for learning what a line is, for what it is to be a line, and for judging how good drawn lines are?

If so, then we can see how Plato might have thought of the form of the good as the common denominator of forms, what they have in com-mon as forms that make them forms: they are the best objects of their kind, or alternatively, they all have in common superlative goodness of kind. This is quite Platonic: if several things have a feature in common (they are all triangular), they participate in the form captured by the definition of that feature (the form triangle), they are triangular because they participate in the form triangle, and are even named after it. By the same principle, if all forms are superlatively good then they have the form of the good in common, they are superlatively good because they participate in the form of the good, and they are even named after it. The good is the form of forms, the form by which these other entities are forms and the best objects of their kind. This is the sense in which "the being and essence of the forms" is due to the form of the good.

Moreover, if what makes forms (the reason why these forms are forms) the best objects of their kind are the features we highlighted – they have all the essential features defining their kind, they are pure, they are always and without any change, and are immune to destruction – then the form of the good must include these general features of forms, and presumably these must be parts of its definition. This too is quite Platonic: common features of triangles that make them triangles (are the reasons why something that has them is a triangle) must be essential features of triangles: they are the being and essence of triangle, and must be included in the definition of the form triangle.[35]

But does not attributing these features to forms imply that forms are self-predicating? The third set of features does not seem to. Being immune to change and to destruction can be true of properties or attributes or structures that are not self-exemplifying – the property of being large, for example. But we saw reason to believe that these features do not by themselves make the forms good, but only on condition that they are good to begin with. So it seems that we need to have the forms possess the other set of features that can be more reasonably said to make the forms good.

It is these other features of forms – having all the essential attributes included in their definition (having them to the highest degree, when this is applicable) and being pure – that tempt us to think that forms are literally self-exemplifying; especially so if we are thinking purely geometrically (visually and of things in space, as the geometers' diagrams suggest), and suppose that there must be objects satisfying the geometers' definitions, axioms, and theorems. If a line is length without breadth and there must be an object of which this is true, then must not there be something which is length and has no breadth? Must there not be something which is *a* line so defined? And similarly, with at least every other thing that is the object of the geometers' definitions, axioms, and theorems?[36]

Perhaps we should resist this temptation, as perhaps Plato himself did. We must remember his insistence that the geometers' diagrams are not the subjects of the geometers' definitions, axioms, and theorems, but only visual aids, a bit of help to our geometrical intuitions and to our grasping the geometers' proofs. We must also remember his repeated assertions that the forms are not perceptible through our senses at all. He certainly appreciated the great power of vision, especially in the case of forms that have visible participants such as beauty, and used that power in his images and metaphors at crucial points. The three great similes are all visual! And he used the painting of the most beautiful man, which is purely visual, to illustrate a standard for judging the beauty of men, even though it is most misleading as a guide to his metaphysics and theory of art!

The visual metaphors and the visual images are not sufficient to attribute to Plato literal self-predication.[37] It would better suit Plato's thought on this point if we thought of figures and structures not purely geometrically and not visually, but digitally as it were: if we thought of the structure or form of a circle and of its definition numerically or algebraically; something not available to Plato since the Greeks had no analytic geometry, and tended to think even of numbers geometrically – if we did that, we would have no temptation to think of the form circle as a perfect circle.

Notice though, that if the form circle were well defined numerically or algebraically, we could still reasonably think of drawn circles as better or worse approximations of the form circle so defined, if they did not completely satisfy the numerical or algebraic definition, the axioms and theorems about circles. And so we could still think of the forms so defined as giving us standards not only of what physical objects are circles but also of how good physical circles are as circles; not by comparison with each other but by comparison with the definition, the axioms, and the theorems. And we could still think of objects completely satisfying the definitions, even though we were not thinking visually. If we could still think of the forms as ideal standards of the goodness of their physical embodiments, then we can again see how the form of the good would have to be their common denominator and the essence of their being forms.

6   Knowledge of Good

We can now see that Plato's forms are indeed abstract and non-perceptible, and the form of the good super abstract and as far from sense perception as anything can be.

So perhaps we can now appreciate more Plato's view that unless his philosopher-kings (or anyone else for that matter) know the form of the good, they will not know that anything else is good. For now we can see how they would not know what it is for something to be superlatively good, as the forms are, or good to some lesser degree or in some lesser way, as actual physical cities and persons and other physical things might be, unless they know what it is to be good to begin with. Unless they know and understand the form of the good, they will not know the features that make any thing superlatively good of its kind or physical objects more or less good.

Moreover, we can see how approaching these issues even in an elementary fashion, as we have here, involves difficult abstractions such as essential features, knowledge of geometrical definitions and proofs, and definitions and proofs of other kinds of things besides figures, such as atoms and heavenly bodies, and extensive knowledge in other sciences. The application of such knowledge to make judgments and rankings of goodness of physical objects would presuppose extensive knowledge in the sciences indeed. And education in the sciences would be not only useful for educating our minds to think abstractly, but also necessary to make judgments about good things of this world: to know or judge truly that some thing in the physical universe is good, or how good it is, we would have to know what kind of thing it is, what that kind is, and how it is related to many other kinds. Think of how much we would have to know, in Plato's view, to make sound and informed judgments about how good an actual house is, or a ship, a city, a specimen of a spider, a human body, or a human being. We would have to know their forms, what it is to be a house, a ship, a city, a spider, a human body, or a human being, as something satisfying its definition, axioms and proofs about it. And to know all this we would have to know some geometry, architecture, ship design, biology, chemistry, and psychology, to name a few! Centuries before we learned from biochemistry how vastly complex the human body is, and how intricate its good state or health is, Plato appreciated the complexity and great abstractness of the knowledge required to make seemingly simple sound judgments about the goodness of forms or the lesser goodness of their physical embodiments.[38]

This view of goodness is extraordinary and, in great opposition to the view of Plato's contemporaries, explicitly stated in the *Republic* by Thrasymachus, Glaucon and Adeimantus, and current in Athenian democratic culture. This view was that the good is pleasure, or the satisfaction of our desires; and we certainly do not need astronomy, harmonics, geometry or arithmetic to know what pleases us or what satisfies our desires. On these other views, knowledge of good is available to everyone, even with little education; everyone is an almost equally good judge of his or her own good, better than others of one's own good, at least after reaching maturity and with a normal education; and with a little more effort everyone is even a good judge of the public or common good, the good of whole cities, states, and nations. Does not democratic theory suppose this? That the voters can make sound judgments not only of what is to their own good but also the public good of the nation as a whole and so be able to cast informed votes for one or another leader proposing one or another public policy?

Plato explicitly refutes the view that the good is identical with pleasure (*Republic*: 505c). He thinks that one who holds this will have inconsistent beliefs since he will have to admit that there are such things as bad pleasures, and so things that are both good and bad.[39]

Plato refutes even the Socratic view that the good is identical with knowledge (*Republic*: 505b). He claims that when asked, "knowledge of what?" those holding this view can only reply, "knowledge of good," thus ending up with the circular and uninformative view that the good is identical with knowledge of the good. If we allowed the Socratics to give a less circular reply, for example, "the good is identical with knowledge of anything and everything," we might end up with a view that is a bit more elitist than democratic theory, but still far less elitist than Plato's. The Socratic method of clearing our heads of inconsistencies and seeking definitions of the virtues and knowledge about our good by dialogue was after all available even to slave boys.

But Plato's view of knowledge of good is elitist indeed. We can see that from Plato's program of higher education for his future rulers: to understand the good, they have to learn the sciences of the day, a difficult undertaking over many years (our post-graduate education) in geometry, number theory, harmonics, astronomy, and so on. But even this is not enough. To understand the good, they must also be educated in something higher and more difficult yet – what Plato calls dialectic. Dialectic deals only with forms, not at all with their embodied particulars in the physical world. (The geometers of the day did not qualify as dialecticians since they used physical images in their proofs and used hypotheses of which they gave no explanation.)[40] The future rulers must reason upwards from less general and abstract forms to more general and abstract forms and try to reach the form of the good at the very top level of generality and abstraction. Only after they do that can they reason downward to the less general and abstract forms; and only after they complete this process are they fit to come back into the cave, the world of physical objects, and rule there.[41]

We get a glimpse of how difficult all this is and how only very few can attain it by the tests Plato proposes for anyone who claims to have come out of the cave and learned the forms and apprehended the form of the good:

> And by a master of dialectic do you also mean one who demands an account of the essence of each thing? ... And does not this apply to the Good – that the man who is unable to define it in his discourse and distinguish and abstract from other things the form of the good, and who cannot in battle run the gauntlet of all tests, and striving to examine everything not by opinion but by essential reality, hold on in his way through all this without tripping in his reasoning – the man who lacks this power ... does not know the good itself or any particular good. (*Republic*: 534bc; Keyt 2006a: 207–11)

7   How Elitist is Plato's Completely Good City?

There is no dispute that according to Plato only very few, very talented, and very educated human beings can attain knowledge of forms and the form of the good – his so-called philosophers. We may call this *intellectual* elitism, and it is supported by an empirical claim that the natural lottery distributes high talents and abilities to the few, not the many. And there is no dispute that Plato thinks only these very few human beings are entitled to rule the city and can rule it well – the paradox of the philosopher-king. We may call this *political* elitism, and it is largely a normative political theory based in part on the previous empirical claim.

But some commentators go beyond this intellectual and political elitism to an *ethical* elitism: in the completely good city only the philosophers can be just and more generally virtuous, largely because (these commentators think) being just requires wisdom and wisdom requires knowing the form of the good.[42]

Ethical elitism seems paradoxical, because in Plato's completely good city the vast majority of the population would or could not be just – certainly the artisan class and the warrior class as well. Even if a just city is not defined by the justice of its citizens but rather by the justice of its institutions, there is still something strange in supposing that a city is completely good and has all the virtues including justice, but the vast majority of its citizens do not have the natural ability to be just (because they do not have the natural ability to acquire knowledge of the form of the good). All this aside from the fact that such a city might be highly unstable since the vast majority of its citizens could not have justice in their souls. And aside from the fact that Plato never says explicitly that being a just person requires knowledge of the form of the good, but only that knowledge that justice is good requires knowledge of the form of the good.

Ethical elitism would also wreck Plato's main argument in the *Republic* that one is better off or happier being just rather than unjust; at least if this argument is meant to answer Thrasymachus' or Glaucon's challenge. Plato's argument is supposed to provide a rational motivation for being just, a greater such motivation than the motivation for being unjust; but now (according to ethical elitism) this argument, even if completely successful, applies only to a tiny minority, the philosophers, since only the philosophers can be and are just. The argument is irrelevant to the motivation of the rest of the citizens; they still may be motivated by the desire for happiness, but now being just plays no role in their motivation. Why then should they be just? There is no evidence whatsoever in Books I and II that Thrasymachus or Glaucon, or indeed Socrates himself, conceived of the challenge to show that justice pays, as so severely limited in scope – to show only that for a few very naturally talented and highly educated individuals justice pays.

To be sure, since Plato has two kinds of justice, justice for the city and justice for the individual, which, though isomorphic to each other, still are two different standards of justice, ethical elitism might not be so paradoxical if we distinguish just citizen from just person. Ethical elitism can allow that all citizens as citizens can be just – they can have political justice, the justice of the polis – when each is doing that social work for which s/he is best suited by nature and education (see *Republic* (434bc) where Plato says or implies that persons who move from a social function they are best at to another function, or who multifunction, are doing injustice). Ethical elitism claims that it is only the philosophers that can have psychic justice; other citizens can have political justice since this does not require that *they* have wisdom.

Even so, ethical elitism still wrecks Plato's argument that justice pays; for in that argument, both in the health–justice analogy of Book IV and in the pleasure arguments of Book IX,[43] it is clear enough that psychic justice is what is at stake. In all these arguments the issue is whether Plato's psychic justice is better or pleasanter for us. And in Glaucon's challenge that is clear enough too: he wants to know whether it is justice in one's soul that makes one happy (*Republic: 358b*). This is how Plato himself sets it up.

There is only one passage that is direct evidence for the view that psychic justice requires wisdom: "Does it not belong to the rational part to rule, being wise and exercising forethought on behalf of the entire soul, and to the principle of high spirit to be subject of this and its ally?" (*Republic*: 441e4–446e6). This comes immediately after the formal principle of psychic justice, deduced from the isomorphism and the formal principle of city justice: "We must remember, then, that each of us also in whom the several parts within him perform their own task – he will be a just man and a man who minds his own affairs" (*Republic*: 441d1–441e4). So it seems that in the former passage Plato is filling in the formal principle of psychic justice by assigning to reason "its own" task (in my language, the optimal matching of psychic part and psychic task), namely ruling, apparently giving his most fundamental reason why that is the best assignment, which together with the other two optimal assignments, make a person just. His fundamental reason is "being wise and having forethought for the entire soul."

This passage (*Republic*: 441e4–441e6) is put together with the subsequent definition of wisdom (442c) as being possessed "by that small part" (reason) and as being "knowledge of what is beneficial for each [part of] and for the whole [soul]." And in turn these two passages are put together with passages from Books VI and VII (*Republic*: 534b8–534c5) to show that in Plato's view one cannot have knowledge of any other good unless one knows the form of the good. Knowledge of the form of the good is a necessary condition for the wisdom in our passage, and since only the philosophers can have the latter, only the philosophers can be just. The confluence of these passages may seem decisively in favor of ethical elitism, and apparently this is how it is perceived by many.

But there are reasons for serious doubts apart from the unpalatable consequences drawn above. Ethical elitism may conflate a thing performing its optional or exclusive function *and* performing it well, and as a result conflates the virtues of justice and wisdom, or supposes that they are so closely related that justice requires wisdom. My eyes are seeing but they may be seeing well or poorly, well by their appropriate virtues, poorly by their vices. I may be pruning my roses with the optimal instrument for doing so, but my shears may be sharp or dull at the edges and I prune well or poorly.

Similarly, my reason may be performing its exclusive functions of judging, reasoning, or calculating, but it may be doing so well or poorly. My reason may be in charge of my life (performing its optimal function of ruling), setting the purposes of my life and choosing effective means to them, but it may be doing so well or poorly; it does it well if it has wisdom and not so well if it does not, but it can be ruling in either case. When my reason rules, my spirit helps to carry out the injunctions of reason, and my appetites are obedient to reason on what, when, and how much to eat, drink and be merry, then I am a just person according to Plato's definition of psychic justice; whether I also have wisdom that enables my reason to rule well is an open, further question. If I have wisdom, my reason rules well. But perhaps my reason can still rule well if it has only true opinion. After all, Socrates tells us that he himself had only (true) opinion about the form of the good (*Republic*: 506b–506d), not knowledge. Is then the Socrates of the *Republic*, Plato's architect and legislator of the completely good city, not a just person?

It may be objected that Plato himself seems to conflate a thing performing its proper function and performing it well and consequently in the relevant cases conflate justice and wisdom. There is a grain of truth to this, but it does not favor conflating justice and wisdom. It is true that on Plato's theory of justice the optimal matching of parts to functions will result in these functions being performed better than they would be without the optimal matching. This is how he argues for the principle of social justice the first time it comes up (*Republic*: 370a–370e): his comparison is between a city organized by division of labor by natural talent versus a city without division of labor or with division irrespective of talent, and his conclusion is that the city's needs will be better satisfied, the corresponding functions better performed, with the first model.

Given the isomorphism, the corresponding conclusion can be drawn about the organization (through experience and education) of the complex human soul: the soul as a whole will perform its functions better with division of psychic labor by psychic parts on the basis of the natural capabilities of these parts, than it would otherwise. In this sense, justice, too, enables a soul or a city to perform its functions better, and in this sense justice, like temperance (a temperate soul will perform its tasks better as a whole because it has no structural conflicts, no internal stasis, but harmony), is a holistic virtue; unlike wisdom and courage that are located in parts of the city or parts of the soul and enable those parts to perform their functions well, that is, perform better than they would without these virtues. But this gives us no reason to conflate justice and wisdom or to suppose that justice requires wisdom, or that Plato conflated these things. It is of course true that a part, the rulers or reason, will perform its function well if it has wisdom, but that performing well involves a different comparison from the performing well that justice enables the whole city or person to do. There is no conflation of justice and wisdom, or of a part performing well by a virtue belonging to that part and a whole performing better by a virtue belonging to that whole.

Aside from the functional theory itself, which plainly distinguishes between what the function of something is and whether it performs that function well, the view I am also supporting, has textual support: namely, that in Plato's definition itself of justice, either of the city or the individual, and at least in its formal parts,[44] there is no reference to wisdom. This is especially true of Plato's account of the justice of the city in *Republic* (433a–434c): in that whole discussion (of formal social justice and its full definition) there is no reference whatsoever to social wisdom; the definition is entirely based on the principle of optimally matching natural capabilities of citizens to the main city functions. Isomorphically, the same thing should be possible for psychic justice. And indeed, in the formal part of the definition of psychic justice there is no reference to wisdom. This is in line with the functional theory, since it assigns functions to persons or parts of persons based on capabilities, exclusive or optimal, and it does not conflate assigning functions with performing those functions well, or Plato's justice with his wisdom. Platonic wisdom is the virtue that enables philosophers to perform their optimal function of ruling the city well and their reason to rule themselves well; it may presuppose the optimal matching of the philosophers ruling the city and the reason ruling the soul (since otherwise the wisdom would not be of effective use in choices), but is not implied by it. This can be seen especially in Plato's accounts of social wisdom and social justice: his account of social wisdom (*Republic*: 428d–429a) presupposes its location in those who are by nature the fewest, those who have already been assigned to ruling the city; while his account of social justice, as already argued, makes no reference to wisdom.

Now it may seem strange to suppose that we can understand someone's justice without any reference whatsoever to any of their cognitive states. But the view I am supporting does not do that; for it allows that the just person can have true relevant beliefs, perhaps even reasonable true relevant beliefs. So it seems a possible interpretation of Plato's view that a person may be just with knowledge of the form of the good, or with true beliefs about the form of the good (as Socrates himself says that he has only beliefs about the form of the good (*Republic*: 506b–506d)), or with true beliefs about what is good in this world for the city or for oneself. And this view has indeed been held by several commentators, and it has been the chief traditional means of combating ethical elitism as an interpretation of Plato's *Republic*.[45]

Some main evidence for this interpretation is Plato's definition of social courage, the courage of the city as located in the defenders of the city; they can be courageous with true belief from the rulers about what the city should fear (*Republic*: 429bc, 430b). This has often been discounted as being only "political" or civic courage (*Republic*: 430c) rather than courage within the soul, and it is indeed true that this is a virtue of the city. But this virtue is located in persons assigned to defend the city, as social wisdom is located in persons assigned to rule the city. These two social virtues are unlike the holistic social virtues of justice and temperance; a city being Platonically just does not imply that its citizens have Platonic justice in their souls, and the same is true of Platonic social temperance (the isomorphism is not strong enough to have this implication for the holistic virtues).

But a city being Platonically courageous does imply that some of its citizens are courageous – namely its defenders. The city is courageous when its defenders preserve in all circumstances correct beliefs from the legislators about what the city should fear; they can do this because they are born high spirited and are educated and trained to so preserve in all circumstances such beliefs. In giving his account of social courage Plato goes into the souls of the defenders twice, first to sketch their education and then to define the quality they have by which the city is courageous. To be sure, this definition does not explicitly refer to the beliefs they must preserve that would be psychic courage, but true beliefs about what they should fear for themselves.[46] The content of the two beliefs, the belief taken from the rulers and the belief taken from reason, have different objects: the former what the city should fear, the latter what a person should fear. But Plato tells us explicitly and forcefully that the rulers and the defenders must identify their interests or good with the interests or good of the city (*Republic*: 412de), and this is essential for doing their job well; and from this we can reasonably infer that what the rulers and defenders should fear for themselves is the same as what they should fear for the city. This is also well supported by Plato saying that the defenders must preserve the belief about what the city should fear "in all circumstances"; the brave man "preserves it both in pain and pleasures and in desires and fears and does not expel it from his soul" (*Republic*: 429cd).

Moreover, it seems wildly paradoxical to suppose that the defenders of the city, who are courageous as soldiers in battle, risking their lives, and indeed preserving beliefs about what the city should fear in "in all circumstances" – that these people would not need to have correct beliefs about what they should fear for themselves. The same holds for the non-holistic virtue of social wisdom, which is located in the rulers: the city is wise by the rulers being wise, and their wisdom in knowledge of what is good for the city in its internal and external relations; but since they too and above all identify their good with the good of the city, the wisdom by which they are psychically wise has to have the same content. It is not possible for the rulers to be wise as rulers without being wise as persons, as it is not possible for the defenders to be courageous as defenders without being courageous as persons.

To all this we may add that even Plato's philosophers have to use a lot of, perhaps entirely, true beliefs rather than knowledge when they rule, since their laws and policies and directives will be about sensible things, and according to the Divided Line no one can have knowledge of sensible things;[47] Many philosophers' "wisdom," at least the wisdom they use when they rule, is going to consist of at most true beliefs rather than knowledge. Indeed, when we look at his two accounts of wisdom in Book IV we see that they are about sensible cities and persons in this world, not about Platonic forms: social wisdom is about "the city as a whole and the betterment of its relations within itself and with other states" (*Republic*: 428d); and individual wisdom is "knowledge of what is beneficial for each [part of the soul] and for the whole, the community composed of the three" (*Republic*: 442c). Cities and souls are not forms, they are changing things in our changing world. Though Plato holds that no one can know anything – perhaps not even have rational true beliefs – without knowing the forms, he still allows other citizens, besides the philosopher-rulers to have relevant true beliefs necessary for some psychic virtues, as we have seen in the case of courage. Similarly, other citizens besides the philosopher-rulers can have the true beliefs necessary for being just in their souls. Plato's completely good city can avoid the paradoxes of ethical elitism, and in that ideal city all the citizens can have a rational motivation for being just.

Even so, we must recognize that Plato's elitism remains very troubling, notably at its very center, that knowledge of good is possible only for very few human beings who are born very smart and are highly educated. It may be reasonable to suppose that our societies cannot be governed well without our rulers having knowledge or rational beliefs about what is good; and that we cannot govern ourselves well without knowledge or rational beliefs about our own good. But Plato sets the bar too high when he argues that we cannot know what is good for our societies or ourselves if we do not know the form of the good – and a knowledge that is "infallible." This extreme elitism about knowledge of our good is very different from elitism about knowledge of physics or mathematics, of astronomy or biochemistry. Unlike knowledge in these other fields, knowledge or at least rational belief about our good is necessary to function well as human beings, for making rational choices and acting rightly. Even though Plato may have been right in claiming that knowledge of good is more complex and difficult than we usually suppose, his knowledge of the form of the good may have been too difficult even for him. And according to his own testimony knowledge of the form of the good was certainly too difficult for his star philosopher in the *Republic*.

Notes

1 See Burnyeat (1999b) and Morrison (2007).
2 See Keyt (2006a) for the richness of Plato's famous ship of state analogy.
3 Plato's theories of early and higher education, like his theory of art, form part of the contingent super-structure of the *Republic*. They depend very much on his more fundamental analysis of the human soul and his theory of forms and knowledge. This super-structure is not a necessary part of Plato's fundamental theories, in my opinion. They can be revised without change in the fundamentals. For some classic discussions, see Nettleship (1962), Cornford (1941), Urmson (1997), and G.R. Lear (2006).
4 Plato's setting tyranny as the polar opposite of his completely good city should give pause to those who assimilate all too easily Plato's political ideal to totalitarian regimes and dictatorships.
5 Rawls (1971: ch. VII, "Goodness as Rationality").
6 Keyt (1991) and Anagnostopoulos (1994: chapters 6 and 7).
7 Rawls (1982). Our comprehensive good includes our ultimate ends about which it is difficult to reach agreement. But agreement on major instrumental goods, such as Rawls' "primary goods" is sufficient for rational choice of principles of justice in the "original position." Or so Rawls argues.
8 To know something is not only to know that it is so and so but also why it is so and so; alternatively, to know that something is true we must have proof or evidence for its truth. For discussion see Irwin (1995).
9 For the features of perfection and purity of forms, see Code (1993) and Rickless (2007: chapter 1).
10 A much-discussed passage. See, for example, Penner (1987) and Rickless (2007).

11   Plato seems to think that physical collections "are and are not" the number they seem to exemplify; because a collection of five men, say, is also a collection of ten feet. Apparently only a collection of five absolutely indivisible units is exactly five, no other number.

12   See Penner (1987).

13   For a recent discussion see Rickless (2007: chapter 1).

14   Fine (1993; 1999).

15   This statement combines what the quoted statement says with other elements of the theory found in the *Phaedo* (100–2). For a discussion of various versions of the "one over many" principle see Fine (1993: chapters 15 and 16).

16   This naming after other things seems to be the same relation as Aristotle's paronymy in *Categories* (chapter 1): brave persons are so named after the bravery they have in them, with a grammatical change from "bravery" to "brave".

17   Aristotle suggests that Plato distinguished not only between, say, the form circle and physical circles, but also between the form circle, which is single and one, and many geometrical circles which are perfect and pure particulars satisfying completely all of Euclid's definitions, axioms, and theorems about circles. Similarly with numbers. The so-called mathematical "intermediates" between forms and physical particulars. See *Metaphysics, Mu, Nu* (Barnes 1984).

18   It is important to note that Plato's theory of forms does not require that all sensible objects have all the "defects" listed: some sensible objects may not have all the defining features of their forms, other sensible objects may have them in a lesser degree than their forms, and yet others may be impure. All the forms are perfect *and* pure, but sensible objects are imperfect *or* impure *or* both. See Santas (2001: 173–4).

19   For the scope of the theory of forms, see Wedberg (1955), and for Plato's doubts about some sets having forms, see Rickless (2007: chapter 2).

20   This is the sample form Plato uses explicitly in the "third man arguments" in the *Parmenides*, and the form large being large seems to be an implicit premise in these arguments. See Fine (1993) and Rickless (2007) for informed discussions.

21   To attribute such self-predications to Plato seems to turn him into a "metaphysical fool," to use Terry Penner's stunning phrase. Plato's language may suggest it at times, but perhaps this evidence can be disarmed. Penner goes over such evidence in the *Republic*, and tries to account for it without self-predication (Penner 2006). On the other hand, Rickless assembles some impressive evidence that Plato, in the middle dialogues, was committed to self-predication, and also argues that self-predication, even for the form large, is not necessarily absurd (Rickless 2007: 33–6).

22   This explaining away of Plato's self-predicating language is similar to the one preferred by Cherniss and Allen: the F is F amounts to an identity statement,

the F is identical with the F. To say that the F is what it is to be F amounts to saying, the F is identical with what it is to be F, where what it is to be F stands for the definiens of the F.

23 This is what Vlastos (1981) and Peterson (1973) called Pauline self-predication; when St. Paul said that love is kind he meant that those who love are kind, not that love itself is kind.

24 Another seemingly deflationary account of self predication is what Fine (1993: 62) calls broad self-predication: the form F is F in the sense that it explains why particular sensible things are F. This avoids the seeming absurdities of literal or narrow self-predication.

25 Socrates tells us three times in the *Phaedo* (102b, 102d, 103e) that sensibles are "named after" the forms (Cooper 1997).

26 Here I follow Shields (2008) and Prior (1983) who distinguish between *paradigms*, as individual exemplars (or individual role models) which are self-exemplifying to a high degree, and paradigms as patterns or structures which are general or universal and are not necessarily self-exemplifying. A person can be an exemplar of virtue, a role model and a paradigm in the first sense; a law can be a standard of behavior, a paradigm in the second sense. A species too (especially once we have its definition) can be a standard for its specimens; mutations can make for "less perfect" specimens, even though some of these mutations might eventually prove advantageous in a given environment, as evolutionists might point out. Plato and Aristotle were not evolutionists but teleologists, and they thought that any gross deviations from species in specimens were defective specimens, which Aristotle noticed and called *terata*.

27 See Rickless (2007: 33–36), where Rickless tries to disarm "obvious" absurdities of self-predication in this way: we tend to find these absurdities because we tend to think in terms of physical entities (largeness in terms of large buildings or stars) and not abstractly enough.

28 This marks a change, hopefully an improvement, over the author's account of the form of the good (Fine 1999b; Santas 2001).

29 See Shields' excellent discussion of Aristotle's criticisms of Plato's being and goodness (Shields 1999: chapters 8 and 9).

30 The allegory of the cave reflects Plato's epistemology and metaphysics and interprets the divided line both statically and dynamically (see Ferejohn 2006). It relates a human journey from inside the cave, the world of images of physical objects at first mistaken for physical objects, to the world outside, the world of mathematical and other Platonic Forms, with the form of the good at the top. A successful traveler will start from the usual human condition (perhaps early life), realize the successive mistakes, and end up with knowledge of the forms and of the good. The rest of Book VII outlines the curriculum of higher education necessary for such a successful journey. Socrates

says that the successful travelers, very few gifted individuals, must come back into the cave and govern the city (see White 1986).

31   What a species is, and how to define a given species, have much changed since Plato and Aristotle. For an informed discussion, including criticisms of Plato's "types in nature" and the nominalists' explaining away species, see, for example, the great essay by Ernst Mayr, "The Biological Meaning of Species," (Mayr 1996). For evolutionists too, specimens can be more or less "successful," but their notion of evolutionary success is certainly different from Plato (and to a lesser degree Aristotle).

32   See also Shields (2008) who tries to show that we can have an intelligible theory of the form of the good without literal self-predication; Plato seems to take the immutability of forms as a good-making characteristic. For dissent see Keyt (1971).

33   For a discussion, see Santas (1988: 32–40).

34   Aristotle, *History of Animals* (Book I, chapter 1).

35   For discussion of this point in greater significant detail see Santas (2001: chapter 5).

36   Aristotle indeed attributes to Plato the view that there are such objects, self-exemplifying perfect particulars, "intermediate" between Platonic forms and physical objects and their images. These, certainly, would be the best objects of their kinds, the best lines, the best circles, and so on. But the intermediates are particulars, not universals, there are many of each kind, not just one, and they are not Platonic forms. For a recent discussion of these mathematical objects, see Arsen (2009).

37   Rickless (2007: chapter 1) and others earlier, have assembled evidence for self-predication that goes beyond metaphors and images. And we may be able to avoid the absurdities of literal self-predications by thinking of self-predication very abstractly: for example, large is not only a special property; a set can be larger than another set; a number can be larger than another number.

38   See Penner's statement: "To know *what beds are* one needs to know what sleep is (the good of beds), and to know what sleep is, one needs to know what human life (the good of sleep) is, and to know this one needs to know what the human good (the good of human life) is, and to know this one will have to know what the good quite generally is" (Penner 2006:246).

39   For Plato's views on pleasure as the human good, see Santas (2006b).

40   For a recent discussion of Platonic (not Socratic) dialectic, see Benson (2006a).

41   How the philosopher's knowledge of forms can help him/her rule the city well, a city which belongs to the physical world about which nothing presumably can be strictly known, is a problem that has puzzled many readers. From the most recent discussion, see Sedley (2007).

42   The best case for this view has been ably made by Bobonich (2002, 41–88).

43 See chapter 9. Some readers think that in these pleasure arguments Plato is
    comparing the philosophers with soldiers and artisans of his good city on
    the assumption that soldiers are the same as timocratic men and the artisans
    the same as the oligarchic characters. I think this is a mistake. Philosophers,
    soldiers, and artisans in the good city are defined by their aptitude for the
    three main social functions of the city; timocratic and oligarchic characters
    are defined by what part of their soul rules; and in the pleasure arguments the
    three characters are characterized by what elements in their souls are domi-
    nant and ruling.

44 The formal part of justice in the city is: a city is just when each of its parts is
    performing its optimal function; the full definition specifies the parts of the
    city and its functions. Similarly, the formal part of justice in the soul is: a soul
    is just when each of its parts is performing its optimal function; the full defini-
    tion of justice in the soul specifies parts of the soul and the soul's function.
    See a fuller discussion of this point in Santas (2001:112–13).

45 Indeed this is the view that Sedley has most recently and ably argued for
    (Sedley 2007).

46 Charles Young brought the importance of this point to my attention.

47 But see Fine (1999b) for an informed and well argued dissenting view that
    Plato allows some knowledge of sensible things, though not without knowl-
    edge of forms.

8

Plato's Criticisms of Democracy and the Democratic Character

Discussions of Plato's criticisms of democracy in the *Republic* have to begin with some important facts.

To begin with, the democracy he criticized was importantly different from modern democracies. The Athens of his day was a direct, participatory democracy, not the representative democracies or republics of modern times. Its dominant political institution was the Assembly, to which every citizen belonged, each citizen with exactly one vote. This is absolute equality in ruling. Other major political institutions, such as the Council and the Jury Courts, were representative, since not every citizen could belong to them at the same time; but they were very equalitarian, by the devices of rotation in office and random selection by lot; these devices allowed each citizen an equal turn (for the Council) or an equal chance (for the Jury Courts) over a life time.[1] As the fathers of the American constitution knew and feared, participatory democracies were far more open to abuses and to mob rule than modern representative democracies whose rulers can be far more educated than the average citizen.[2]

Second, Plato was acutely aware that he was allowed to criticize democracy because he lived in one. It was the democracy's freedom of speech that made it possible for him to lecture and write critically about democracy. Moreover, his very writing style highlighted oppositions, gave them a fair hearing, and carried on reason's dialogue with them; this could exist and flourish only in a democratic culture. Plato's criticism of ancient direct democracies came from someone who, if not an admirer of democracy, must have prized living in one that allowed him to dream and speak of something he thought better.

Finally, much as we moderns may prefer democracy to other practically available forms of government, we are hard put to deny that democracies, ancient and modern, have displayed faults and imperfections of many kinds. Can we then learn from Plato's criticisms at least how democracies might become better, more just and/or more conducive to the good of all their citizens?

We begin with examining Plato's handling of three subjects relevant to his criticisms of democratic constitutions: private property and wealth, knowledge for governing, and freedom. After that, we examine his criticisms of what he calls a democratic person.

1 Political Equalities and Economic Inequalities

Plato correctly identifies the main principles of democratic constitutions as equality and freedom. And his central criticism is that democracy prizes equality and freedom far too much and the knowledge required for ruling well far too little. In a famous passage, he first showers it with irony and sarcasm: twice he calls it "most beautiful" (*Republic*, Book VIII: 557c). Then he notes that it disdains his fundamental principle of social justice, and ends with: "it is a delightful form of government, anarchic and motley, assigning a kind of equality to equals and unequals alike." (Book VIII: 558c4–558c6).

His reasons against treating equals and unequals alike can be found in his arguments for his own principle of social justice. He objects to democracy allowing unequals in ability and expertise for ruling to rule equally, as direct democracy did in the Assembly, and even in the Council and Courts. He objects to the absolute or arithmetical equality in ruling of the ancient participatory democracies. His principle of social justice allows for proportional equality in ruling, ruling in proportion to ability and education for ruling. Reasonably enough, it would seem, he thinks that a city would be better ruled if ruling were matched to high ability and extensive education for it.

However, even the greatest ability and highest possible education is not enough for governing well. Plato takes up private property and wealth because it can corrupt rulers to put their interests above the interest of the whole city. Democracies have to be concerned about that too; but they also worry that great economic inequalities, which they usually allow, undermine the political and other equalities that they value so much. On private property and economic inequalities, Plato's proposals and current democratic practices can be instructively compared.

Let us look at Socrates' proposals about private property and about extremes of poverty and wealth, in *Republic*, Books III and IV.[3] His concern is about the corrupting effects of private property and wealth on guarding and ruling the city, and extremes of wealth and poverty on the providers of the city.

In Book III Plato is primarily concerned with the native qualities that make one best suited to defend and rule the city and with the early education of such persons with a view to the best performance of these functions:

> They must then to begin with be intelligent in these matters and capable, and furthermore careful of the interests of the city. That is so. But one would be most likely to be careful of that which he loved. Necessarily. And again, one would be most likely to love that whose interest he thought to coincide with his own, and thought that when it [the city's interest] prospered he too would prosper, and if not, the contrary. (Republic, Book III: 412c–412d7)

Next he proposes a series of tests and trials for the guardians and the rulers, trials of pleasure and pain, desire and fear, to insure that they would in all circumstances preserve the conviction that they must do what is best for the city and that what is best for the city is best for them and not otherwise. He ends with the myth of the metals rounding out their education. In sum, Socrates has outlined the rulers' and guardians' native qualities, the engendering of beliefs and desires about what is best for the city, and tests and trials to preserve these beliefs in all circumstances as to act in accordance with the desire for the good of the city.

But then (*Republic*: 415e–417b) we learn that the correct native qualities and the right education are not enough. There is still a danger that the guardian dogs will turn into wolves. "Must we not guard then by every means in our power against our helpers treating the citizens in such a way and, because they are stronger, converting themselves from benign assistants into savage masters?" (416b1–416b3). Their education, even if it is really a good one, is not enough of a safeguard. "In addition, to such an education a thoughtful man would affirm that their houses and the possessions provided for them ought to be such as not to interfere with the best performance of their own work as guardians and not to incite them to wrong the other citizens" (416c5–416d1). If they had private property, private houses, land of their own and money, they would be "householders and farmers instead of guardians," they would become not helpers but "enemies and masters" of their fellow citizens, and end up in shipwreck for themselves and the city (417ab). Therefore, they must not have private property, private houses, land or money.

This argument should give pause to those who think that Plato's ideal city-state is totalitarian. We know of no totalitarian regimes whose rulers were willing to live without private property, private houses, land, or even wages. What we nowadays call totalitarian regimes Plato knew as tyrannies. And he famously classifies and ranks his ideal city as the polar opposite of tyranny and his philosopher as the polar opposite of the tyrant. His extreme firewall between private property, wealth *and* ruling is in answer to the problem posed by Thrasymachus' view, the perpetual human problem of rulers ruling in their own interest.

Whether the extreme economic measures he proposes are necessary for ruling well seems to be an empirical issue.[4] Is it true?

In the absence of experiments, we can only go by historical and contemporary experience. Plato's proposals here are clearly a recognizable version of separating institutionally political and military power from property and wealth. These are radical reforms, relative to the Athenian practices of his day, for the economic and political institutions of the city. And they are immediately comparable to less extreme attempts in modern democracies for some such separation by means of blind trusts, financial disclosure requirements, conflict of interest laws, and campaign rules for raising and spending money.

Plato's proposals here are extreme. His guardians' manner of life is more Spartan than their counterparts in Sparta. And Plato knows it. Though his Glaucon assent to them emphatically, his Adeimantus immediately makes a serious objection. To deprive the guardians – rulers and soldiers – of all these things would make them unhappy; for these are the very goods the possession of which is thought to make men happy (the opening liens of Book IV: 419e–420a). Indeed, these are the goods that Thrasymachus' heroes and men with the ring of Gyges go after. The objection is fundamental, since Plato agrees that everyone pursues his/her own happiness, and his guardians would have more power than anyone else to pursue these goods.

But his Socrates does not retreat. He challenges the conception of happiness that underlies the objection. After observing that they set out not to make any one class in the city especially happy (as Thrasymachus' cities do), but to make the whole city as happy as possible – for they thought that only in such a city would they find justice – he challenges the conception of happiness used in the objection. He would not be surprised, he says, if his guardians were "most happy," and suggests that their happiness will be found not in the possession of fine houses and lands, but in being "the best craftsman in their own work ... And so, as the entire city develops and is ordered well, each class is to be left to the share of happiness that its nature comports" (Book IV: 421c3–421c6; Shorey 1935). The rulers will have a ruler's happiness, to be found primarily in the best performance of their work as rulers (as those who by nature and education are best suited to rule), and/or in the satisfaction of being best craftsmen in their own work; the soldiers similarly will have a soldier's happiness, and the craftsmen and traders the kind of happiness appropriate to their nature and work.

This answer supposes not only that part of happiness is to be found in doing well what one is by nature suited to do best, but also that such a happiness of one class does not compete with the happiness of another.

But are such extreme proposals realistic? Are there people who would be "most happy" without any of the goods most people enjoy and Socrates excludes? No rulers that we know of have been satisfied to live in the conditions of deprivation Socrates described. Nor have any known states required their rulers to live so. Even in states where the means of production are publicly owned, personal property is allowed; and even where not, rulers live in palatial public houses (e.g. the former Soviet Union). We know of actual democracies that have been compatible with public ownership of the means of production, such as socialist England after the Second World War; but it allowed personal private property for all, including rulers, and even considerable wealth. John Rawls, our most fundamental recent defender of democratic theory, considers such public ownership compatible with his democratic principles of justice, but not with the abolition of personal private property.[5]

On the other hand, Plato makes an important point. Democracies acknowledge that a close link between ruling and great wealth pose a danger to ruling well, which by their own rights must conform as much as possible to political equality in ruling and equality of maximum civil liberties. Wealthy men are not excluded from office, but on attaining office they have to disclose their wealth, their wealth may have to go into a blind trust, and they have to rule behind a veil of ignorance – ignorance of how their public decisions will affect their wealth. The unending attempts and fights for political campaign reform in the United States, for example, acknowledge the same danger.

But these democratic measures to separate wealth from ruling are feeble compared to Plato's, and have been a largely ineffective means to their declared end: an end to political corruption and equality in ruling and in civil liberties. For example, about a third of the US House of Representatives are millionaires in annual income, not just assets, and the same is true of the Senate,[6] while US Presidents are millionaires when they run for office or can become so the moment they leave office (by selling their memoirs). But only one percent of the population they represent are millionaires. Even when they are not millionaires, people running for office need millions for their campaigns and most of them most of the time have to indebt themselves to millionaires.[7]

There must be some ground between these extremes that would not make Plato's city less Platonically just or a democratic city less democratic. John Rawls recognizes the ineffectiveness and resulting unfairness of the current relevant democratic practices and his proposals are somewhere in between those practices and Plato's proposals on property and wealth.[8] Plato can accept the idea that his guardians can rule well even if they had some modest property or lived in better public quarters, and still hold on to the essence of his theory of social justice; while democracies can move closer to Plato on the link between ruling and wealth and still remain democratic.

The other proposal that Socrates brings up next is to set limits to wealth and poverty for the rest of the population, the providers, who are allowed private property in the completely good city, indeed allowed a free market (Book IV: 421d–422b).[9] His argument proceeds on the basis of the abstract functional theory and empirical assumptions about what is needed for the artisans to perform their function well. A potter who grew rich, Socrates claims, would no longer mind his craft; he would become idle, negligent, and a worse potter. But a potter who was poor would be unable to obtain tools and other things he needs, and once more would not be able to do his work well. "From both causes, then, poverty and wealth, the products of the arts deteriorate and so do the artisans ... Here then is a second group of things, it seems, that our guardians must guard against and do all in their power to keep from slipping into the city without their knowledge ... Wealth and poverty" (421e4–422a1). Wealth saps motivation in craftsmanship; a tanner does his job well, becomes rich, gets bored with tanning, and runs for office. On the other hand, Socrates may sculpt well, but has no money to buy marble.

Democracies acknowledge the need to set wealth ceilings and poverty floors. Measures such as inheritance taxes presumably were designed to prevent extreme concentrations of wealth over generations; "the negative income tax" and Rawls' *difference principle* are clearly designed to elimi-nate extremes of poverty.[10] Democracies' reasons may be different from Plato's: extremes of wealth and poverty produce inequalities in ruling and in the enjoyment of civil liberties. Even in a rich democracy, such as the United States, more than ten percent of the population fall below the offi-cial poverty line, and their participation in elections and governing is most likely very unequal to the wealthy. John Rawls draws a distinction between liberty and the worth of liberty;[11] for example, all citizens have an equal right to free speech, but the wealthy have greater access to the means of exercising this right in newspapers, radio, and television. Or, take the right to travel: all citizens can have it equally, but its exercise will vary widely with variation of means – the poor go nowhere. The democratic ideals of free-dom and equality cannot be effectively realized with extremes of wealth and poverty. Rawls proposes constitutional measures to compensate for the unequal worth of liberty caused by inequalities in income and wealth.[12]

Plato's reforms on extremes of wealth and poverty seem too Spartan; this is an empirical issue, and Plato may well be wrong. How much wealth or poverty is too much? Given the enormous differences in size, numbers, and technologies between ancient Greek city states and modern nation states, his view on how much is necessary or best to do one's job well, and how much is too much, might need considerable revision.

In the modern democracies there seems to be no significant agreement on the limits of wealth and poverty. Rawls' difference principle ties the prospects of the less fortunate in talents and social and economic resources at birth to the prospects of the more fortunate in these respects. It still allows great inequalities in property and wealth; to allow for incentives and productivity and for the more talented and hard-working to be compen-sated for costs of their additional education and training. But the upward movement of the more fortunate is allowed only so long as it brings with it an improvement in the less fortunate.[13] Sad to say, the difference princi-ple is the most controversial of all Rawls' principles and the objections do not come from the poor, even though arguably it seems fair and its con-crete implementation far more fair than the present state of affairs – great wealth seemingly at the expense of great poverty.

In any case, Plato's ideal city and the democracies can agree that prop-erty and wealth and extremes of wealth and poverty can significantly affect ruling as well as affect significant social and economic functions, and that both constitutions need to regulate them. Plato seems correct in sup-posing that doing well the social task that a citizen can do best is one important human good and one important component of the citizen's happiness; but he may have been considerably mistaken in the empirical assumptions he makes about how much of the usual material goods are necessary or effective for doing one's job well; whether one is a ruler, a soldier, or an artisan. His completely good city and its citizens might require more of these goods and still remain Platonically just. But he is right to point to the dangers of wealth and poverty, and democracies are subject to these dangers and need to lean more in his direction.

In the *Republic* Plato integrates his politics and economics in a different way from modern democracies. He proposes far greater economic equalities than dreamt up by any democracy, though in an almost paradoxical mixture with political inequalities. The deeper bases for these economic equalities are his functional theory, the primacy of doing well what one does best as part of the human good, and the parallels between ruling and the other arts and sciences. Modern democracies, too, try to moderate economic inequalities, but their deeper basis is clearly political equality; economic inequalities are based on economic realities (e.g. motivational incentives and costs of training) and are to be mitigated mainly for the sake of maintaining political equalities and the meaningful exercise of liberties. If we take Rawls' well-ordered society as a modern democratic ideal, a democracy highly approximating it would eliminate the worst existing economic inequalities through the institutional requirements of the difference principle (such as a negative income tax) and of the principle of fair equality of opportunity.[14] Such a society would lean in Plato's direction, although for different reasons.

2 Platonic Knowledge and Democratic Ruling

Plato's ideal city is usually thought to be anti-democratic and politically elitist with respect to the knowledge required for ruling the city well: the wisdom of what is good for the city as a whole in its internal and external relations (Book IV: 428b–429a).[15] It is the possession of this virtue of social wisdom that entitles some of the citizens to rule over others, not the consent of the ruled; though the virtue of civic temperance implies consent by all citizens that the wise should rule, and presumably brings harmony between rulers and ruled and makes the ideal city stable.

This much is clear enough in Book IV. And by itself it is not necessarily elitist or even anti-democratic. Maybe all the citizens in a direct democracy, or at least their elected representatives in modern republics, can acquire such wisdom with appropriate education; and maybe the best way to find out if the ruled consent (in a temperate city) is by elections of some kind. It depends on whether some of Plato's empirical assumptions are true; for example, whether he is correct about the natural lottery, symbolized by the myth of metals (Book III: 415), that nature distributes talents and abilities very unequally at birth. Maybe, contrary to what he thought, there is enough gold in everyone's souls, though not necessarily in the same proportions to the other metals, so that everyone can acquire wisdom.

Now, the democracies can lean in Plato's direction: literacy tests for voting would not be objectionable if there were no citizens so poor they could not afford an education (and assuming the tests were applied impartially); absent the poor, the requirements for voting might include a high school education. Why would it be anti-democratic to require informed voting under such conditions? And absent the poor, the requirements for running for office might go beyond residency and age, to a certain level of education. We have such requirements for other professions, most relevantly for judges who must have an education in the law; why not for ruling? Even if it is the consent of the ruled that entitles some to rule over others, surely the wisdom of Book IV would be one of the rulers' virtues?

But the metaphysics and epistemology of Books V, VI, and VII make these overtures of moderation and conciliation difficult. The apparently common-sense view of political wisdom, in Book IV, turns out to be an illusion. Socrates draws a very strong distinction between knowledge and opinion, requiring the metaphysics of the forms. The wisdom of Book IV requires knowledge of the Form of the Good, without which no other thing can be known to be good, not even justice. And such knowledge in turn requires great native intelligence and demands higher education in the sciences; so it is clear that only a small minority of human beings can attain such knowledge. Plato's metaphysics of the Form of the Good puts an enormous political burden on knowledge of the good of the city. Somebody has to know the Form of the Good in order to rule a city well – that is the political burden. But nobody does! Plato sets the bar of knowledge of the good so high that according to him even his Socrates of the *Republic* – the very character who proposes all the important ideas of this great work – has no knowledge of the Form of the Good but only opinions (Book VI: 506c2–506c3). It seems reasonable to suppose, as Socrates does at the end of Book I, that we do not know that justice is good for us unless we know what justice is; and reasonable to suppose that we don't know that justice is good unless we know what good is. But it is quite different, far more demanding, and far too doubtful that we need to know the Platonic Form of the Good to know that justice is good.

Plato has worked up a potent combination of (1) too sparsely distributed high intelligence, (2) too high a standard of knowledge for ruling, and (3) this knowledge as the basis for governing. To make government even more exclusive, Plato's conception of philosophers in the *Republic* has proved to be too narrow: according to the argument at the end of Book V, those who do not recognize, or deny that there is, a form Beauty, the Beautiful itself, as distinct from beautiful colors and shapes and bodies and sunsets, these people are not philosophers but only lovers of opinion. Thus nominalists – those who deny or do not think necessary to postulate universals – are not philosophers! William of Okham and Nelson Goodman are not philosophers!

Perhaps the most important insight of the *Republic*, that good governing requires great intelligence and great education – so much more true today with our huge populations and very complex societies – tends to get lost in Plato's prolific metaphysics, demanding knowledge, and narrow conception of philosophy.

Though philosophers might love Plato's dream of philosophers being kings, or even the harder task of educating existing kings to be philosophers, perhaps we should ask whether Plato's ideal of good government can remain essentially intact with a less demanding standard of knowledge and a less prolific metaphysics. Perhaps we can have Plato's theory of justice and the human good with a weaker metaphysics and epistemology: without forms, or with forms as properties without self-predication, and with knowledge as justified true belief, perhaps highly probable belief rather than certainty.[16]

Of course the *Republic* would not be the great and comprehensive work it is without its middle books (V, VI, and VII); they are part of the very essence of the work, and show that Plato thinks we cannot do ethics and political philosophy well without some assumptions or theories about knowledge and reality. And this is certainly one tradition in moral philosophy. But do the assumptions need to be so strong?

The other tradition is clearly stated by John Rawls, who claims that his theory of justice is "political, not metaphysical."[17] Without going all the way to Rawls, and without attacking the unity and integrity of the *Republic*, we can still consider whether Plato's central idea of good government can remain intact, with a lower standard of knowledge and a less prolific metaphysics, and can thus come closer to democratic ideals.[18]

The way the *Republic* is written allows to some degree for such an *imaginary* isolation of Plato's ethical and political theory without his metaphysics and epistemology. The theory of what justice is and the defense of justice are put forward by Socrates in Books II, III, IV, the first half of V, and the later books VII, and IX. Socrates develops his theory of justice in the first group without any essential reference to the theory of forms or knowledge of forms. Even after the forms and knowledge of them has been elaborated in the middle books, these theories are not used explicitly in the classification and rankings of unjust cities and persons in Book VIII. To be sure, though not explicitly used, the metaphysics and the epistemology may be thought necessary for the main arguments in the defense of justice in Book IX.[19] Still, the only later passage in which the theory of forms is explicitly used to explain the nature and value of works of art is a small stretch of Book X. So it would seem that Plato himself allows that his theory of justice in the city and in a person can be understood without the theory of forms; and similarly for at least some of his defenses of his justice (see chapter 9) against the rival theories of Glaucon and Thrasymachus, and against the timocratic, oligarchic and democratic theories of justice.

It might be argued that Plato's justice is more deeply understood and better defended if we bring in and integrate with it his metaphysics and epistemology (and perhaps the grand metaphysical teleology of the *Timaeus*). The "longer road," deferred in Book IV and taken up in Book VI, points to such integration.[20] And this interpretation of the work maintains its unity and integrity. But still this longer road is not adequately explained because of the obscurity of Plato's good and because no one ever traveled such a road. It is highly doubtful that Plato's theory of political justice can be better defended on the basis of his prolific ontology, demanding knowledge, and narrow conception of the philosopher. And there are serious doubts about the practicability of any theory of justice that depends on them. In any case, I do not propose cutting out the middle books of the *Republic*, but only a thought experiment that brackets them.

Some might question how significant the remainder from this isolation experiment is. Well, two principal questions of the work, what justice is and whether we are better off being just rather than unjust, are in fact answered mostly in passages that make no explicit reference to or use of the forms or knowledge of them. Further, we still have significant oppositions to the theories of justice of Thrasymachus and Glaucon. Further yet, Plato's conception of unjust states and unjust individuals in Book VIII remains intact: Plato's political justice is still not honor based, not wealth based, not freedom and equality based, and not power based. With respect to the function of ruling the city, the ideal city is still an "epistocracy" (the rule of knowledge)[21]; but with a lower standard of knowledge as justified or probable true belief and without Plato's prolific metaphysics – something closer to Aristotle's view of the subject matter of ethics and politics as what is true for the most part.

If we thus moderate Plato's wisdom to the claim that ruling well requires some attainable and publicly understood knowledge of what is good and what is good for the city, as medicine, for example, requires such a type of knowledge about what is good for the body (rather than Plato's stronger claim that it requires knowledge of the *Form* of the Good), then we can have something that seems more reasonable and acceptable, and democracies can lean in a significant way in Plato's direction. For example, given the absence of poverty and given universal education, the qualifications for various offices can be raised so that at least a minimum of relevant knowledge (or education) is required, as the qualifications for physicians or attorneys have been raised over the years. Democracy allows this now for civil service positions. Absent poverty and free public education, ruling with higher qualifications for office, can still be based on the consent of the governed.

Another constitutional device leaning in the direction of epistocracy would be plural voting. John Stuart Mill and John Rawls both believed that such practices are compatible with democratic justice: instead of one citizen, one vote, we have one citizen at least one vote; some citizens have more than one vote in proportion to their education (rather than their knowledge).[22] There are several reasons for such proposals. To begin with perhaps the least important, the ideal of equal political liberty, with the precept of "one elector one vote" and all that this implies about representation, is extremely difficult to attain, even to approximate: representation in the United States Senate, for example, completely disregards the implication of this precept – that members of legislatures, with one vote each, represent the same number of electors – and even the US House of Representatives, designed to be truly representative, only approximates it.

The main reason for scholocracy (the rule of the educated) is the idea that the better educated would rule better or more wisely. So, where there are populations in which some are better educated than others (a universal condition, it seems), the more educated have more votes so that their opinions will have greater influence. Mill perhaps was influenced by the Platonic analogies between ruling and other arts; he thought that in a common enterprise in which everyone has an interest, such as ruling, and such other arts as medicine and navigation, everyone should have a say; but not necessarily an equal say, since some can have more relevant knowledge than others and they can act better for everyone's benefit, including the benefit of those with a lesser say.[23] Rawls, with his priority of liberty, which prohibits trade-offs between liberties and other primary goods, would restrict the range of benefits that unequal political liberties might provide to an increase (or at least not a decrease) of the other liberties. And to Mill's condition that plural voting must be for the benefit of all, including those with the lesser votes, Rawls adds the condition that it must be acceptable to those with lesser votes.

His statement on this is worth quoting:

> Government is assumed to aim at the common good … To the extent that this presumption holds, and some men can be identified as having superior wisdom and judgment, others are willing to trust them and to concede to their opinion greater weight. The passengers of a ship are willing to let the captain steer the course, since they believe that he is more knowledgeable and wishes to arrive safely as much as they do. There is both an identity of interests and a noticeably greater skill and judgment in realizing it. Now the ship of state is in some ways analogous to a ship at sea; and to the extent that this is so, the political liberties are indeed subordinate to the other freedoms that, so to say, define the intrinsic good of the passengers. Admitting these assumptions, plural voting may be perfectly just. (Rawls 1971: 205)[24]

In any case, we can perhaps agree that to accept scholocracy is to lean significantly towards Plato's direction; and that scholocracy is still democratic if every citizen has at least one vote, and if it is acceptable to those with the lesser votes.

3   Plato's Criticisms of Democratic Freedoms

Plato's criticisms of democratic freedoms are not easy to find or understand well. As far as I can tell, there are at least three main such criticisms in the *Republic*: one of psychic freedom of the democratic man that we shall soon take up; one of free choice of profession, to be discussed now; and the censorship of poetry.[25]

Let us look to his criticism of free choice of occupation, especially free choice of going into politics, since part of his theory of justice is hard to modify without giving up that theory.

That there is no such free choice of occupation in the completely good city becomes clear when Socrates proposes that a principle they used all along is what (social) justice is: "that each one man must perform one social service in the city for which his nature was best adapted" (Book IV: 433a5–433a6). But Socrates thinks he has to give reasons for this identification – that this is social justice and not some other thing. His last argument for this is the most relevant here. If a cobbler undertook the work of a carpenter or a carpenter the work of a cobbler, or one of them did both, the two chief violations of the principle, this would not injure the city a great deal.

> But when I fancy one who is by nature an artisan or some kind of money maker, tempted and incited by wealth or command of votes or bodily strength or some similar advantage, tries to enter into the class of the soldiers, or one of the soldiers into the class of the counselors and guardians, for which he is not fitted, ... or the same man undertakes all these functions at once ... then this kind of substitution or multitasking is the ruin of the city ... this is the greatest harm to the city and the thing that most works it harm ... and what works the greatest harm to the city is injustice. (Book IV: 434a9–434c4).

This makes it clear that doing what one wants to do (as one's occupation) is not permitted if one wants to do anything for which he is not best suited by nature and education; similarly, if one wants to do several occupations at once, or wants to move from an occupation she is best suited for to one for which she is less suited. All these things are prohibited directly by the principle of social justice, which remarkably in our passages is applied to "child, woman, slave, free, artisan, ruler and ruled" (*Republic* 433d2–433d4).

But why do such violations bring the greatest harm to the city? No reason is given in the present passage. We have to go all the way back to the passages where Socrates first proposed the principle of division of labor by talent and education to see his reasons for it: division of labor (rather than each one doing all necessary things to satisfy all his/her needs) makes production of food, shelter, and clothing easier; people are born with different natures suited for different occupations; people are better at doing one thing (occupation) well rather than several at once;

and doing well at an occupation requires education and time free from other concerns. As Socrates sums it up: "The result, then, is that more things are produced, and better and more easily when one man performs one task according to his nature, at the right moment and at leisure from other occupations" (Book II: 370c3–370c5). Notice that Socrates is not saying quite generally that one cannot do several "things" at once or successively; he is talking about division of labor along occupation lines; and occupations, unlike smaller tasks, require education and considerable time. He is saying that one cannot do several occupations as well as one; and, given the natural lottery assumption (that nature distributes talents and abilities unequally), that one cannot perform as well in an occupation for which she is not suited by nature as in one for which she is. When the model is expanded beyond provisioning to defending and ruling the city, the same reasons work as well. This is why violations of this principle are harmful to the city.

It is difficult to dispute Socrates' reasons in a major way. Division of labor enhances productivity enormously.[26] When the division is along occupation lines (rather than the fine division of labor in an assembly line of a modern factory), it requires extensive education, training, and a considerable part of one's lifetime. One can dispute the natural lottery assumption to some extent, but when it is applied only to the three major social functions (providing, defending, and ruling), it may be mostly true: can we claim that all human beings can be equally good at provisioning their city, defending it, and ruling it, if they are given similar educations? Perhaps only an extreme behaviorist would.

And why are interchanges of the three functions or multifunctioning the greatest harm to the city? Socrates does not say explicitly. The most likely reason is that the principle of organization (division of social labors by talent and education) is the foundation for the other virtues – at least a necessary condition for them: if, for example, those best suited to defend the city were ruling the city, they would not be doing it as well, and it would be difficult if not impossible for them to acquire the virtue of wisdom – they would have no gold or enough gold in their souls. Considerable mismatching of talents, educations, and occupations might well result in no one doing his job well – perhaps in gross incompetence.

Socrates' arguments, however, overlook an important possibility: if a society has free choice of occupation and citizens have the freedom to choose whatever occupation they want, the good results that Socrates claims for his principle of justice might still obtain in the long run, if information and appropriate educations are available, and incentives are provided for choosing occupations according to one's abilities and education. But to allow for this possibility would be to give up the principle of division of labor by talent as a principle of justice, for this principle *requires* that occupations are matched to talents as a matter of justice. Democracies can allow for the value of the results of matching occupations to talents, but they do not require such matching as a matter of justice; if some of their citizens pursue a career other than what they are best at, they might be regarded as foolish, irrational or inefficient, but not unjust. Plato could not allow for this possibility, free choice of occupation even with good results, without giving up his theory of social justice.

But how can he argue against this possibility? And why do the democrats insist on free choice of occupation?

Plato might argue that if his principle of justice is adopted for the city, those officials charged with assigning occupations to citizens would be more competent to make such choices than the citizens themselves; and if this is so, then in his city the good results are more likely to obtain and more uniformly than in a city with free choice of profession. Provisioning the city, defending it, and ruling it would be better done than in a society with free choice of these professions. But this argument is rather opaque, because he does not say who would be making such choices, what their education would be, and why they are more likely to make correct choices than educated citizens themselves. Moreover, if we look forward to modern nation states, the enormity of numbers makes this argument dubious: in effect Plato would have a command system for choice of profession, and in economics at least – in provisioning the city – such systems fare poorly. An alternative system of free choice of profession, with information, appropriate education, and incentives for choosing the career one is best suited for, might do as well.

This might seem like a dispute about the instrumental value of a command system of choice of profession versus a social structure that allows free choice of profession by individuals – the value depending on how well each promotes the same good end of matching talents to careers.

But unlike the previous cases we considered – where Plato could accept revisions in his empirical or metaphysical or epistemological assumptions and still maintain the essence of his theory of justice – here the stakes are too high for both Plato and the democrats. We have seen that free choice of profession is incompatible with Plato's principle of social justice, and this is too essential a change for him to accept. At the same time, the democrats want to argue that free choice has value on its own and that this tips the scales decisively.[27] Indeed Rawls is explicitly not content to leave the fate of liberty to standard empirical assumptions as the utilitarian or teleological theories do, but embeds maximum equal liberty and the priority of liberty into first principles. Here the distinction between justice and empirical assumptions finds its limits; the dispute cannot be resolved by modifying – hopefully in the direction of truth – empirical assumptions used to construct the theory of justice or in its applications.

4   Plato's Democratic Character: Freedom and Equality in the Human Psyche

Plato's characterization of the democratic city is correct, but his definition of the corresponding democratic person, as one in whose soul there is equality and freedom of desires, seems to be obviously incorrect, and it has been rejected by the tradition[28]. This makes his criticism of this character seem worthless since it is a criticism based on a misconception of what a democratic person is.

In Book VIII, where Plato describes, classifies, and ranks unjust constitutions and persons, he proceeds from each unjust constitution – timocracy, oligarchy, democracy, and tyranny – to the corresponding individuals whose soul mirrors the city. Plato's apparently incorrect definition of a democratic person is a consequence of his correct definition of a democratic city and the assumption of the isomorphism between the two. The isomorphism is the source of the incorrect definition of the democratic character. And this definition can be contrasted to the subsequent tradition's conception of a democratic person, as one who subscribes to a democratic constitution or its leading principles of freedom and equality.[29]

Plato does not set out the inference from his description of the democratic city to his description of the democratic person as explicitly as he does in the case of the inference from city justice to psychic justice. He proceeds more informally as follows.

Democracy comes into being, he tells us, when everyone in the city is granted an "equal share in both citizenship and offices and for the most part these offices are assigned by lot" (557a). As we saw, the equality of citizens is satisfied in the Assembly, the Council and the Jury Courts.

In the principle of freedom Plato includes freedom of speech, the freedom to do as one pleases in his life – including the freedom to choose any career one pleases and to move from any vocation into politics.

Plato then characterizes the democratic person by two conditions, which seem to be applications of the principles of political equality and freedom to the human psyche, and so parallel to the two conditions by which Plato correctly characterized the democratic city.[30]

We see one condition by contrast to the other three types of unjust persons. The oligarchic person, for example, has a dominant desire to accumulate wealth, because he thinks that wealth is the major instrumental good for appetite satisfaction that he takes to be his good. This enables him to order and organize his appetites and desires rationally. Similarly with the timocratic person who thinks victory and honor are his good, and even the tyrannical persons. All these persons may be mistaken, as Plato holds, in thinking that wealth or honor or power is the good and in making reason nothing but an instrument for gaining these ends; but all the same, these priorities do bring some order and instrumental rationality into their lives.

By contrast, the democratic person has no dominant end or stable dominant desire by which to bring order into his desires and make choices accordingly; nor does he think that any one (or subset) of the things he desires is *the* good. Consequently, lacking the kind of priorities reason can set in Plato's just person, and the kind of priorities the other unjust persons have,[31] the democratic person adopts the political principle of equality to his desires, regards them all as equal and equally worthy of satisfaction.

The second condition is that the democratic person does not observe the distinction between "necessary" and "unnecessary" appetites and pleasures, which Plato draws as follows: necessary appetites are those which we cannot get rid of by training and education, those which are necessary for survival, and those whose satisfaction promotes one's own good; for example, the desire for bread is one whose satisfaction is necessary for survival, while the desire for lean and fat-free food is one whose satisfaction promotes the goods of health and strength (558d–559e). Unnecessary appetites are those that exceed what is necessary for survival, those that can be eliminated by training or education, and those that are harmful to the body and the soul (559bc).[32] The democratic person refuses to distinguish between good and bad desires and to restrain any of them on such grounds. He is thereby deprived of another way of bringing order into his life, the way Plato's just person brings order into his life, namely, by ordering his desires on the basis of criteria external to desires themselves, such as the goodness of their objects independently of their being desired.

All this Plato sums up:

> he establishes and maintains all his pleasures on a footing of equality for-sooth, and so lives turning over the guard house of his soul to each as it happens along until it is sated, as if it had been drawn by lot for that office, and then in turn to another, disdaining none but fostering them all equally ... and does not admit or accept that some pleasures arise from good desires and others from those that are base, and that we ought to practice and esteem the one and control and subdue the other ... and avers that they are all alike and to be equally esteemed ... and lives out his life in this fashion indulging the appetite of the day. (561bc; Shorey 1935)

In this passage we can see that Plato comes very close to applying the democratic egalitarian devices of rotation in office and election by lot to the psyche of the democratic person, presumably to bring some order into it and make choices possible. Though our texts here are not as clear as in the case of justice,[33] Plato seems to think of the psychic equality of desires as corresponding to the political equality of citizens, and the psychic refusal to restrain any of them as corresponding to the political refusal to restrain the freedom of citizens (except by the similar freedom of other citizens).[34]

Here we can perhaps see that Plato's definition of a democratic person is not totally mistaken. We may still have a hard time seeing why a democratic person has to apply the principles of political equality and freedom of citizens to his psyche; why a democratic person is not simply a person who subscribes to the principles of political equality and freedom of citizens, as the Socrates of the *Crito*, surely no democrat of the psyche, seems to be. But we can at least see why Plato's democratic person might prefer to live in a democracy: he would prefer a democratic constitution to any of the others because it gives him greater political freedom to do as he pleases: in a democracy he has fewer political constraints on his attempts to satisfy his desires, and he has at least as much political freedom to do so as anyone else. In Plato's ideal city, and in timocracies, oligarchies, and tyrannies, Plato's democratic person would have no such freedom (or equality); unless he was a philosopher-king, which he could not be, or happened to be a general in charge, a wealthy person, or a tyrant. Further, democracy prizes the very values he applies to his own soul, freedom and equality; whereas in an oligarchy, for example, he would be in disagreement with the dominant value of that society, wealth being the dominant value.

If we assume the isomorphism, as Plato does, we can see that there would be reciprocal relations between a democratic city and a democratic person: a democratic person would have to be pretty exactly what Plato says he is. And if he is as Plato defines him, then we can see why he would prefer a democratic constitution.

5 Plato's Criticisms of his Democratic Character

Plato's criticisms of the democratic person, though not entirely explicit, assume the two conditions by which Plato defined him: psychic equality of desires and freedom of desires from reason's or spirit's constraints.

His first objection is that since the democratic person has no dominant desire but treats them all alike, he has no rational way for making choices when his desires *conflict* with each other and cannot all be satisfied at once, perhaps not even successively. Examples of conflicts of desires abound: say, he wants to smoke, and he want to be healthy, he wants to take a vacation and finish his book, and so on. In case of such conflicts, how is he to choose? The objection takes it as a *fact* that our desires some-times do conflict, and suggests that the theory of democracy, when applied to the psyche, has no way of guiding choices in such cases. So at best, the theory is *incomplete*; and if such conflicts are frequent, as they appear to be, the theory may be devastatingly incomplete. I will call this the conflict of desires problem.[35]

The second objection is that some desires are for things *known* to be *bad* for us: for example, if we happen to have no desire for food we may hasten our death; if we have desires for fatty foods, their satisfaction may be bad for our health. The desires for smoking, for fatty foods, for avoiding school, are all desires for things known to be bad for us. And if this is so, it is a mistake to treat all desires as equal. I call this the bad desires problem.[36]

Plato himself, as far as I can tell, suggests no reply on behalf of his demo-cratic person to the bad desires objection: the distinction between necessary and unnecessary appetites, based as it seems to be on a theory of good inde-pendent of desire, would provide a solution, but it amounts to abandoning the freedom of desires (from psychic constraints) and their equality.

To the conflict of desires problem Plato does suggest a solution, and with heavy irony implies that it is very much mistaken. The solution is for the person, when faced with conflict of desires, to apply *to her psyche* the democratic *political* devices for solving conflicts among citizens: to the conflicts in his own psyche he applies the devices of rotation in office and selection by lot. When his desires conflict, he tries to satisfy them in turn. And further, if there is a conflict about which desire to satisfy *first*, he uses selection by lot. The lucky desire is satisfied first, the unlucky second, and so on.

Plato seems to think that the application to the psyche of rotation and selection by lot is a *reductio ad absurdum* of the democratic person's method of making choices. He is probably right in supposing that it is absurd to treat all desires as equal, as these two devices do. After all, it is clear enough that desires differ extrinsically with respect to their objects, such as survival, health, food, pleasure, knowledge, wealth, honor, and so on. And they differ inherently with respect to their intensities, durations, and cycles of recurrence. The desire for food occurs with periodic regularity, it can be very intense, and its generic object (food) is necessary for survival and health. None of this is true of the desires to go to the theater, attend the assembly, or travel abroad. As a general strategy, to rotate the satisfaction of these four desires over, say, a four day period is simply irrational if not outright mad. And to select by lot which of these is to be satisfied first, second or third is even worse.[37]

But now we are faced with another problem: we may have made sense of Plato's criticism of *his* democratic person; but if a democratic person is one who subscribes to the political principles of the equality and freedom of citizens, and not necessarily one who applies these principles to his very psyche, what is Plato criticizing? The obvious answer is, of course, that he is criticizing the democratic man as he conceives him. But what about him is he criticizing?

My suggestion is that he is criticizing a version of a desire satisfaction theory of the human good.

One piece of evidence is that Plato seems to correlate every constitution with some theory of the good of the individual, and seems to attribute such a theory to the corresponding person. In an oligarchy, for example, wealth is the dominant value, institutionalized by putting a high property qualification for office; wealth is also the dominant value of the oligarchic person, it is the major instrumental good, correlated with his dominant desire to accumulate wealth. Similarly, honor is the dominant value of timocracy and the dominant value of the timocratic man; power for tyrannies and the tyrant. The same is true, I think, for Plato's theory of the ideal city and the ideal person: his political theory of justice and the other social virtues is correlated – based on I would say – with his theories of functional and formal good and reason's unique ability to discover them.

If we now ask, what theory of the human good Plato correlates with the political theory of democracy, a very plausible answer is that it is the good as desire satisfaction: because in the relevant passages the satisfaction of desire is precisely what Plato's democratic person prizes and goes after.[38]

A second piece of evidence is that Plato takes away from his democratic person the distinction he draws between necessary and unnecessary appetites, though he seems to allow that distinction to all his other types of character.[39] If we interpret this distinction as importing criteria for the goodness of a desire from outside desires, then what we seem to have left appears to be a person who seems to think that his good is the satisfaction of his desires and tries to make his choices accordingly.

A third piece of evidence is that the chief objections Plato has to the way of life of his democratic person, what I called the conflict of desires and the bad desires problems, are indeed among the chief problems that any theory of the good as desire satisfaction faces.

If the suggestion is correct, we can look on Plato's criticisms of the democratic person as criticisms of theories of the good as the satisfaction of desire, and even ask how sound they are.

Now to begin with, a desire satisfaction theory need not adopt the democratic political devices of rotation in office and selection by lot to solve the psychic problem of which of the conflicting desires to satisfy. These political devices seem rational applied to the polis and irrational applied to the psyche, but a desire satisfaction theory has no commitment to such irrationalities. A person who holds a desire satisfaction theory of good need not be a democrat in Plato's sense. And if he is a democrat in the normal sense (one who subscribes to the principles of freedom and equality of citizens), he does not have to adopt rotation in office and selection by lot in order to make choices in his life. So Plato's criticisms of psychic rotation and psychic selection are not sound criticisms of all versions of a desire satisfaction theory of the good or of a person who is a democrat in the normal sense.

Moreover, the problem of bad desires which Plato brings up against the desire satisfaction theory, is indeed severe *if* the theory is that a person's good consists in the satisfaction of her *actual* desires, the desires she happens to have at any given time and over a lifetime. But this is a *naive* version of the desire satisfaction theory of human good.

The moderns who favor desire satisfaction theories, from Rawls to Brand to Elster to Broome, all admit that *actual* desire satisfaction theories of good are false: because, they admit, it is a widespread and well-known fact that human beings sometimes desire things which are known to be bad for them. The desire to smoke is a well-known example.

The moderns propose a different solution to these problems (of bad desires and conflicts of desires) from Plato's democratic solution: the solution is to define good not in terms of the satisfaction of actual desires, but in terms of the desires a person *would* have under certain conditions, the satisfaction of *hypothetical* desires.

Thus Rawls tells us not that the good is the satisfaction of desire, but that it is the satisfaction of *rational* desire. Rationality, in turn, he explicates by a series of conditions: the counting principles and deliberative rationality.[40]

Here is Broome's condition:

A person's good consists in the satisfaction of all the desires (preferences) she *would have* if she were *well informed and rational*.[41]

This definition, which seems to be an *idealization*, is supposed to overcome the objections to the view that the good is the satisfaction of desires.

Broome treats this theory as overcoming the bad desires objection and the conflicts objection. Presumably, being well informed answers the bad desires objection; and being rational answers the conflict of desires objection, since rationality requires at least consistency.

It is not clear, however, that they do or how far they do, and there is certainly disagreement whether they do.

It is also not clear, for example, how information about facts would enable us to decide, within the desire satisfaction theory, that some of the things we desire are bad for us. Suppose we desire to smoke and we learn that smoking will cause an early death. How can this affect our choices on the modern theory? Presumably it will affect our choice only if we want to avoid an early death. But now we have reduced the problem of bad desires to a problem of conflicts of desires: we want to smoke and we want to avoid an early death, but how do we decide which desire to satisfy?[42] Elster, for one, has argued that rationality, what he calls "thin rationality" – that is to say, *consistency* and *information* – does not exclude known immoral desires or desires for things bad for us: one can have consistent immoral desires and make no factual errors; and consistent desires for things bad for us. Elster mentions, voluntary suicide, homicide, and genocide as all being consistent with rationality as consistency and information.[43]

Again, how is rationality supposed to resolve conflict of desires? Rationality requires consistency of preferences, for example, transitivity of preferences; so that we have no conflicting or inconsistent preferences. Presumably, this is supposed to answer the conflict of desires objection. But if conflicts occur in our *actual* desires or preferences, how are we supposed to eliminate the conflict and become consistent? By eliminating which desires, which preferences? If we admit consistency into the desire satisfaction theory, it is not clear how *to reach* consistency, how to decide which of the actual conflicting desires to eliminate (or satisfy).[44]

Now one might suppose that Plato would agree with the idealized version of the desire satisfaction theory: in his terms, he might agree that the satisfaction of desire is good if it is guided by reason. But though true, this is misleading, because he has a different notion of the powers and functions of reason from the moderns (as well as a different theory of the good – the functional-formal theory now out of favor). Plato believes that human reason is capable of knowing what is good in itself; it is capable of knowing functional good and ultimately the forms and the form of the good. So rationality includes the capacity to know ultimate human good. It is not simply instrumental rationality or simply formal rationality, or a conjunction of the two.[45]

That is why Plato thinks that not only the democratic person, but also the timocratic, the oligarchic, and the tyrannical, are all both unjust and unhappy: they all share the characteristic of putting reason to a purely instrumental use: to discover means to victory, to honor, wealth, the satisfaction of desires no matter what they are, or power. Only Plato's ideally just person assigns reason to its correct functions: to discover what is ultimately good, as well as correct means to it; and for that reason to deserve the role of ruling the soul.

But the moderns seem to use a much thinner notion of rationality, formal and instrumental rationality that does not include the capacity to know things good in themselves or intrinsic goods or ultimate goods.[46] So there remains a very substantial disagreement between Plato and the moderns on rationality; and consequently on their idealized versions of desire satisfaction. On Plato's view, desire – desire which is not itself the result of reasoning – has nothing to say about what is good, either ultimately or instrumentally; these are reason's functions. This is certainly true of appetite; while the so-called desires of reason are reason's tendencies toward the good, or desires based entirely on reason and reasoning, not desires in the modern sense.

On the modern view, reason only operates on desires, given from outside reason, to make them rational: that is, consistent, a formal cognitive and value-neutral function; and, with the help of the senses, well informed about their objects and their causes and effects, an empirical cognitive and value-neutral function. That is all. But the problems Plato raised for his version of a democratic person, the problems of bad desires and of conflicts of desires, keep intruding into the modern versions of desire satisfaction theories of the human good, which use this limited notion of reason. Whatever the present state of affairs with respect to these problems, Plato may have been the first to recognize and articulate these problems.

Notes

1   See Keyt (1991) for a discussion of how much more equalitarian ancient direct democracies were.
2   See the excellent discussions of how the fathers of the American Constitution feared direct democracies and all the devices they used to avoid such constitutions and to construct representative institutions (Allen 2006; Miller 2007).
3   In Book V proposals about common property and common family for the upper classes are repeated and amplified, but for somewhat different reasons, namely, promoting unity and preventing strife within the ruling classes.
4   Many important arguments in the *Republic* combine abstract theory and empirical assumptions. This division of labor in Plato's arguments is not always noted by critics. Plato is sometimes criticized without adequately locating what is supposed to be his mistake: is it the abstract theory, or a metaphysical, or an empirical premise used in the application that is at fault? If we can locate the mistakes, in the abstract theory or in the empirical or metaphysical substantive assumptions, we can determine where the theory needs revision, and in what science we need to search in order to find truths to replace the mistakes.
5   Rawls (1971: 53, 57).
6   Reported by *Agence France Presse*, June 30, 2004, on the basis of annual financial disclosed statements by US congressmen (the figures are for the year 2003). These figures vary from year to year, but it is clear enough that a far greater proportion of US congressmen are wealthy than the general population.
7   In nineteenth century England J.S. Mill was worried about a similar problem when he spoke of "the anomaly of a democratic constitution in a predominantly plutocratically constituted society." See Burns (1968: 286), "J.S. Mill and Democracy, 1829–61."
8   Rawls (1971: 242–51).

9   *Republic* (421–2) and Weinstein (2004).
10 The difference principle states that "the higher expectations of those better situated are just if and only if they work as part of a scheme which improves the expectations of the least advantaged members of society." (Rawls 1971: 65). For Rawls's extended discussion of this principle see Rawls (1971: 65–73).
11 Rawls (1971: 179–80).
12 Rawls (1971: 196–200).
13 Rawls (1971: 65–73).
14 Rawls (1971: 57–81, 83–96).
15 Here we are concerned with Plato's political elitism – that only his philosophers, those who know the form of the good, can rule well; not the ethical elitism that we rejected in chapter 7 – that only his philosophers could have justice in their souls and the other psychic virtues.
16 Aristotle's conception of ethics and politics, as dealing with what is true for the most part (see Anagnostopoulos 1994), might serve as an example of a view that retains Plato's insights into good government without the prolific metaphysics and too high epistemic standards for ethics and politics. And though Aristotle is a logical realist, and opposes nominalism, there is no evidence that he thought nominalists are not philosophers (see, for example, his arguments against the Megarians).
17 Rawls (1985), "Justice: Political, not Metaphysical."
18 For a similar attempt to distinguish and examine "the rule of reason" in Plato's *Republic*, apart from his controversial metaphysics and epistemology, see Miller (2005: 50–83).
19 David Keyt has pointed out to me that the third argument that justice pays in Book IX, the argument about real and illusory pleasures (especially pp. 585d11–585e4) may contain a reference to forms. I am inclined to agree, at least in the sense that the argument may be best understood by reference to knowledge of the Platonic forms.
20 See Penner (2006), "The Forms in the *Republic*."
21 Estlund (2003). Epistocracy is, literally, the rule of knowledge.
22 Rawls (1971: 203–6) includes a critical discussion of plural voting proposals by Mill. See also Burns, "J.S. Mill and Democracy, 1829–61" (1968: 318–28) and Estlund , "Why Not Epistocracy," (2003: 61). Estlund calls a democracy with more than one vote for the educated a "scholocracy" – the rule of scholars.
23 Mill, *Essays on Politics and Society* (1977: 466–81).
24 The ship of state analogy, of course, was made famous by Plato in the *Republic* (488–9). For a more recent discussion, see Keyt (2006a). For a democratic objection to plural voting see Estlund (2003). For a discussion of Estlund's objection see Santas (2007). Another objection, owed to David Keyt, is that political decisions often involve war and peace and have human costs. Why should a mother of two sons of military age have fewer votes than a single man

with a PhD? Perhaps she should not, and others besides the better educated should have more than one vote. Plural voting itself does not exclude unequal weighing of votes for other groups besides the educated. It is worth noting, though, that the weighing of votes in favor of the educated is not based on representation of their interests, but on the idea that it promotes better governing for all – a common interest.

25 For Plato's criticism of poetry see, for example, Urmson's classic article (1997), Asmis (1992), Janaway (2006), and Moss (2007).

26 Smith, *The Wealth of Nations* (1937: 3–22).

27 See argument by Rawls (1971: 73, 184–5, 205–6).

28 Plato characterization of democracy agrees in essentials with Aristotle's account of democracy in *Politics* and the *Athenian Constitution*. His definition of a democratic person seems unique and wrong. For a characteristic reaction see, for example, Annas (1981: 301): "But the kind of person he depicts has no obvious connection with democracy." A democrat, rather, is one who subscribes to the political principles of democracy, liberty and equality, or to a constitution which satisfies these principles.

29 Parallel to the subsequent tradition's definition of a just person, roughly, as one who subscribes to the principles or laws of a just society.

30 Plato not only characterizes or defines the four unjust cities and corresponding characters, but he also gives some accounts of how a just city can turn into a timocratic one, a timocratic into an oligarchic, and so on; and he does the same for the corresponding characters. In each case he speaks of the "origin and nature" of each, as Glaucon did in the case of contractarian justice in Book II. Here I abstract from Plato's discussion of the origin of the democratic city and person from the oligarchic ones, except in so far as these accounts help us to understand his conception of the nature of the democratic city and man.

31 See, for example, the contrast to the oligarchic man in 559d–560e.

32 It is not clear to me whether Plato has two or three classes of necessary appetites; in particular whether those which cannot be eliminated by education or habituation are the same as those that are necessary for survival. See White (1979). Whatever the case, I take the distinction to import criteria from outside desire for distinguishing between good and bad desires.

33 We can set out the argument by which Plato infers his characterization of the democratic person from his characterization of the democratic city, as follows: (1)(a) if things are called by the same name, they will be alike in the respect in which they are called the same; (b) we call cities and persons democratic. Therefore, (c) democratic cities and persons do not differ at all with respect to being democratic. (2) A democratic city is a city in which (a) all citizens have equal political shares, and (b) all citizens have equal maximum freedoms to do and live as they please. (3) The principle of equal political shares is implemented through

(a) all citizens being members of the Assembly with one vote each; (b) rotation in office and (c) selection by lot in the Council and the Jury Courts. The principle of equal maximum freedoms is implemented through the fewest possible legal limits on freedom to do as one pleases. (4) What corresponds to citizens in a democratic city are (parts of the soul or) desires in a democratic person. (5) Therefore, a democratic person is a person in whom (a) all desires have an equal shares in ruling, and (b) all desires have equal maximum freedom to be satisfied (from 1c and 2ab). (6) Therefore, the democratic person is a person in whom (a) each desire has one vote (equal claim to satisfaction), (b) desires take turns (rotation) for satisfaction, and (c) desires are selected for satisfaction by lot.

34   There is a question here about what corresponds to citizens: just the desires of the appetitive part, or the "desires" of spirit and reason as well? This may depend on how we are to understand Plato's division of the psyche, and also how to understand desires in the theory of the human good as the satisfaction of desires (see Scott 2000).

35   Plato presents us with vivid descriptions of such conflicts in his democratic person (see, e.g. 560ff.).

36   In so far as Plato admits incontinence or weakness of will in the *Republic*, as he is commonly supposed to do on the basis of his division of the psyche and the story of Leontius, he admits that a person may desire something which even *he* knows or believes is bad for him.

37   In the case of other types of personality, particularly the timocratic, oligarchic, and tyrannical, Plato proposes other ways of solving conflict of desires: having one dominant desire or end. And in the case of his ideal type of person, he proposes another way yet: putting reason in charge and letting it decide what is good as an end (as well as a means).

38   It might be that the theory of the good that Plato attributes to his democratic person is hedonism, rather than a desire satisfaction theory. It is not entirely clear that Plato distinguishes the two, either in the *Gorgias* or the *Republic*, but I think the objections he makes have a much better target in desire satisfaction theories rather than hedonistic ones.

39   Though they might draw it differently. For example, the oligarchic man, to whom Plato explicitly allows the distinction, draws it by reference to his dominant value, wealth, or possibly even only his dominant desire for wealth. This is different from the way Plato actually draws it, which presumably is the way the Platonically just person draws it. The essential point is that Plato's democratic person refuses to draw this distinction, either as Plato's other unjust persons do or as his just person does; and so he is deprived of these ways of bringing order and rationality into his choices.

40   Rawls admits that the counting principles and even deliberative rationality are not sufficient for making rational choices in all cases (1971, chapter VII, sections 63 and 64).

41 Broome (1996: 133).

42 Receiving of the information will also not itself lead to the extinction of one of the desires, even if we could decide which is bad for us to satisfy, if weakness of will occurs; even when we know the better we can still desire the worse. We may have all the pertinent negative information and still desire the object.

43 See Elster (1985: 15ff.).

44 There are some modern arguments that inconsistency, lack of transitivity of preferences, for example, is bad for one. What do these arguments show? They might be taken to show that in addition to desire satisfaction, consistency is also a good; but in so far as they do that they bring in value from outside desire, and desire satisfaction is then no longer the only source of value (thus the title of chapter VII of Rawls 1971: "Goodness as Rationality", rather than his earlier phrase for the theory, the good as "the satisfaction of rational desire"). Or they might be taken to show that consistency is a necessary means to maximizing the satisfaction of desires. But such arguments still leave us with the problem of how to bring about consistency: by eliminating which desires and which preferences?

45 For a fine discussion of the differences between the ancients and the moderns on the scope of the powers of human reason, see Frede (1996). It is not entirely clear, though, that the relevant differences are just on scope. It may well be that the relevant differences are differences about the nature of goodness. Plato may have a theory of goodness such that human reason, endowed with the powers Hume attributes to it, can apprehend goodness; whereas on Hume's theory of good this may not be so. Metaphysical differences, say, between nominalists and logical realists, may come in here too.

46 See Rawls (1971, section 60 (the opening section of chapter VII)) and Elster (1985) on notions of "thin" practical rationality. Roughly speaking, thin notions are required by the idea that if we explicate goodness in terms of desire and rationality, we cannot turn around and explicate rationality in terms of goodness. That would be a vicious circle.

9

Plato's Defense of his Social and Psychic Justice

Why does justice need defense? Is it not an ideal universally admired and often fought for?

One reason is that in the *Republic* justice was attacked by Thrasymachus and even by Plato's brothers. "I cannot stand by and hear justice reviled without lifting a finger," Socrates says (367). It was reviled by Thrasymachus when he argued that justice is in the interest of the rulers, and not good for the rest of us, at least when the rulers' interest conflicts with ours. Justice was downgraded as a good by the more reasonable view of Plato's brothers, who argued that while minimal egalitarian justice is better for us than a state of nature, even so it is better yet for any one of us to be unjust when we can get away with it. Socrates says he lost faith in his powers when Plato's brothers were not satisfied with the proof he gave against Thrasymachus that it is better to be just; but it is a sin to stay aloof and not come to the defense of justice so long as one has breath and strength. So he will try again.

But Thrasymachus and Glaucon's attacks on justice are not a peculiarity of Plato's writing that we can safely ignore. Such attacks are a universal human problem, because justice, unlike prudence which is good for me almost by definition, is not always in my everyday interest: It seems that I would be better off economically if I paid less tax than my fair share; that I would be better off if I did not go to war and let others defend the country; maybe I would be better off if I did not get caught and punished for breaking almost any law.[1]

Plato would remind us that there is also the prior question of what justice is, and the question what justice is being attacked and what justice defended. A good point: yes, if we know what justice is, we know what is being attacked and what defended; but if what justice is, is also in question, then the best we can do is take up different conceptions and systems of justice and consider attacks and defenses of each of them; that is what Plato does in the *Republic*, and it is what Rawls does in *A Theory of Justice*.[2] Still, no matter what justice is, it seems that practicing it is not always in my interest: in Thrasymachus' view justice is systemically contrary to my interests if I am not a ruler; Glaucon's justice cuts down my freedom and so do the equalities of democratic justice; even in Rawls' "well ordered society," with his admirable principles of justice, I might be better off breaking some just laws if I were born in a lower economic class and I could get away with it; even those born rich might be better off breaking some of Rawls' just laws if they could get away with it and if getting even more riches is good for them. Plato might claim that anyone would be better off with his own justice than with the justice of Thrasymachus or the justice of Plato's brothers. But Plato's own justice needs defense too: the artisan class might reasonably complain that by law it is kept from the experience of ruling the city (or even ruling themselves; since they are to be guided by the rulers even on what their own good is), and his upper classes might well complain about being deprived of private property and family.

All justice needs defense, it seems. And in all important books about justice, from Plato to Rawls, we find defenses of justice by writers who try to define justice, defend their definition, and also argue that justice is good for us. The defenses take different forms, but all of them have these two components: the writer offers us a definition or principles of justice and argues that it is correct or at least better than other definitions or principles of justice; and the writer also argues that given his definition or principles, his justice is better for us than injustice. Thus Rawls formulates and elucidates his two principles of justice (1971: chapter II) and argues that they would be chosen in the original position over other principles of justice (chapter III); and then in the last chapter of *A Theory of Justice* he also argues for the "congruence" of his justice with our good.

Plato initiated this two-part defense of justice in the *Republic*. He presents us with three major answers to the question what justice is – that of Thrasymachus, of Glaucon, and of Socrates – and argues that Socrates' account is the correct one; and then he argues that Socrates' justice is better for its citizens than his injustice.

These two questions are intimately related, but we must try our best not to confuse them: one requires a comparison among different principles and systems of justice – to decide which is correct or the best one; the other assumes one of principle(s) and system of justice as correct and compares just and unjust conduct according to it. Both comparisons might make reference to our good, and that can be a source of confusion. Still, they are crucially different comparisons: in the first comparison, the crucial question is, would I be better off under the justice of Thrasymachus or Glaucon or Socrates (*I being any human being*)? The crucial question in the second comparison is, would I be better off being just rather than unjust under one or another of these systems (*I being any citizen under that system*)?

Some have argued, however, that Plato does not succeed in defining justice at all – that he mistakes something else for justice. So we have an even more prior question, whether Plato's justice is justice at all; and since he splits the question, what justice is, into two, the justice of the city and of the person, we need to ask: is Plato's political justice then justice at all, or something else, such as efficiency? And, is Plato's psychic justice at all justice, or something else, such as mental health?

We begin with this prior issue, then go to the comparison of different kinds of justice, and finally to the comparison of just and unjust conduct according to Plato's justice.

1   Is Plato's Social Justice Justice at all?

Did Plato miss his target? His Socrates tried to define social justice, the justice of a city state. Did he end up defining something else instead? Did he unwittingly fail to keep to Bishop Butler's dictum that justice, like everything else, is what it is and not another thing?

It is sometimes said, for example, that what he ended up defining is efficiency, not justice. As Adam Smith masterfully argues in the first three chapters of *The Wealth of Nations*, division of labor, together with trade, enhance labor productivity enormously and create wealth for nations. Perhaps this is what Plato got hold of, division of labor and trade, saw its benefits for all concerned, and pronounced it to be justice.

Notice that if Plato did indeed miss his target and defined something else, say efficiency, as justice, this would adversely affect the second part of his defense of his justice: if he defined what is really efficiency as justice, then the beneficial effects of his justice would really be the effects of efficiency, and thus his defense of his political justice would indeed suffer Sachs' fallacy of irrelevance. We want to know whether social justice is good for us; telling us that social efficiency is good for us is by itself no defense of social justice.

Now there is a large grain of truth in the objection that what Plato got hold of is efficiency. We saw that when Socrates began the construction of his completely good city – on the assumption that a completely good city would include social justice – he indeed used division of labor and trade as structures that would make the city perform its function of providing for our individual insufficiencies better than no division of labor (*Republic*: 369b–370d). But he next invoked the natural lottery assumption, that humans are born with different talents and abilities, and to division of labor and trade he added the distribution of labors according to inborn talent or ability (and subsequent appropriate education). He even built the natural lottery assumption into his myth of the metals. So his principle of social justice is not simply division of labor and trade, but division of labor according to inborn talent, and appropriate education, for the three main social needs and the social functions of provisioning, defending, and ruling the city. Plato's principle in effect requires and regulates the distribution of social careers on the basis of natural talents and education. Division of labor and trade are different and independent of Plato's principle of social justice, as Smith indeed noted: they can be found and practiced apart from distribution of labor according to talent, and as such they enhance productivity immensely. Plato's principle of social justice does include division of labor; it has efficiency built into it, but it goes beyond efficiency to regulating the distribution of careers.

So did Plato make the mistake of taking efficiency to be justice? At most, he thought that efficiency, as division of labor and trade, is part of justice. But he did not mistake efficiency by itself for justice. We can see this if we consider that in his view it is possible for division of labor by itself to result in injustice: if someone best suited to run a leather factory were governing the city and someone best suited to govern the city were running a leather factory, division of labor would be satisfied, but according to Plato's principle of justice this division would be unjust (*Republic*: 434).

It is instructive to compare here Rawls' treatment of efficiency, as Pareto optimality, and its relation to his principles of justice. Pareto optimality, applied to the distribution of primary goods, such as income and wealth (and burdens such as taxation and defense), states that a distribution is optimal or efficient if there is no redistribution which makes at least one person better off and no one worse off.[3] For example, a new tax law that redistributes the tax burden is Pareto optimal if as a result there is at least one winner (one whose tax burden is decreased) and no losers (no one's tax burden is increased). As Rawls correctly argues, there are many different distributions which are Pareto optimal; including a distribution in which one person has everything, since any redistribution would make him worse off, at least if we assume a fixed quantity of goods and a zero-sum game. But clearly not all such Pareto optimal distributions are just or equally just. So efficiency, as Pareto optimality, is not by itself justice. And Rawls does not built efficiency into his principles of justice, as Plato did. But he correctly points out that we want our institutions to be efficient as well as just; efficiency is also a virtue of institutions, though posterior to justice; so in the best case scenario we want to have justice with efficiency. Thus, for example, a new tax law would have to pass not only the test of Pareto optimality but also the test of the difference principle.

But even if Plato did not mistake efficiency for justice, still it is possible he missed the mark and his principle is not a principle of justice at all, never mind a correct one or a better one than that of Thrasymachus or Glaucon. How will we settle this?

Plato is aware of the issue, and his Socrates gives some arguments that social justice as he defined it is indeed justice – that it would be recognizable by his contemporaries (and hopefully by us) as justice (*Republic*: 433b–434c). But they are not convincing arguments. We can use some better tests that were not available to Plato and his pioneering book on justice, namely, what Aristotle would consider to be a principle of social justice, and what some twenty-four centuries later, Rawls would consider a principle of justice.

Aristotle tells us that (particularly social) justice has two branches, the justice of distribution, and the justice of punishment. We are concerned here with the first of these. Aristotle says that the justice of distribution is concerned with the distribution of divisible goods, such as "honors [offices], wealth," and safety. Any principle that regulates the distribution of these goods is a principle of social justice. But of course, different such principles regulate the distributions differently; democratic principles of justice regulate the distribution of offices in a far more egalitarian way than oligarchic principles and differently from aristocratic principles. All these are principles of justice. Which is correct or better than the others is a separate issue.[4]

Plato's principle of social justice passes Aristotle's test: it regulates the distribution of one of Aristotle's goods, namely offices, directly as well as other careers such as defending the city and provisioning the city. Moreover, as we saw in chapter 8, it regulates the distribution of wealth; though it does so indirectly, with the aid of some empirical assumptions, such as the assumption that poverty prevents artisans from doing their crafts well, too much wealth weakens the motivation to practice what one is best suited to do, as well as the assumption that private property and wealth would tempt the rulers to look after their private good rather than the good of the whole city.

Rawls, too, has a test whether a given principle is a principle of justice: that is, whether it can play "the role of principles of justice." That role is to "provide a way of assigning rights and duties in the basic institutions of society and [to] define the appropriate distribution of the benefits and burdens of social cooperation" (Rawls 1971: 4). Plato's principle of social justice also passes this test. Of course what is distributed is not exactly the same in Plato and Rawls, but this is a difference in their theory of goods: Rawls' principles regulate, through the major institutions of the basic structure of society, the social primary goods of rights and liberties, income and wealth, positions of authority and opportunities. But there is a considerable overlap: Plato's principle does regulate the distribution of political rights such as the right to rule, burdens such as defense, and, indirectly, property and wealth.

As we shall see, Plato's psychic justice, what he thinks is a just *person*, presents a greater problem on this issue – whether it is justice at all.

2   Is Plato's Political Justice Better for me than the Justice of Thrasymachus or the Justice of Plato's Brothers?

Plato's principle of social justice is indeed a principle of justice and not of something else. Whether it is correct or adequate, or whether it would be chosen over other principles of justice in a state of nature or in Rawls' original position is another matter – and these are now the issues before us.

Within the *Republic* the question can perhaps be treated best in a comparative way. In this work Plato presents us with three major theories of social justice and he is commonly thought to favor the theory of Socrates over the theory of Thrasymachus and over the theory he puts in the mouth of Plato's brothers. So we can look to his reasons against the other theories, and his reasons for preferring the justice of Socrates.

We have already examined his reasons against Thrasymachus' theory of justice as the interest of the rulers (chapter 2). He attacks the positivist assumption on which the argument for that theory rests, that justice is to be found entirely embedded in the positive laws of a given society. And he also attacks the empirical generalization that such a law-embedded justice in every society always favors the rulers; though this attack is limited by the fact that Socrates employs arguments by analogy to other arts, besides ruling; whereas what is called for is an empirical investigation of the generalization.

We have no such *explicit* criticism of Glaucon's theory of justice, either of the contractarian method or the results that Glaucon produces by applying the method. Now the results that Glaucon produces, the results of the choice in the state of nature, are in fact very minimal: everyone agrees to give up equally his/her freedom to harm others in return for equal security from being harmed by others.

Plato would certainly not object to limiting the citizens' freedom to harm others; after all, his Socrates gave a famous argument in the first book that it is never just to harm a human being;[5] though he would extend the concept of harm beyond the typical harms found in Glaucon's theory – such as theft, property damage, bodily injury, and homicide, the harms men with a Ring of Gyges do – to harming another person's *character* and harms to another person's *soul*. Nor would Plato object to the two equalities explicitly stated in Glaucon's theory: namely, limiting equally among citizens the freedom to harm others, and providing security from harm equally to all citizens.

But Glaucon's minimalist theory tells us very little about how government would be constituted, its powers and limits, what the main economic institutions would be, their powers and limits, and so on. In so far as Glaucon's theory might be a foundation for a democratic theory of justice, we can look to Plato's criticism of this democracy (see chapter 8). Generally, Plato would object to an inference implicit in Glaucon's theory, namely that all freedoms, besides the freedom to harm others, remain with the citizens, since these are not freedoms they give up in the original contract. And he would certainly object to the democratic basis for selection of rulers, consent of the citizens determined by election. He thinks that ruling requires great expertise and only experts in a given field can tell reliably who are other experts in that field; the average citizen has a hard time telling a real expert from a mere pretender; and yet this is what citizens are asked to do when they vote on who is to rule them. Democrats might argue that all citizens are qualified to rule, especially in direct non-representative democracies; but this is manifestly false, especially in modern and very complex nation states.[6]

On the whole, Plato defends his social justice partly by explicitly refuting the justice of Thrasymachus and by implicitly objecting to the justice of Plato's brothers.

3   Is Plato's Political Justice Good for *All* the Citizens?

Plato has Socrates give a positive defense of his own theory of social justice, in the opening pages of the central Book IV, in reply to a major objection he puts in the mouth of Adeimantus.

As we have seen (chapter 8), one of the major institutional reforms Socrates proposed for the completely good city is that its rulers and soldiers not be permitted to hold any private property whatsoever (*Republic*: 415–19).

What would Socrates reply, Adeimantus asks, if

> anyone objects that you are not making these men very happy ...? For the city really belongs to them, and yet they get no enjoyment out of it as ordinary men do by owning lands and building fine big houses ... and winning the favor of the gods by private sacrifices and entertaining guests and enjoying too these possessions you just spoke of, gold and silver and all that is customary for those who are expecting to be happy.

Socrates at first strengthens the objection by pointing out that the rulers and the soldiers serve for board wages

> and do not even receive pay in addition to their food as others do, so that they will not even be able to take a journey on their own account, if they wish, or make presents to their mistresses, or spend money in other directions according to their desires like the men who are thought to be happy. (*Republic*: 419–20; Shorey 1935)

This is a powerful objection, partly because the reform Socrates has proposed is indeed extreme, not only putting some firewall between political or military power and wealth, but abolishing private property and wealth altogether for the classes that have political and military power. The objection is also powerful because it uses a conception of happiness common to most human beings, a happiness to which private property and wealth are major means.

Plato has Socrates make a two part reply:

> [1] while it would not surprise us if these men [rulers and soldiers] thus living prove to be the most happy, yet [2] the object on which we fixed our eyes in the establishment of our state was not the exceptional happiness of any one class but the greatest possible happiness of the whole city. For we thought that in a state so constituted we should be most likely to discover justice as we should injustice in the worst governed state, and that when we had made these out we could pass judgment on the issue of our long inquiry [whether we would be happier being just]. (420bc; Shorey 1935, modified)

A revealing reply. First, Socrates challenges radically the common conception of happiness as requiring private property and wealth, since he says that his rulers and soldiers could be "most happy" without these things. And at the end of his reply he seems to substitute for "the common conception of happiness" a happiness that comes from members of each class "being the best craftsmen in their own work" (421c). Though Socrates may be wrong in rejecting altogether even a minimum of private property and wealth as a requirement of happiness, he is not wrong in pointing out that being best at what we are by nature and education best suited to do is a major human good, and thus a major means or major constituent to human happiness. Even John Rawls, who opposes perfectionist theories of good and of justice, agrees that exercising and developing our human faculties, talents, and abilities, is an important human good (Rawls 1971, chapter VII, section 65). Doing well what we can do best is a major source of human happiness, no less than private property and wealth which can be acquired by luck as well as by merit and can be lost by bad fortune. Being best at what we are suited to do is the result of work and merit and it can never be taken away from us. Plato's theory of social justice selects being best at what we are naturally fitted to do as the main good to be distributed to the citizens of the completely good city. A balanced view of the complete human good will take both that good and property and wealth into account.

In the second part of his answer, Socrates says that social justice is to be found in an arrangement of the institutions of the city that promotes the happiness of "the whole city," not only or primarily the happiness of any one class in it. Three times he repeats that in designing the city, they aimed all along at the happiness of the whole city, not the greatest happiness of any one class, supposing that it is in such a city that justice would be found. This is in obvious contrast to, and rejection of, Thrasymachus' view that justice is what promotes the interest of the ruling party. Socrates was certainly correct in this part of his reply, and he is supported by the whole tradition on justice, from Aristotle to John Rawls and Brian Barry. Aristotle explicitly rejects the justice of Thrasymachus in his rejection of "deviant constitutions" (*Politics*, Book III), which aim at the good of the rulers instead of the good of all the citizens. Barry says that there are two main traditions on what justice is, justice as mutual advantage and justice as impartiality – and claims that even Rawls does not always distinguish them.[7] However that may be, in both traditions it is assumed that the good of all the citizens is at stake – mutual advantage among all the citizens, and impartiality (whether in procedures or in the distribution of the benefits and burdens of social cooperation) among all the citizens.[8] Thrasymachus' theory of justice fails both the test of mutual advantage and the test of impartiality, because it fails the test of benefit to all the citizens. Socrates claims that his theory of justice passes that crucial test, indeed, that it was designed from the beginning to meet it. It should be noted that Glaucon's theory of justice also passes this test.

The crucial and controversial question here is not whether justice should aim at the good of all the citizens, but how that good is to be construed; in Socrates' reply, how is "the greatest [happiness] of the whole city" (420b) to be understood?

At one extreme, does Plato understand the good (or happiness) of the whole city to be the *sum total* of the good of each of its citizens? Not likely. Such a conception (1) presupposes that the good or happiness of one citizen can be *added* to that of another until we reach the sum total of the happiness of all the citizens; and (2) it allows that such a sum total of good can be increased simply by increasing the good of only one citizen or one of the three classes. There is no sign in our passage or elsewhere in Plato that he would accept (1). Some goods, most evidently property and wealth, can be measured and added up (think of the gross domestic product of a country – the sum total of its goods and services), but Plato's upper classes do not even possess this good; other goods, such as knowledge, health, and being the best craftsman at what one does best, might be most difficult to measure, and might not in any case be commensurable.[9]

Nor could Plato accept (2), since it could even allow a city satisfying Thrasymachus' principle to be a just city: we can imagine a baseline of goods distributed among all the citizens, and then by successive changes increase only the good of the rulers and thus increase total good. But in our passage Socrates objects exactly to that as being just.

At the other extreme, some have thought that by the good of the whole city (1) Plato understands a good of some entity other than the citizens, and a good of that entity that would be over and above the good of the citizens. Some have even added that (2) Plato has an organic view of the city and its good: his ideal city is (or is like) an organism, an organism is not simply a sum total of its parts, and the good of the organism is not simply the sum total of the good of its parts.

The most direct and revealing passage for this organic view of the state is in Book V (462c):

> That city then is best ordered in which the greatest number use the expressions 'mine' and 'not mine' of the same things and in the same way. Much the best. And the city whose condition is most like that of the individual man.

How sweeping this passage is can be seen if we remember that the "same things" to which these expressions are to apply are not only property and wealth, and not only children and parents and husbands and wives, but also beliefs about what is good and bad and feelings of love and hate, hope and fear. In context, Plato is saying that a city is best governed when the greatest number in it (all if possible) share property and wealth, parents and children, husbands and wives, brothers and sisters;[10] they all believe the same things are good, they all love the same things and all hate the same things. Only in this way, he thinks, will the social unity of a city approximate the natural unity of a person, and only such a city will be best ordered and be the best city. However, the overriding concern here is not some metaphysical notion of unity, but the avoidance of political conflict and instability that leads to civil war, especially within the ruling class.[11]

Now there is a large grain of truth in the idea that a city is not simply the totality of its citizens, nor its good the totality of the good of its citizens. For one thing, there is the territory, organic and inorganic, that the whole city occupies and what is good for its continued existence and its capability to sustain human beings. For another, there are the future citizens of the city and their good to consider, since the lifetime of a city usually far exceeds the lifetimes of the citizens comprising it at any given time. There are also institutions and structures that may be good for citizens and require goods for their maintenance – for example, courts and legislatures. And Plato is well aware of these basic points and their bearing in determining the good of the whole city. But there is no sign in the passage (*Republic*: 419–20) of an organic view of the city or of its good. Nor do the above grains of truth require an organic view of the city and of its good. An artifact or a machine is also not the sum total of its parts; we have to add how the parts are arranged or put together, how their functions relate to each other and to the function of the whole machine; and the machine can easily outlive any one or even all of its original parts. All these grains of truth apply to a house, a ship, an automobile, or an airplane.

There is no hint in our passage that there is some super good attached to some super entity, the state, or that this good is absolutely prior to the good of the citizens. In the good of the whole city Plato certainly includes the good of each and every citizen, though not as a sum total of these goods. And the remaining good of the whole city – the good of its territory, its physical structure and its institutions – may be reducible or wholly dependent on the good of its present or future citizens. In his insistence that justice be good to each and every citizens, and in his insistence that justice is better than injustice to each and all the citizens, Plato's theory of justice is in fact very individualistic.

The modern view that Plato's completely good city is some form of totalitarian society stems from other parts of his theory, notably his criticisms of democracy and his censorship of the arts. This modern view is much contradicted by Plato's placing tyranny as the *polar opposite* of his completely good and just city. One has to understand this polar opposition before the modern criticism can stick. Plato would have a hard time understanding Popper's criticisms; yes, Plato thought of his just society as antidemocratic, but the direct democracy Plato criticized is far removed from our representative democracies and does not exist anywhere among modern nation states, just as his ideal city does not. The moderns tend to think that if a regime is not democratic then it is totalitarian. Plato's completely good city is the rule of knowledge, not the rule of power, or honor, or wealth, or freedom and equality.[12]

But the views of justice of Thrasymachus and of Plato's brothers press upon Plato a crucial question relevant to justice: what if the good of one citizen conflicts with the good of another? How does Plato's appeal to the good of the whole city deal with that problem? These other views of justice answer this question, and so does Rawls' view; indeed any theory of justice must answer this question, since such conflicts are a fundamental reason why we need justice. On Thrasymachus' view, conflict between rulers and ruled is always resolved in favor of rulers, and that consideration, too, is dominant in conflict among the ruled; Glaucon's view is incomplete on this issue, other than conflicts in freedom and security. How does Plato's appeal to the good of the whole city as the good of each and every citizen answer this question, if it does?

Plato must have an answer for both kinds of goods in our passage: for the good of being the best craftsman at what one is naturally suited to do best, which all the citizens can have; and for the good of property and wealth (and private families) that the artisans are allowed to have but the rulers and soldiers are not.

Now the first of these goods does not appear to be a competitive good whose distribution would give rise to conflicts among citizens and would be a zero-sum game: my being the best craftsman at what I am suited to do best, say soldiering, does not in any direct way compete, and is not in conflict with, your being the best craftsman at what you are suited by nature to do best, say, mathematics; we can both excel without the excellence of one taking away from the excellence of another. With respect to this important good there is no conflict among the citizens. All the citizens can have this good, and they can have it equally; they can all excel to the limit of their ability at what each is naturally suited to do best. Notice though that the good in question is not ruling the city – that is not distributed equally and not every citizen can have it; nor is it defending the city, or provisioning it. The good in question is being the best craftsman at what one is best suited by nature and appropriate education to do. If this good is not competitive and its pursuit by citizens does not give rise to conflicts, then a theory of justice need not put limits to its pursuit.

And similarly for the happiness that derives from this good. As Socrates says at the end of his long reply: "And so, as the entire city develops and is well ordered, each class is to be left to the share of happiness that its nature comports" (421c). The happiness in question is the happiness of the citizens of each of the three classes, it is the happiness that comes from being "the best craftsmen in their own work" (previous sentence), and "one's own work" is apportioned on the basis of natural ability for ruling, defending, or provisioning the city. The distribution of this happiness of citizens follows the distribution of social careers that is based on their natural abilities. There is happiness appropriated to the rulers that can be derived only from being best craftsmen at ruling, happiness from being best at soldiering, and happiness appropriated to being best at provisioning the city. No class can derive happiness from being best at something else since it is not best at something else; and no class' happiness conflicts with another class' happiness.

There is an important qualification, though. To excel at what I am by nature suited to do best I must be allowed and have the resources to *educate* my natural abilities. It is no accident that the *Republic* contains long stretches on education: the primary good that Plato's social justice directly distributes, excellence in careers based on innate abilities, absolutely requires education of those innate abilities; unlike some other goods that can be inherited or acquired or lost by luck, without education Plato's primary good is unrealizable. Even Mozart, who was born a musical genius, needed a technical education in music and was lucky enough that his father was a fine technical musician and provided it. But resources for education, both human (teachers) and non-human (classrooms and equipment) can be moderately scarce, there can be competition for them, and their distribution can be and usually is a zero-sum game. So the issues of conflict and distribution of resources for education enter indirectly into the distribution of excellence in careers. Once more, Plato's appeal to the good of each and every citizen is correct, but how does it answer questions of distribution of resources for education?[13]

If we were coloring a statue, Socrates says, and we were accused of not applying to the eyes, the most beautiful part, the most beautiful pigments, we should reply: "Don't expect us, wonderful friend, to paint the eyes so beautiful that they will not be like eyes, nor the other parts, but observe whether by assigning what is proper to each we make the whole beautiful" (420d). Similarly, we must not "attach to the guardians a happiness that will make them anything but guardians," nor to potters or farmers a happiness that will make them anything but potters or formers (420d–421b). We must not apportion to any of these three classes anything that would make them less excellent at their own work, or anything but rulers or soldiers or providers.

The analogy is suggestive: even if gold, say, were the most beautiful color, it does not follow that we should paint the eyes of a statue gold – for gold is not a color for eyes at all and so golden eyes would not be like (i.e. statue) eyes, and so not beautiful (statue) eyes. By coloring eyes with a color that is both beautiful and a color for eyes we render beautiful *eyes*, and by coloring the other parts thus appropriately we render the whole statue beautiful. Beauty here is an analogue for goodness. As the whole statue is rendered beautiful by apportioning to each part a beauty appropriate to it, so the whole city is rendered happy by apportioning to each part (each social class in this case) a happiness appropriate to it. There is not a super good (or a super happiness) attached to a super entity (the state), but the good of the parts, though not as a sum, but as a good for each part appropriate to that part.

But we need not rely only on the analogy. As we saw in chapter 8, Socrates had argued earlier (end of Book III) that if we allow private lands and houses to the rulers or soldiers, this would create a conflict of interest in them (the interest of their property and the interest of the whole city, also argued in Book V) and would thereby detract from excelling at ruling or defending the city; and it would also divert them from their ruling to taking care of their property and so to not being (only) rulers but also farmers. These are Plato's main reasons for the severe exclusion of private property and wealth for rulers and defenders.

His answer to the question of just distribution of resources for education could follow similar lines. Since an appropriate education is required for being the best craftsman at one's own work, the distribution of educational resources for a given career would follow what is required for excellence in that career and what is required for developing the natural talent required for practicing it. Ruling a city may be more complex than making shoes, and excellence in the former may be more demanding than in the latter. Moreover, more complex abilities and talents may be required for ruling, and if so, the education of these abilities may take longer ("the longer way" of the higher education of reason, in Book VII). Educational resources then must be apportioned accordingly. And Plato does just that: the education of the rulers takes a lot longer and is far more complex than that of the soldiers, and of the soldiers than that of the providers.

Finally, Plato allows private property and wealth, and private family too, to the rest of the citizens, the providers and traders who, in fact, are the vast majority of the population of the ideal city. And Plato does not dispute that conflicts can arise among the citizens in the pursuit of these goods. Plato's ideal city allows a market economy for the majority of its citizens, as Joshua Weinstein has shown.[14]

How does his appeal to the good of the whole city, then, draw limits to the pursuit of such goods and provide for their just distribution among the providers and traders? As we have seen in chapter 8, Plato provides only economic ceilings and economic floors that exclude great wealth and poverty. And, again following his fundamental principle of justice and the chief good it directly distributes (careers), he sets ceilings and floors based on what is required for being the best craftsman of one's own work: having enough for equipment and materials for excellent craftsmanship, and not so much that one is no longer motivated to perform well. He appears to have no further principle for regulating the distribution of private property and wealth for the artisan class; within the economic ceiling and floor, any further distribution he seems to leave to a market economy; he does not even provide economic criteria for floors and ceilings, as Rawls does.[15]

Of course, this goal, being best at one's own work, might also be achieved if all property and wealth were publicly owned, and no one was poor or wealthy. In allowing private property and wealth to the majority of citizens and a market economy for provisioning the city, Plato may be conceding that a market economy is more efficient than a command economy with all public property (means of production and even personal property). Even more likely, he appears to be conceding that most human beings would not be happy if deprived of private property and private family. He still needs to show, though, that his rulers and soldiers could and would be happy without private property and private family; his Socrates said that he would not be surprised if they would be "most happy," but he does not think that being best at what one can do best is the sole source of happiness. How does he complete his defense of justice? We shall soon see his answers in the health–justice analogy, and the value of pleasure in the just life.

4 Plato's Defense of his Just Person: The Sachs Problem

Whether what Plato defines as justice in our souls is justice at all is a more difficult issue.

David Sachs' paper, "A Fallacy in Plato's *Republic*," had enormous impact and still dominates discussions about Plato's defense of justice. Sachs took it for granted that Plato's defense of justice had to answer Thrasymachus' and Glaucon's challenge, that one would be better off or happier being unjust rather than just (if one could get away with injustice by deception or violence). But, Sachs argued, the way Plato defines a just person – as one whose soul is so constituted that reason rules, spirit helps reason carry out its decisions, and appetite is obedient to reason – provides no assurance that such a just person would refrain, to begin with, from the unjust actions that Thrasymachus and Glaucon argued would be profitable if one could get away with it. Even if it is better for a person to have a soul so constituted, this is irrelevant to Thrasymachus' and Glaucon's challenge.

Sachs allowed that Plato tries to forestall this objection, in *Republic* (442), where Socrates asks whether the just person as they have defined him/her would be "specially likely" to embezzle money entrusted to him or commit sacrilege or theft or treachery or be guilty of adultery or neglect of parents or gods, and gets a negative answer. These are the so-called "vulgar" or "commonplace" tests that his definition of a just person must pass (as there are some tests his political justice must pass, as we just saw). But, Sachs correctly pointed out, all we get in this passage are Glaucon's convenient answer to Socrates' question: that the person they defined would be least likely to do such things. There is no argument, just assertion. Since then many have tried to supply needed arguments, but no satisfactory consensus has emerged.[16]

Sachs' charge of irrelevance still stands: yes, we may be better off, perhaps mentally healthier and more rational if our souls are Platonically constituted. But why is that justice? And if it is not, being thus better off is no defense of justice but of something else, mental health or rationality perhaps.

Now clearly, what makes Sachs' objection possible and indeed powerful is that Plato defines a just person not by any causal or logical connection to just laws, just constitutions, or principles of social justice, but as a state of the soul structurally similar, or isomorphic to his just city state. As a city state is just when it is so organized that each citizen is assigned to that social function for which s/he is best suited by nature and education to perform, so a person is just when her soul is so organized that each part of it is doing that psychic function for which it is best suited by nature and education to perform. It is hard to see how from this definition of a just person (and the particular assignments of psychic functions to psychic parts) we could validly infer that such a person would refrain from the profitably unjust actions of Thrasymachus' and Glaucon's heroes; it is even equally hard to see how we could infer that such a person would choose to perform that social function for which s/he is best suited by nature and education, or how such a person would refrain from the supreme Platonic social injustices, multi-careering or choosing a career she likes but is not best at. Sachs' objection can be pressed even within Plato's own ideal theory, as an objection that applies within the completely good city, in addition to the case of a Platonically just soul, one perhaps like Socrates, living in a Platonically unjust society, like democratic Athens!

To be sure, Plato connects his just soul to just actions: once a man has attained a just soul (and perhaps even the other virtues), he tells us in *Republic* (443e),

> he should then and then only turn to practice ... in the getting of wealth or the tendance of the body or it may be in political action or private business, in all such doings believing and naming the just and honorable action to be that which preserves and helps to produce this condition of soul ... [the structural psychic condition of reason ruling, spirit defending, and appetite provisioning].

This is the reverse of what we might expect and the reverse of what would be helpful for the Sachs problem, namely, that a just soul is one disposed to act justly, acting justly being independently specified by just principles, just constitutions, and just laws. Instead, Socrates definition of just acts makes Sachs' objection even more powerful: for actions so defined have no definitional connection to acts of social justice. His psychic justice may not produce social justice, nor may his social justice produce psychic justice.

Had Plato defined a just person as every subsequent theorist of justice, from Aristotle to Rawls, as a person with a strong and usually effective desire to act according to principles of social justice, just constitutions, and just laws, Sachs' objection would simply have no hold! Indeed, Thrasymachus and Glaucon themselves, in the *Republic*, think of a just person that way, as one who would refrain from commonly thought unjust actions – all the unlawful actions that men with the Ring of Gyges would most pursue.

Now in his paper Sachs ignored or abstracted from Plato's theory of social justice; perhaps he thought it irrelevant to his issue, it had been and still is out of favor as anti-democratic, and few, if any, would want to defend it. Sachs also ignored or abstracted from Plato's theory of the other personal virtues, temperance, courage, and wisdom. This isolation enabled Sachs to focus his objection and make it sharp and powerful. But when it came to Plato's answer, this isolation deprived Plato of weapons at his disposal for a good reply. Since then commentators have tried to bring in other parts of Plato's overall theory to answer the objection, though no one perhaps has brought in all that is needed.

How did Plato think of the issue, given that he portrays the answer to Socrates' question by Glaucon as if it were obvious and needed no argument? There is evidence in our passage that Plato thought of the issue in a holistic manner, rather than the isolated way Sachs posed the problem:

> For example, if an answer were demanded to the question concerning that city and the man whose birth and breeding was in harmony with it, whether we believe that such a man, entrusted with a deposit of gold or silver, would withhold it and embezzle it, who would you suppose would think that he would be more likely so to act than men of a different kind? No one would, he [Glaucon] said. (442e)

The issue is about the ideal city and a person who was born and educated in it and is "in harmony" with it: would s/he refrain from such acts in the ideal city? Now the ideal city would certainly have laws prohibiting such acts – laws prohibiting the standard crimes (theft, property damage, bodily injury, homicide, breaking contracts, and so on), as any system of social justice would. In this part of justice, criminal justice, different theories and systems of justice overlap; no society could survive without outlawing such standard acts of harming others. So if a person is educated in the ideal city, whether a future ruler, soldier, or provider, it would be part of such an education that such actions are (socially) unjust, should be avoided, and would be punished.

Plato's theory of social justice would imply that such actions are unjust, and the Platonic education in the ideal city would provide a causal link between a citizen's character and the refraining of such acts. Further, since (primary and secondary) Platonic education in the ideal would include education in all the virtues (whether or not Plato had a unity of virtue thesis in the *Republic*), the issue is whether one born and educated in the ideal city so as to have all the virtues would refrain from such unjust acts: whether one who had been educated to be Platonically wise, brave, temperate, and just, would refrain from theft, unfaithfulness, sacrilege and so on, "more so than men of a different character" (443a).

This is the most favorable interpretation to Plato of how he thought of the issue, and the most plausible reply is the one that Glaucon gave. A citizen educated in Plato's ideal city would be likely to refrain from such actions.

But what would be the cause of such refraining? At the end of our passage Plato replies:

> And is not the cause of this [refraining from such actions] to be found in the fact that each of the principles [parts of the soul] within him does its own work [the psychic function of] in the matter of ruling and being ruled? Yes, that and nothing else. Do you still then look for justice to be anything else than this power that produces such men and cities? No, by heavens, he said, I do not. (443b)

The answer we previously gave, that Platonic education would provide a causal link from character to action, may provide some assurance that persons so educated would refrain from such unjust actions. But it is not sufficient to show that the cause of this refraining is nothing but the functional structure of the educated person's character, namely, that his soul is so constituted that reason rules, appetite is obedient to reason on what appetites should be satisfied, by what and how much, and spirit helps reason to carry out its decisions. The cause might sometimes be, for example, the person's having learned that such actions are unjust and are usually found out and punished; one might act justly out of fear of punishment.

Moreover, even if we assume that a citizen in Plato's ideal city has *all* the psychic personal virtues, it would seem that this psychic state is logically compatible with actions that are socially unjust (commonly criminal and/ or Platonically socially unjust). Suppose in such a city a citizen's reason rules, appetite obeys, and spirit helps reason execute its decisions in situation of danger; further, there is harmony among them on this ordering; further yet, reason has psychic wisdom, knowledge or true belief about what is good for each part of the soul and the whole soul. Even in this paragon of the virtues, what would exclude reason thinking *truly* that some act of Platonic *social* injustice is good for the person when s/he could get away with it? Only if it is absolutely true that every act of Platonic social justice is good for one and every act of Platonic social injustice bad for one. But the most Plato has shown in his theory of social justice is that doing well what one is naturally and educationally best at is good for one and better than any other occupation; that much Plato can rely on here without danger of circularity. But for other acts of social injustice, embezzlement by a trader for example, Plato has no such proof or even much evidence.

Plato concedes that his educational programs, even the long, broad, and deep education of his rulers, would not be sufficient to ensure that they would always act justly socially and virtuously within the ideal city. For, as we saw in the last chapter, Plato deprives his rulers and soldiers entirely of private property and private family, on the ground that, even with their education, if they had such private interests and loves they might not always pursue the good of the city as a whole. This seems very much to concede the possibility of his rulers being psychically just and virtuous and socially unjust.

If we consider the issue outside the framework of Plato's ideal state, whether a citizen with all of Plato's psychic virtues would ever act unjustly in a non-ideal state, Plato's answer is even less convincing. It may well be that in any of Thrasymachus' just states, or in Glaucon's just state, or in a timocracy, an oligarchy, a democracy, and certainly in a tyranny, acts of social injustice – social injustice by the standards of these constitutions – would truly be better for one when s/he can get away with it. And in such cases the Platonically virtuous person's reason would and should truly choose such actions.

In sum, even if we fill the gaps in Plato's assertion that his Platonic psychic justice really is justice, by bringing in his education in his ideal state to supply a causal link between character and action, and even by bringing in his other three psychic virtues, his paragon's psychic virtues are still logically compatible with occasional acts of social injustice even in the ideal state; and even when such a person acts justly, the cause may occasionally not be the psychic state Plato calls justice. Sachs' objection still stands: Plato's just psychic constitution has not sufficient causal connection to his social justice, and no relevant logical or definitional connection with it either. The isomorphism between his psychic and social justice, even together with his educational program, is not sufficient for what is required – that the psychic state of justice is so defined as to be incompatible with acts of social injustice.

The fault lies in Plato's defining the psychic state he calls justice independently of social or political justice; and it can only be closed by defining a person's justice as a disposition to act in accordance with principles of justice, just constitutions, and just laws. Plato's problem here provided the impetus for the subsequent tradition, beginning with Aristotle, to do exactly that.

But the psychic state Plato defines as justice, isomorphic to his ideal of social justice, is an ideal of prudential rationality, especially when we add wisdom, the virtue of reason, as knowledge or true belief of what is good for one; and when we add yet the other virtues, especially temperance as harmony among the three parts on the rule of reason, it is also an ideal of mental and emotional health. It is hard to dispute Plato's paragon of the virtues of the soul as something that is good for us, maybe better than any other ordering or constitution of the soul. The Platonically well-ordered state and the Platonic well-ordered soul are reflections of each other, the one good for the citizens the other good for their souls. Even with Plato's failure to provide the logical and causal link necessary between the two, at least in the case of justice, Plato's primary motive for the isomorphism is evidently the defense of justice: a social order good for all its citizens and a parallel psychic order good for all human beings.

5   The Defense of Justice as the Health of the Soul

At the very end of Book iv, Socrates faces directly for the first time Glaucon's challenge, to show that justice in our souls is better for us, better *in itself*, aside from rewards and punishments. He tries to show this by an analogy between his psychic justice and health.

Plato tried out this kind of analogy before, most notably in the *Gorgias* (464–6, 504, 517, 520, 521). Here Socrates says that body and soul each have good conditions, which are health and (he claims) justice and temperance, respectively. He then draws up an elaborate analogy between the arts of the body, gymnastics and medicine, and (what he claims are) the arts of the psyche, legislation and (corrective) justice: as gymnastics is to the body so legislation is to the psyche, and as medicine is to the body so (corrective) justice is to the psyche. Gymnastics and medicine aim at producing or restoring the good condition of the body and health; legislation and corrective justice aim at producing or restoring the good condition of the soul, justice and temperance. But in the *Gorgias*, this justice remains undefined.

Since Plato has now defined justice, his analogy is between his psychic justice, as defined, and health; and since he has also used a theory of functional good to construct his theory of justice, we now know what he means by justice in our souls and what he might mean by the claim that this justice is better for us. There can be no better context for understanding and assessing this analogy than his theory of justice and his theory of functional good in the *Republic*.

Let us see how Socrates draws the analogy:

> Doing justice and doing injustice do not differ at all from the healthful and
> the diseaseful: the former are in the soul as the latter are in the body. Doing
> just acts engenders justice [in the soul of the agent] and doing unjust

injustice. But to produce health is to establish the elements of the body in the relation of dominating and being dominated by one another according to nature, while to cause disease is to bring it about that one rules or is ruled by another contrary to nature. Likewise, to engender justice [in the soul] is to establish the elements of the soul in the relation of ruling and being ruled according to nature, while [to cause] injustice is to cause one to rule or be ruled by another contrary to nature. Virtue then is a kind of health ... and vice disease. (444cd)

Socrates claims just actions are to psychic justice as healthful actions are to health: both are actions that produce and maintain the corresponding psychic and bodily states, and analogously for injustice and disease. He then uses the analogy to argue that since health is the good of the body, and certainly better than disease, and justice is to the psyche as health is to the body, justice must be the good of the psyche, and certainly better than injustice.

This argument has not generated much conviction among readers of the *Republic*; their reactions have been very much unlike Plato's Glaucon, who immediately concedes that injustice in our souls makes life even less worth living than a ruined body, even if we could do as we pleased.

One reason may be that Plato's analogical relation of psychic to social justice does not assure that a person who has psychic justice will be socially just, or act justly towards others. Plato's definition of psychic justice may bring *that* justice closer to health, since the health of a person can be conceived functionally, by how well his body and its parts function, *independently of relation to other persons*. But this only reinforces our reaction, and inclines us to agree with Sachs, that Plato's psychic justice isn't justice, something more like mental health. So even if there is the analogy Plato claims between *his* justice and health, it does not show what he claims it shows – that it is good or better for us to be just in the sense of being disposed to act justly toward others, to be just by the standard of social justice. Now, though this difficulty affects the health analogy, we cannot expect any interpretation of that analogy by itself to solve it, because it is a difficulty whose cause is the *other* analogy, between social and psychic justice.

Plato's analogy seems implausible to begin with: we think of health as a natural condition of the body, at least up to a certain age, and of the deterioration of health in old age also as natural, a biologic rhythm of the body. But we think of justice as something we have to be instructed and habituated in, a man-made virtue; while the fall from justice, if it occurs, has no particular association with old age or any rhythm of psycho-biological normality. But in our passage Plato says explicitly that both justice and health are "according to nature" and both injustice and disease "contrary to nature."

Further, Plato has not defined health; he has given us far more information about his conception of justice than he has about his idea of bodily health. The analogy directs us to think of psychic justice as being like health; but given the relative amounts of information he gives about the two, we are more likely to take his justice as a guide to how he thinks about health.

His theory of functional good and virtue might help us to understand his conception of health and the analogy, since it can be applied to both body and soul and thus both justice and health can be thought of functionally: health is a virtue of the body as justice is a virtue of the soul and each enables its possessor to function well. This assumption is very much confirmed by the long discussion of the human body in the *Timaeus*. Here the parts and organs of the body are conceived functionally or teleologically: each part and organ exists in order to do some particular work (teleological), or at least has some particular work to do (functional),[17] which is its exclusive or optimal function. When all the parts and organs are performing their functions and doing so well, the organism is healthy; when some are prevented from performing their functions, by excessive food intake or violence, for example, we have illness and disease. The functional theory of good seems very much implicit, or taken for granted, in this conception of health. The examples of functions for eyes and ears Plato gives to illustrate his definition of exclusive function in the *Republic* are part of a bigger, teleological conception of the physical universe, including living things, of course.

If the functional theory of good is implicit in both his conceptions of health and psychic justice, his analogy becomes more understandable: the good of justice and health is the same good, functioning well, applied to the human body and soul and their parts. And Plato's claim, that both justice and health are according to nature and injustice and disease are contrary to nature, now becomes more understandable. According to the functional theory psychic justice is both a natural and an artificial (man-made) virtue: the division of the soul and the exclusive functions of parts are natural or inborn; but the matching of reason to ruling, spirit to defense, and appetite to obeying reason, is the result of legislation and education, and so it is artificial or man made.

Similarly, we are born with bodies that already have a physical division of parts and labor, with eyes and ears and stomachs and hearts and brains having their exclusive work, and this division is certainly natural. But well functioning and health also require learning and proper nutrition and exercise; we even have to learn to see well, the brain has to develop by use; and any of the bodily systems can malfunction and might require human intervention. The ancient arts of gymnastics and medicine were devoted to promoting, maintaining, and restoring health. For example, one of the three branches of ancient medicine, dietetics, had rules and regimens for attaining this end; and these can be thought of as parallel to the laws of justice, as Socrates in fact thinks of them in the *Gorgias*.[18] In so far as health is the result of such medical practices, it is an artificial or man-made condition. So both justice and health are natural and artificial conditions, the results of nature and human art or science.

The larger idea of nature and artifice that underlies these conceptions is non-evolutionary and teleological, as the *Timaeus* makes clear. Organisms themselves are the work of divine art. According to Plato, we are divine artifacts. What we take as natural is really the work of the Divine Craftsman imposing the order and goodness of the forms on matter. *Our* division between the natural and the artificial is a division between the regularity and order we find in the world independently of human intervention *and* the results of our human intervention, industry, science and art. But for Plato it is a division between divine creation and human creation; with the important qualification that divine creation was limited in its results by the nature of matter – the results of divine creation were good but not perfectly so. Justice as Plato defines it is the result of divine creativity and human intervention; and so is health, he thinks. He observes the order of nature and postulates divine creativity according to forms to explain it. The evidence for human intervention for both justice and health is easier to find – in the arts of education, legislation and medicine.

Plato has a continuing analogy going, among city, psyche, and body. All three are conceived functionally or teleologically as complexes with naturally divided parts which are naturally suited, or adapted as evolutionists would now say, for some function or other, exclusive or optimal, needed by the complex. And they all share the idea that when the parts are doing the functions for which they are naturally suited and doing them well, the whole complex functions well and is in its best state: justice and virtue for cities and persons and health for organisms.

6   The Defense of the Just Life as the Pleasantest

Plato discusses hedonism – the view that pleasure is the human good – in several dialogues, and all his hedonists ("the many" of the *Protagoras*, Callicles in the *Gorgias* and Protarchus in the *Philebus*) share some assumptions. They all hold that pleasure itself is the only thing that is good by itself (or good as an ultimate end); all other things that are good are good as a means or sources of pleasure. They do not admit that any pleasures themselves are bad. They evaluate and rank pleasures on the basis of magnitude alone – their duration and intensity. And they all suppose that a person who feels pleasure knows or is the ultimate judge whether s/he feels pleasure.

Plato is not a hedonist: his evaluations and rankings of pleasures in *Republic*, Book IX, presuppose his earlier proof in that the good is not identical with pleasure: "What about those who define the good as pleasure? Are they any less confused than the others? Aren't even they forced to admit that there are bad pleasures? Most definitely. So, I think, they have to agree that the same things are good and bad. Isn't that true? Of course" (*Republic*: 505c).[19]

Still, he thinks that pleasure has some value, that some pleasures are better than others and that some lives are better off or happier than others in so far as they contain the better pleasures.

This is what he argues in *Republic* (Book IX: 580–87), as part of his whole argument that the just man is happier than the unjust. He compares three lives with respect to pleasure: the life of the just man who pursues knowledge as his ultimate end (Plato's philosopher) is pleasanter than the life of the unjust man who is ruled by spirit and pursues honor (the timocratic person); and the latter's life is in turn pleasanter than the life of the more unjust man who is ruled by appetite and who pursues wealth as the ultimate end of his life (the oligarchic person). And this is partly because the first life contains more valuable pleasures (the pleasures of gaining knowledge) than the pleasures of the second (the pleasures of victory and honors), which in turn contains more valuable pleasures than the pleasures of wealth or appetite satisfaction.[20]

This presupposes that pleasures have some value and that some pleasures have more value than others. But Plato evaluates and ranks pleasures differently from the hedonist. He disagrees that the value of pleasures depends entirely on their magnitude (in intensity or duration), as the hedonists of the *Protagoras* suppose. And he disagrees that a man who thinks he feels pleasure can make no mistake about that, as all hedonists suppose; though they can concede that a man can make a mistake about the magnitude of prospective imagined pleasures or the magnitude of remembered pleasures. It is Plato's task then to explain what other bases there are for evaluating pleasures and how a man can be deceived in thinking that he feels pleasure. Here we shall consider how he carries out this project in the *Republic*.

Plato proposes two criteria for evaluating and ranking pleasures: purity of a pleasure or its non-mixture with pain; and truth or reality of a pleasure as distinct from falsehood or the appearance of pleasure. He also discusses the nature of pleasure, what pleasure is, something he thinks necessary to do before we can evaluate pleasures.

His argument attempts to show that the life of the just man of knowledge is the most pleasant by showing that the pleasures of knowledge are pure and true (or real), whereas the pleasures of eating, drinking, and having sex (the main pleasures of appetitive part of the soul and of the man of wealth) and the pleasures of victory and honors (the pleasures of the spirited part of the soul and the main pleasures of the military man) are neither pure nor true (or real).

Now, purity might be thought compatible with the hedonist's basis for evaluating and ranking pleasures. Indeed, Bentham counts it, though he points out that purity is not strictly speaking a property of a pleasure itself, but rather of the act which produces pleasure; all pleasures themselves are pure, but some may be produced in such a way that there is a chance that the pleasure may be followed by pain and these are the impure pleasures (Bentham 1789: chapter IV). Further, a hedonist would rank pure and impure pleasures by magnitude alone, the net balance of pleasure over pain; thus an impure pleasure might be more valuable or rank higher than a pure pleasure if the net balance of pleasure over pain in the mixed pleasure was greater than the pure pleasure.

Plato, however, does not seem to be thinking of purity in the hedonist's way. First, he has a theory of what the pleasures that arise from the satisfaction of bodily appetites are, from which it follows that these pleasures are always mixed; or at least that pains are necessary conditions of the pleasures, not just a probable effect of the acts that produce them. And second, he seems to think that pure pleasures are always more valuable than mixed pleasures, apparently no matter what the quantitative relations are between them.[21]

In the *Gorgias* (491e5–494d1) we already have a picture of what a large class of impure pleasures are. Callicles thinks of pleasure as the satisfaction of bodily appetite, he admits that appetite itself is painful, and he thinks that the intensity of a pleasure is directly proportional to the intensity of the appetite it satisfies. He thinks primarily of bodily appetites and pleasures, and seems to accept a physiological model of appetite and pleasure: appetite occurs when the body is depleted or deficient of something (say, one is thirsty or hungry) and pleasure occurs when the body is replenished and the desire (e.g. for drink or food) satisfied – a model that seems to fit well with hunger and thirst and perhaps even some sexual longing.

In the *Republic* (585d8–586c7) Socrates himself proposes a similar model of desire and pleasure, but he modifies it in two significant ways. First, he applies the depletion-replenishment model not only to desires and pleasures that arise in the soul through the body but also to some of the soul's own desires and pleasures: "And is not ignorance and folly in turn a kind of emptiness in the condition of the soul? It is indeed. And he who partakes of nourishment and wisdom fills the void and is filled?" (*Republic*: 585b) If the ignorance and folly are felt as painful and a desire arises for filling this emptiness with wisdom, then the gaining of wisdom will be pleasant and this pleasure will not be pure; but perhaps, unlike hunger and thirst and sexual longing, folly and ignorance are not always felt as painful; if for no other reason, because the person may not be aware of his ignorance or folly, as is often demonstrated in Plato's early dialogues.

Second, Plato does not think that all pleasures that arise in the soul through the body are to be understood on the empty-filling model: he explicitly mentions pleasures of smell as pure pleasures that can be very intense (*Republic*: 584b6–584b9)[22] These are not preceded by any deficiency in the body or soul, even though in a very general sense we sometimes lack them and so can desire them.

We can think of the human body in health or illness; some bodily pleasures then occur when health is restored or deficiency remedied. Similarly, we can think of the soul as having the health or soundness of the soul, such as virtue and knowledge, or as being corrupted by vice or ignorance; and in such cases, once more, we can think of pleasure as occurring when virtue is restored or knowledge gained. But we can also think of human beings not as being deficient as human beings, but as being imperfect beings relative to gods. There are things we do not have, even though these lacks are not deficiencies: coming to know an elegant mathematical proof, the appreciation of a peaceful scene, the smelling of a gardenia, the listening of

Mozart's fortieth symphony – all these one might not have and might enjoy partly because one did not already have them, though they are not restorations to health or the remedying of any psychic deficiency.

Now why should pure pleasures always be ranked above mixed pleasures, no matter what the quantities of these pleasures and pains are? Plato might have thought, perhaps, that a life of pleasures and no pains – a life of pure pleasures only – is rationally preferable to a life of some pleasures and some pains, even if the net balance of pleasure over pain in the life of mixed pleasures exceeds the sum total of pleasures in the life of pure pleasures. One's aversion to pain might be considerable, or one's tolerance of pain might be near zero; and in such circumstances the choice of a life of pure pleasures over a life of mixed pleasures might well be rational for such a person, assuming it is possible. But there is no evidence in our texts that Plato thought of the matter in this way.

Rather, he seems to want to evaluate pleasures on the basis of things other than the pleasures themselves or their intrinsic properties, in the way in which we normally evaluate another psychic phenomenon, desires: we usually evaluate and rank our desires by evaluating and ranking the objects of our desires. We evaluate the desire for a certain food or drink, for example, by finding out whether that food or drink is good for us; if it is, the desire is a good desire, if not, it is not. And this is how Plato evaluates desires generally, as he does, for example, in his distinction between necessary and unnecessary appetites (*Republic*: 558d5–559d2). Now what makes it possible to evaluate desires in this way is that desires come, ready made as it were, with a certain structure: a desire must be a desire for something, it must have an object. Indeed, it is standard Platonic theory (e.g. *Symposium*: 199e6–200b5) that desire is always for something. This structure gives us a handle, as it were, for evaluating our desires.

But pleasure does not seem to have any such structure: it may have causes and conditions under which it arises, but it does not seem to have, as part of its nature, an object. At any rate not as evidently as desire does. Plato's essential thought, in the *Republic* (and the *Philebus*) is that pleasure does really have an object, and it should be evaluated by evaluating that object: it is no more appropriate to evaluate and rank pleasures by their intensities, as the hedonist does, than it is to evaluate desires by their intensities. Purity is indeed a basis for evaluating a pleasure, but the purity of a pleasure is due to the purity of its object; it is because the object of a pure pleasure is better than the object of an impure pleasure that pure pleasures should be ranked above impure pleasures.

To determine what are better and worse objects Plato relies on his meta-physics: forms are better than their sensible participants, which are in turn better than the images of sensible participants – the metaphysics (and episte-mology) of the Divided Line in the *Republic*, Book VI. Thus the pleasure of learning or knowing Platonic forms is pure because Platonic forms are pure and flawless specimens of their kind, whereas their sensible participants are flawed in some way or other; thus the pleasures of knowing the forms will rank above even the pure aesthetic pleasures whose objects are, say, colors or sounds – the pleasures of viewing beautiful paintings or listening to music.

Even for the mixed pleasures Socrates finds a basis for evaluation and ranking that comes from outside the pleasures themselves (that is, other than their intrinsic properties of intensity and duration), but this time it is not reliance of heavy Platonic metaphysics, but on the medicine of the day and its psychic analogues. Using the depletion-replenishment or restorative physiological model of pleasure, Socrates points out that the replenishment of a depletion may be appropriate or not for the depletion, good or bad for the person filling the emptiness; certainly something true of foods and drinks – they can be good or bad for our health, excessive or defective in amounts, too frequent or not frequent enough, and so on. The medicine of the day routinely evaluated the "physical pleasures" (the satisfactions of bodily appetites) on the basis of health and disease; enjoying the foods and drinks that are good for us makes for good enjoyment; enjoying harmful foods and drinks make for bad enjoyment. And something similar, Socrates teaches, may be true of filling the emptiness of ignorance and folly; igno-rance can be filled with false opinion, for example, and even though one might enjoy the false belief, he is in a fool's paradise (*Republic*: 585e, 586e). Presumably, then, it is on the basis of the goodness or badness of the object that fills the emptiness that the pleasure is to be evaluated, and Plato might have thought that here he is evaluating the pleasure not hedonistically, but by something other than the pleasure itself, for example, health.[23]

The other property on which Plato relies to evaluate pleasures in the *Republic* is truth or reality. This unusual, difficult and obscure view has been discussed most extensively in the secondary literature (see, for exam-ple, Gosling and Taylor (1982), D. Frede (1992, 1993)), and we can take it up only briefly here. There are at least two different issues.

First, Plato claims that sometimes we mistake relief from pain for pleas-ure. He thinks that besides the two states of pleasure and pain there is a psychological state in the middle which is neither pleasant nor painful – a neutral or zero hedonic point. When our body becomes depleted – let us say dehydrated – we may feel the depletion as pain; this is like a movement downward from zero and this is real or true pain. When our body gets replenished we are moving from pain back to zero, but because of the contrast to the pain that is leaving us we mistake this relief from pain for pleasure. But this relief from pain is not pleasure but only a "phantom" of a pleasure (*Republic*: 586b7–586b9). Apparently Plato thinks that relief from pain is similar to pleasure, as an image is similar to its object, and we mistake this similarity for identity. Real or true pleasure is felt when there is a movement upwards from zero – as when we are in neither pleasure nor pain and then enjoy the smell of a rose, the exhibit of an elegant mathematical proof, or the beholding of beauty itself. These are real or true pleasures, Plato claims, and they should be ranked always above apparent or false pleasures, which are relief from pain.

A second issue is Plato's apparent application of truth and falsity to pleasure and pain. Especially since Hume, the moderns think that truth and falsity can be applied to psychic states that represent something, such as beliefs, expectations, and memories; these can be true or false by comparison to the realities they represent. But, they say, pleasure and pain are not representational psychic entities; they do not represent anything by comparison to which they can be true or false. The Humean and the hedonist might concede of course that an expectation of pleasure may be false; and a memory of pleasure can be false too, but that is a different matter; such cases do not show that pleasures themselves can be false, but only that these pleasures will not or did not in fact obtain or were different in magnitude.

It is not clear how strictly we can take Plato's application of the Greek terms for truth and falsity to pleasure; sometimes the same words can mean real and apparent; and though one might still dispute that the distinction between real and apparent can be applied to pleasures, it is a different kind of dispute, and not necessarily a confusion or even category mistake. In any case this dispute, whether truth and falsity can be applied to pleasures, may not affect Plato's view that we sometimes can mistake relief from pain for pleasure. Even if pleasure and pain are not representational psychic entities, as they do not seem to be, we could still mistake relief from one as being the other. Plato speaks of such mistakes in the *Republic*: we can mistake a beautiful sound or color for beauty itself, on account of their similarity.

There remains perhaps an air of paradox about Plato's evaluation and ranking of pleasures by purity and truth. We saw that he does not use purity in the way the hedonist does, by taking it into account in the calculations of the net balance of pleasure over pain; nor does he conceive it in the way a hedonist does, by whether or not a pleasure is preceded or followed by pain; rather he claims that the purity of some pleasures depends on the purity of their objects. In any case, it is clear enough that purity and truth of pleasures are not for Plato quantitative criteria; so that not only is he not a hedonist, but even in evaluating pleasure as one of the good things of life, he wants to do it qualitatively rather than by magnitude and number.

Notes

1   See White (1979: Introduction) for a fine discussion of this issue in ancient and modern times.
2   See Penner (2005) for the view that what is being attacked or defended in the *Republic* is what justice really is, not Thrasymachus' justice or Glaucon's justice or even Socrates' justice (if it happens to be mistaken). For a reply see Santas (2003).
3   Rawls (1971: chapter II, section 12, pp. 67–72).
4   See Keyt, "Aristotle's Theory of Distributive Justice (1991), for a clear, indeed definitive discussion of these points.
5   For an analysis of this argument see Santas (2010).
6   For instructive discussion of these issues, see Allen (2006) and Miller (2007).
7   Barry (1989: part III).
8   See Rawls' acceptance of the principle that inequalities must be to the advantage of everyone and his difference principles as an partial interpretation of "the advantage of everyone" (Rawls: 1971: chapter II, sections 12, 13).
9   See Santas (2006b) for Plato's attraction to pleasure as the human good, in the *Protagoras*, when he thought that pleasure is measurable and would make sources or causes of pleasure commensurable goods, having previously thought, in the *Euthyphro*, that the good, the just, and the beautiful, are not subject to the arts of measurement.
10   But notice that the providers are allowed private property and private family, so at most Plato could think of this extreme unity only within the class of rulers and soldiers.
11   See a parallel concern about social unity in Rawls (1988). The concept of primary goods is constructed and used so as to assure social unity, as agreement on justice, in the face of disagreements about final ends or ultimate good. Of course the unity Rawls seeks is not at all Plato's extreme unity of even beliefs and feelings. See Aristotle's criticisms of Plato's unity in *Politics*, Book II.
12   This issue is far more complex. See Taylor (1997) for a useful discussion of the issues.
13   Aside from conflicts about resources, there can also be problems about matching talents to needs; what does justice require when there are a lot fewer mathematicians born than we need?

14 Weinstein (2007).

15 Rawls (1971: chapter III, section 15) defines an economic floor, the class of the "the least advantaged," in two different ways, something his difference principle needs for application.

16 See Singpurwalla (2006) for a review and discussion of the main lines of answer to Sachs, by many writers: for example, Vlastos (1981), Reeve (1988), Dahl (1999), Kraut (1992), Penner (2005), Keyt (2006b).

17 The teleology assumed here can be strong: each part or organ comes into being or exists for the sake of its function. Or weaker: each part or organ serves a particular function, aside from how it came to exist. Since Plato has a divine craftsman creating the order of the material universe, he may have the stronger teleology, which is not compatible with the theory of evolution.

18 Both social and psychic justice may require man-made laws and regulations, and learning, but these are based on *physis* (nature); as dietetics, one of the three branches in ancient medicine concerned with the regulations of nutrition, was man made but based on nature – the needs of the body.

19 In the *Philebus* Plato has Socrates also refute hedonism, but in a new way, by an isolation test. See Frede (1992), and for a fuller discussion of Plato's views on pleasure, see Santas (2006b).

20 Usually writers think this is a comparison between Plato's just person and two of Plato's unjust persons – the timocratic person and the oligarch; Bobonich (2002) argues that it is a comparison within Plato's completely good city among his philosophers and his soldiers and his artisans; this is partly because Bobonich thinks a person can be just only if he has wisdom, wisdom in turn requires knowledge of the form of the good, and only philosophers have such knowledge, hence only philosophers can be just.

21 He explicitly tells us so in the *Philebus* (53b10–53c3): "Any pure pleasure, however small or infrequent, if uncontaminated with pain, is pleasanter and more beautiful than a repeated pleasure without purity." Not only more beautiful; but even pleasanter, though apparently here pleasanter does not mean that it is of greater intensity or duration or frequency!

22 In the *Philebus* (51d7–51d10) he adds pleasures of hearing (e.g. listening to music) and sight (e.g. watching a sunset or looking at a beautiful painting); indeed all the aesthetic pleasures – literally the pleasures of sense perception – might be of this kind.

23 The hedonist might reply, as in *Protagoras*, that the value of health in turn depends on the pleasures it enables us to enjoy or the pains to avoid; so that this is not ultimately evaluating pleasures non-hedonistically. But Plato may be relying here on his arguments against the identity of good and pleasure, which, if successful, open up some space for other things besides pleasure to be good in themselves.

Bibliography

Adam, James (1902) *The Republic of Plato*, 2 vols, Cambridge.

Allen, R.E. (1965) *Studies in Plato's Metaphysics*, New York.

Allen, R.E., tr. (2006) *Plato, The Republic*, New Haven.

Anagnostopoulos, Georgios (1994) *Aristotle on the Goals and Exactness of Ethics*, Berkeley.

Anagnostopoulos, Georgios, ed. (2009) *A Companion to Aristotle*, Oxford.

Andersson, T.J. (1971) *Polis and Psyche: A Motif in Plato's Republic*, Stockholm.

Annas, Julia (1981) *An Introduction to Plato's* Republic, Oxford.

Anton, John P., ed. (1980) *Science and the Sciences in Plato*, Delmal, NY.

Anton, John P. (2008) "The *Republic* as Philosophical Drama," *Philosophical Inquiry*, vol. xxx.

Arsen, Hera (2009) *Was Plato a Mathematical Platonist?* PhD Dissertation, Irvine, CA.

Asmis, Elizabeth (1992) "Plato on Poetic Creativity," in R. Kraut, ed., *The Cambridge Companion to Plato*, Cambridge.

Aune, Bruce (1997) "The Unity of Plato's *Republic*," *Ancient Philosophy*, 17.

Barker, E. (1946) *The Politics of Aristotle*, Oxford.

Barnes, J., ed. (1984) *The Collected Works of Aristotle*, Princeton.

Barry, Brian (1989) *Theories of Justice*, Berkeley.

Benson, Hugh (2006a) "Plato's Method of Dialectic," in H. Benson, ed., *A Companion to Plato*, Oxford.

Benson, Hugh, ed. (2006b) *A Companion to Plato*, Oxford.

Bentham, J. (1789) *The Principles of Morals and Legislation*, London.

Bloom, A. (1968) *The Republic of Plato*, New York.

Blosser, N. (1997) *Dialogform und Argument: Studien zu Platons Politeia*, Stuttgart.

Bobonich, Christopher (2002) *Plato's Utopia Recast*, Oxford.

Broome, John (1996) *Weighing Goods*, Oxford.

Burns, J.H. (1968) "J.S. Mill and Democracy, 1829–61," in J.B. Schneewind, ed., *Mill*, Garden City, NJ.

Burnyeat, M. (1999a) "Culture and Society in Plato's *Republic*," *The Tanner Lectures on Human Values*, 20, Salt Lake City.

Burnyeat, M. (1999b) "Utopia and Phantasy: The Practicability of Plato's Ideally Just City," in G. Fine, ed., *Plato 2: Ethics, Politics, Religion and the Soul*, Oxford.

Code, Alan (1993) "Vlastos on a Metaphysical Paradox," in T. Irwin and M. Nussbaum, eds, *Virtue, Love and Form*, Edmonton.

Cohen, Mark (1999) "The Logic of the Third Man," in G. Fine, ed., *Plato 1: Metaphysics and Epistemology*, Oxford.

Cohen, Mark and Keyt, David (1992) "Analysing Plato's Arguments: Plato and Platonism," in J. Klagge and N.D. Smith, eds, *Methods of Interpreting Plato and his Dialogues*, Oxford.

Cooper, John M., ed. (1997) *Plato: Complete Works*, Indianapolis/Cambridge.

Cooper, John M. (1999) *Reason and Emotion*, Princeton.

Cooper, John M. (2004) *Knowledge, Nature, and the Good*, Princeton.

Cornford, F.M. (1941) *The Republic of Plato*, Oxford.

Coumoundouros, A. and Polansky, R. (2009) "Function, Ability and Desire in Plato's *Republic*," *Philosphical Inquiry*, vol. xxxi, Winter–Spring, no. 1–2.

Cross, R.C. and A.D. Woozley (1964) *Plato's Republic*, London.

Dahl, Norman (1999) "Plato's Defense of Justice," in G. Fine, ed., *Plato 2: Ethics, Politics, Religion and the Soul*, Oxford.

Daniels, Norman (1975) *Reading Rawls*, New York.

Denyer, Nicholas (2007) "Sun and Line: The Role of the Good," in G.R.F. Ferrari, ed., *The Cambridge Companion to Plato's Republic*, Cambridge.

Deveveux, Daniel (2006) "The Unity of the Virtues," in H. Benson, ed., *A Companion to Plato*, Oxford.

Dixsaut, M., ed. (2005) *Edudes sur la* Republique *de Platon*, vols 1 and 2, Paris.

Elster, Jon (1985) *Sour Grapes*, Cambridge.

Estlund, David (2003) "Why not Epistocracy?" in N. Reshotko, ed., *Desire, Identity and Existence*, Edmonton.

Everson, S., ed. (1990) *Companions to Ancient Thought 1: Epistemology*, Cambridge.

Ferejohn, M.T. (2006) "Knowledge, Recollection, and the Forms in *Republic* VII," in G. Santas, ed., *The Blackwell Guide to Plato's Republic*, Oxford.

Ferrari, G.R.F, ed. (2000) *Plato: Republic*, tr. Tom Griffith, Cambridge.

Ferrari, G.R.F. (2003) *City and Soul in Plato's Republic*, Sankt Augustin.

Ferrari, G.R.F., ed. (2007) *The Cambridge Companion to Plato's Republic*, Cambridge.

Fine, Gail (1993) *On Ideas: Aristotle's Criticisms of Plato's Theory of Forms*, Oxford.

Fine, Gail (1999a) "Knowledge and Belief in *Republic* 5–7," in G. Fine, ed., *Plato 1: Metaphysics and Epistemology*, Oxford.

Fine, Gail, ed. (1999b) *Plato 1: Metaphysics and Epistemology*, Oxford.

Fine, Gail, ed. (1999c) *Plato 2: Ethics, Politics, Religion and the Soul*, Oxford.
Frede, Dorothea (1992) "Disintegration and Restoration: Pleasure and Pain in Plato's *Philebus*," in R. Kraut, ed., *The Cambridge Companion to Plato*, Oxford.
Frede, Dorothea, tr. (1993) *Philebus*, Indianapolis.
Frede, M. (1996) "The Affections of the Soul," in M. Frede and G. Stryker, *Rationality in Greek Thought*, Oxford.
Freud, S. (1953) *The Standard Edition of the Complete Psychological Works of Sigmund Freud*, ed. J. Strachey, London, vols I–XXVI.
Gill, C., ed. (1990) *The Person and the Human Mind: Issues in Ancient and Modern Philosophy*, Oxford.
Gosling, J.C.B. and Taylor, C.C.W. (1982) *The Greeks on Pleasure*, Oxford.
Griswold, C.L., ed. (1988) *Platonic Writings, Platonic Readings*, New York.
Grote, George (1988) *Plato and the Other Companions of Socrates*, 4th edn., 4 vols, London.
Guthrie, W.K.C. (1975) *A History of Greek Philosophy*, vol. 4, Cambridge.
Hardy, J.H. and Rudebusch, G., eds (2010) *Foundations in Ancient Ethics*, Göttingen.
Hoffe, O., ed. (1997) *Platon: Politeia*, Berlin.
Hull, D.L. and Ruse, M., eds (1998) *The Philosophy of Biology*, Oxford.
Hume, David (1955) *Treatise of Human Nature*, ed. L.A. Selby-Bigge, Oxford.
Irwin, T. (1989) *Classical Thought*, Oxford.
Irwin, T. (1995) *Plato's Ethics*, Oxford.
Irwin, T. and Nussbaum, M., eds (1993) *Virtue, Love, and Form*, Edmonton.
Janaway, Christopher (2006) "Plato and the Arts," in H. Benson, ed., *A Companion to Plato*, Oxford.
Joseph, H.W.B. (1935) *Essays in Ancient and Modern Philosophy*, Oxford.
Jowett, B. and Campbell, L., eds (1894) *The Republic of Plato*, 3 vols, Oxford.
Kahn, Charles (1996) *Plato and the Socratic Dialogues*, Cambridge.
Keyt, David (1971) "The Mad Crartsman of the *Timaeus*," *Philosophical Review*, 80.
Keyt, David (1991) "Aristotle's Theory of Distributive Justice," in D. Keyt and F. Miller, eds, *A Companion to Aristotle's Politics*, Oxford.
Keyt, David (2006a) "Plato and the Ship of State," in G. Santas, ed., *The Blackwell Guide to Plato's Republic*, Oxford.
Keyt, David (2006b) "Plato on Justice," in H. Benson, ed., *A Companion to Plato*, Oxford.
Keyt, David and Miller, Fred, eds (1991) *A Companion to Aristotle's Politics*, Oxford.
Keyt, David and Miller, Fred, eds (2007) *Freedom, Reason, and the Polis: Essays in Ancient Greek Political Philosophy*, Cambridge.
Klagge, J.C. and Smith N.D. (1992) *Methods of Interpreting Plato and his Dialogues*, Oxford.

Klosko, G. (1986) *The Development of Plato's Political Theory*, London.

Kraut, Richard, ed. (1992) *The Cambridge Companion to Plato*, Cambridge.

Kraut, Richard, ed. (1997a) *Plato's Republic: Critical Essays*, New York.

Kraut, Richard (1997b) "The Defense of Justice in Plato's *Republic*," in R. Kraut, ed., *Plato's Republic: Critical Essays*, New York.

Lear, Gabriel Richardson (2006) "Plato on Learning to Love Beauty," in G. Santas, ed., *The Blackwell Guide to Plato's Republic*, Oxford.

Lear, Jonathan (1993) "Plato's Politics of Narcissism," in T. Irwin and M. Nussbaum, eds, *Virtue, Love, and Form*, Edmonton.

Lear, Jonathan (1997) "Inside and Outside the *Republic*," in Kraut, R., ed., *Plato's Republic*, New York.

Lear, Jonathan (2005) *Freud*, New York.

Lear, Jonathan (2006) "Allegory and Myth in Plato's *Republic*," in G. Santas, ed., *The Blackwell Guide to Plato's Republic*, Oxford.

Lorenz, Hendrik (2005) *The Beast Within*, Oxford.

Lorenz, Hendrik (2006) "The Analysis of the Soul in Plato's *Republic*," in G. Santas, ed., *The Blackwell Guide to Plato's Republic*, Oxford.

Mayhew, R. (1997) *Aristotle's Criticisms of Plato's Republic*, Lanham.

Mayr, Ernst (1976) *Evolution and the Diversity of Life*, Cambridge, MA, Part VI, Ch. 35.

McPherran, Mark (2006) "The Gods and Piety in Plato's *Republic*," in G. Santas, ed., *The Blackwell Guide to Plato's Republic*, Oxford.

Mill, J.S. (1977) *Essays on Politics and Society*, ed. J.M. Robson, Toronto.

Miller, Fred (1995) *Nature, Justice, and Rights in Aristotle's Politics*, Oxford.

Miller, Fred (2005) "Plato on the Rule of Reason," *The Southern Journal of Philosophy*, 43.

Miller, Fred (2007) "The Rule of Reason in Plato's *Statesman* and the American *Federalist*, in D. Keyt and F. Miller, eds, *Freedom, Reason, and the Polis*, Cambridge.

Mitchell, Basil and Lucas, J.R. (2003) *An Engagement with Plato's Republic*, Ashgate.

Modrak, Deborah K.W. (2008) "Desires and Faculties in Plato and Aristotle," *Philosophical Inquiry*, vol. XXX, Summer–Fall, no. 3–4.

Moravcsik, J. (1992) *Plato and Platonism*, Oxford.

Moravcsik, J. and Temko, P., eds (1982) *Plato on Beauty, Wisdom and the Arts*, Totowa, NJ.

Morrison, Donald (2007) "The Utopian Character of Plato's Ideal City," in G.R.F. Ferrari, ed., *The Cambridge Companion to Plato's Republic*, Cambridge.

Moss, Jessica (2007) "What is Imitative Poetry and why is it Bad?" in G.R.F. Ferrari, ed., *The Cambridge Companion to Plato's Republic*, Cambridge.

Murdoch, I. (1997) *The Fire and the Sun: Why Plato Banished the Artists*, Oxford.

Murphy, N.R. (1951) *The Interpretation of Plato's Republic*, Oxford.

Nagel, Thomas (1975) "A Theory of Justice," in N. Daniels, ed., *Reading Rawls*, New York.

Nettleship, Richard (1962) *Lectures on the Republic of Plato*, London.

Nussbaum, M. (1986) *The Fragility of Goodness*, Cambridge.

O'Connor, David K. (2007) "Rewriting the Poets in Plato's Characters," in G.R.F. Ferrari, ed., *The Cambridge Companion to Plato's Republic*, Cambridge.

Ostenfeld, E.N., ed. (1998) *Essays on Plato's* Republic, Aarhus.

Penner, Terry (1987) *The Ascent from Nominalism*, Dordrecht.

Penner, Terry (2005) "Platonic Justice and What we Mean by 'Justice'," *Plato: Internet Journal of the International Plato Society*, 5.

Penner, Terry (2006) "The Forms in the *Republic*," in G. Santas, ed., *The Blackwell Guide to Plato's Republic*, Oxford.

Peterson, Sandra (1973) "A Reasonable Self-predication Premise for the Third Man Argument," *Philosophical Review*, 82.

Preston, Beth (1998) "Why is a Wing like a Spoon: A Pluralist Theory of Function," *Journal of Philosophy*, 95:5, May.

Price, A.W. (1989) *Love and Friendship in Plato and Aristotle*, Oxford.

Price, A.W. (1995) *Mental Conflict*, London.

Price, A.W. (2008) "Reasoning About Justice in Plato's *Republic*," *Philosophical Inquiry*, xxx: 3–4.

Prior, William (1983) "The Concept of Paradeigma in Plato's Philosophy," *Apeiron*, 17.

Popper, K. (1945) *The Open Society and its Enemies*, vol. 1, London.

Reale, Giovanni and Scolnicov, Samuel, eds (2002) *Dialogues on Plato – The Idea of the Good*, St Augustine.

Rawls, John (1971) *A Theory of Justice*, Cambridge, MA.

Rawls, John (1988) "Social Unity and Primary Goods," in A. Sen and B. Williams, eds, *Utilitarianism and Beyond*, Cambridge.

Rawls, John (1985) "Justice as Fairness: Political, not Metaphysical," *Philosophy and Public Affairs*, 14.

Rawls, John (1999) *The Law of Peoples*, Cambridge, MA.

Rawls, John (2000) *Lectures on the History of Moral Philosophy*, ed. B. Herman, Cambridge, MA.

Reeve, C.D.C. (1988) *Philosopher-Kings: The Argument of Plato's Republic*, Princeton.

Reeve, C.D.C. (1997) "The Naked Old Women in the Palaestra," in R. Kraut, ed., *Plato's Republic*, New York.

Reshotko, N., ed. (2003) *Desire, Identity and Existence*, Kelowna, BC.

Rickless, Samuel (2007) *Plato's Forms in Transition*, Oxford.

Rosen, Stanley (2005) *Plato's Republic: A Study*, New Haven.

Rowe, C.J. (2006) "The Literary and Philosophical Style of the *Republic*," in G. Santas, ed., *The Blackwell Guide to Plato's Republic*, Oxford.

Rowe, C.J. and Schofield, M., eds (2000) *The Cambridge History of Greek and Roman Political Thought*, Cambridge.

Sacks, David (1997) "A Fallacy in Plato's *Republic*," in R. Kraut, ed., *Plato's Republic: Critical Essays*, New York.

Santas, Gerasimos (1979) *Socrates*, London.

Santas, Gerasimos (1988) *Plato and Freud*, Oxford.

Santas, Gerasimos (1999) "The Form of the Good in Plato's *Republic*," in G. Fine, ed., *Plato 1: Metaphysics and Epistemology*, Oxford.

Santas, Gerasimos (2001) *Goodness and Justice: Plato, Aristotle, and the Moderns*, Oxford.

Santas, Gerasimos (2003) "Penner, Plato, and Sachs on Justice and Happiness," in N. Reshotko, ed., *Desire, Identity, and Existence*, Kelwna, BC.

Santas, Gerasimos, ed. (2006a) *The Blackwell Guide to Plato's Republic*, Oxford.

Santas, Gerasimos (2006b) "Plato on Pleasure as the Human Good," in H. Benson, ed., *A Companion to Plato*, Oxford.

Santas, Gerasimos (2007) "Plato's Criticisms of Democracy in the *Republic*," in D. Keyt and F. Miller, eds, *Freedom, Reason, and the Polis*, Cambridge.

Santas, Gerasimos (2010) "The Socratic Method and Ethics," in J. Hardy and G. Rudebusch, eds, *Foundations of Ancient Ethics*, Göttingen.

Saxonhouse, A.W. (1997) "The Philosopher and the Female in the Political Thought of Plato," in R. Kraut, ed., *Plato's* Republic, New York.

Schneewind, J.B. (1968) *Mill*, Garden City, NY.

Schofield, M (1999) *Saving the City: Philosopher-Kings and Other Classical Paradigms*, London.

Schofield, M. (2007) "The Noble Lie," in G.R.F. Ferrari, ed., *The Cambridge Companion to Plato's Republic*, Oxford.

Schofield, M. and Stryker, G., eds (1986) *The Norms of Nature*, Cambridge.

Scott, D. (2000) "Plato's Critique of the Democratic Character," *Phronesis*, 45.

Sedley, David (2007) "Philosophy, Forms, and the Art of Ruling," in G.R.F. Ferrari, ed., *The Cambridge Companion to Plato's Republic*, Oxford.

Sen, A. (2006) "What Do We Want from A Theory of Justice?" *The Journal of Philosophy*, May, ciii: 5.

Sen, A., and Williams, B., eds (1988) *Utilitarianism and Beyond*, Cambridge.

Shields, Christopher (1999) *Order in Multiplicity*, Oxford.

Shields, Christorpher (2006) "Plato's Challenge: the Case Against Justice in *Republic* II," in G. Santas, ed., *The Blackwell Guide to Plato's Republic*, Oxford.

Shields, Christopher (2007) "Forcing Goodness in Plato's *Republic*," in D. Keyt and F. Miller, eds, *Freedom, Reason, and the Polis*, Cambridge.

Shields, Christopher (2008) "Surpassing in Dignity and Power: the Metaphysics of Goodness in Plato's *Republic*," *Philosophical Inquiry*, vol. xxx, Summer–Fall.

Shorey, P. (1935) *The Republic*, 2 vols, Cambridge, MA.

Sidgwick, H. (1981) *The Methods of Ethics*, 7th edn, Indianapolis.

Singpurwalla, R.G.K. (2006) "Plato's Defense of Justice in the *Republic*," in G. Santas, ed., *The Blackwell Guide to the* Republic, Oxford.

Skyrms, Brian (1998) *Evolution and the Social Contract*, Oxford.

Smith, Adam (1937) *The Wealth of Nations*, London.

Smith, N.D. (1983) "Plato and Aristotle on the Nature of Women," *Journal of the History of Philosophy*, 21.

Smith, N.D. (2000) "Plato on Knowledge as a Power," *Journal of the History of Philosophy*, 38:145–68.

Sorabji, R. (1996) "Rationality," in M. Frede and G. Stryker, eds, *Rationality in Greek Thought*, Oxford.

Taylor, C.C.W. (1997) "Plato's Totalitarianism," in R. Kraut, ed., *Plato's Republic: Critical Essays*, New York.

Urmson, James (1997) "Plato and the Poets," in R. Kraut, ed., *Plato's Republic: Critical Essays*, New York.

Vigetti, di M. (1998–2003) *Platone: La Republica*, vols 1–5, Napoli.

Vlastos, Gregory, ed. (1971) *Plato*, 2 vols, Garden City, NJ.

Vlastos, Gregory (1981) *Platonic Studies*, 2nd edn, Princeton.

Vlastos, Gregory (1991) *Socrates, Ironist and Moral Philosopher*, Ithaca.

Vlastos, Gregory (1994) *Studies in Greek Philosophy*, 2 vols, Princeton.

Waterfield, R. (1994) *Plato: Republic*, Oxford.

Wedberg, Anders (1955) *Plato's Philosophy of Mathematics*, Stockholm.

Weinstein, Joshua (2004) *Thumos and Tripartition in Plato's* Republic, PhD Dissertation, Hebrew University.

Weinstein, Joshua (2007) "The Market in Plato's *Republic*," *Classical Philology*.

Weiss, Roslyn (2007) "Wise Guys and Smart Alecks in *Republic* 1 and 2," in G.R.F. Ferrari, ed., *The Cambridge Companion to Plato's Republic*, Cambridge.

White, N.P. (1979) *A Companion to Plato's Republic*, Indianapolis.

White, N.P. (1984) "The Classification of Goods in Plato's *Republic*," *Journal of the History of Philosophy*, 22: 393–42.

White, N.P. (1986) "The Rulers's Choice," *Archiv fur Geschichte der Philosophie*, 68.

White, N.P. (1992), "Plato's Metaphysical Epistemology," in R. Kraut, ed. *The Cambridge Companion to Plato*, Cambridge.

Williams, Bernard (1997) "The Analogy of City and Soul in Plato's *Republic*," in R. Kraut, ed., *Plato's Republic: Critical Essays*, New York.

Young, Charles, "Justice," in G. Anagnostopoulos, ed., *A Companion to Aristotle*, Oxford.

Yunis, Harvey (2007) "The Protreptic Rhetoric of the *Republic*," in G.R.F. Ferrari, ed., *The Cambridge Companion to Plato's Republic*, Cambridge.

Index

distributive justice, 41, 60–1, 191–2
Divided Line, 132, 137, 152, 216
Divine Craftsman, 211
division of labor and inborn abilities
    and gender, 111
    and health analogy, 211
    and social functions, 10, 61–2, 63,
        70–1, 77, 93, 102, 109–10, 147,
        150, 171–3, 190, 199–200
division of souls, 11, 76–7, 78,
    79–93, 203
    gender neutrality, 117

economic inequalities and democracy,
    159–65
education, 7, 24
    and analysis and tripartite division of
        soul, 11
    and distribution of goods, 200, 201
    and division of labor, 62, 63
    and just society, 58, 205–7
    for knowledge of the good, 144,
        145–6
    and plural voting, 169–70
    and pursuits, 110–11, 113
    and reason, 123
    and virtues, 94, 206–7
    women and higher education, 117
    see also higher education of rulers;
        knowledge
efficiency and justice, 189–91
election by lot, 176, 178, 184–5
elenchus ("say only what you believe
    rule"), 31
elitism and good city
    education and knowledge of the
        good, 145–6, 165–70
    ethical elitism, 146–53
    political elitism, 11, 146, 165
Elster, Jon, 180–1
emotion *see* passions
epistemology, 7

isolation of theory of justice from,
    167–70
metaphysical epistemology, 11,
    125–37, 216
see also knowledge
epistocracy, 6, 122, 169
equality
    democracies and private property
        and wealth, 159–65
    of desires in democratic character,
        175–6, 177–8
    freedom to harm others and social
        contract, 37–8, 39, 40–1,
        50, 60, 72, 193
    of participatory democracy, 158,
        174, 193–4
    and physical equals, 130
    of women, 110–17
eros, 117, 140
Estlund, D., 183*n*.21
ethical elitism, 146–53
ethics, 10
Euclid, 128–9, 130–1, 135, 139–40
Euthyphro, 13*n*.14, 34*n*.15, 218*n*.9
exclusive functions, 30, 63–4, 65, 66,
    83, 88, 96, 148

family life: abolition of private
    families, 24, 62, 122, 199
feminism and Plato, 114–17
Ferejohn, M., 155*n*.30
Ferrari, G. R. F., 13*n*.18
Fine, Gail, 154*n*.15, 157*n*.47
    155*n*.24,
Forms, Theory of, 6, 11, 116, 216
    Diotima instructs Socrates in *eros*, 117
    isolation of theory of justice
        from, 167–70
    level of knowledge required, 144, 166
    and physical particulars, 11, 126,
        127–37, 139, 144
    see also Good, Form of

satisfaction of desires (*Cont'd*)
  bad desires problem, 177,
    179–80, 182
  democratic character and
    conflict of desires,
    177–82
  and pleasure, 213–14
  and theory of the good, 144–5,
    179–80
Saxonhouse, A. W., 118*n*.10
Schofield, M., 14*n*.26
scholocracy, 169–70
science and knowledge of the good,
    144, 145, 166
Scott, D., 185*n*.34
self, justice toward, 29–30
self-interest
  justice in the interest of rulers,
    16–33, 41–4, 187, 193,
    196, 199
  and state of nature, 38
self-predication of forms, 133–7, 142,
    143, 154*nn*.21&22&23
    &24&26&27&37
Sen, A., 74*n*.9
Shields, Christopher, 47, 155*n*.26,
    156*n*.32
Simonides, 15
Singpurwalla, R., 219*n*.16
Smith, Adam, 62, 189, 190
Smith, N. D., 118*n*.10, 119*n*.17
social contract theory of
    justice, 4, 36–44, 50–1, 61,
    101, 187, 188, 189
  comparison with Thrasymachus'
    justice, 41–4, 72
  contractarian method, 37–8
  equality and freedom to harm
    others, 37–8, 39, 40–1, 50,
    60, 72, 193
  state of nature, 37, 38–40, 42–3,
    46–7, 50, 72–3, 193

social courage, 68–9, 70, 151–2
social justice, 55–73, 90, 94, 149
  defense of, 102–3, 187–218
  and division of labor, 10, 61–2, 63,
    70–1, 77, 93, 102, 109–10, 147,
    150, 171–3, 190, 199–200
  and gender difference, 111–14
  and natural difference, 109–10,
    112
  and psychic justice in health analogy,
    208–11
  in ruling forms, 159
  and Sachs problem, 204–6
  see also division of labor
social temperance, 69–70, 72, 93
social wisdom, 68, 70, 122, 150, 152,
    165–6
society, justice of *see* just cities
    (society); social justice
Socrates, 1, 2–3
  Apology, 34*n*.10, 45
  beauty and goodness, 200–1
  in *Crito*, 34*n*.10, 37, 40
  and defense of justice, 187, 192
  desire and pleasure, 214, 216
  dialogue style and characters, 2–5
  dissatisfaction with dialogue with
    Thrasymachus, 5, 31–3
  division of labor, 10, 61–2, 63,
    70–1, 93, 109–10, 171–3, 190,
    199–200
  in *Euthyphro*, 13*n*.14, 34*n*.15
  functional theory of good and
    virtue, 30–1, 63–7, 70–1
  and Glaucon's choice of lives
    experiment, 49–51
  and Glaucon's classification of
    goods, 45, 46, 53
  harm and justice argument, 15–16,
    171, 172, 193
  health and justice analogy, 208–11
  ideal and approximations of, 121